AF505652

Signs of War

Signs of War: From Patriotism to Dissent

Edited by

Anne-Marie Obajtek-Kirkwood and Ernest A. Hakanen

First published in 2007 by
PALGRAVE MACMILLAN™
175 Fifth Avenue, New York, N.Y. 10010 and
Houndmills, Basingstoke, Hampshire, England RG21 6XS.
Companies and representatives throughout the world.

PALGRAVE MACMILLAN is the global academic imprint of the Palgrave Macmillan division of St. Martin's Press, LLC and of Palgrave Macmillan Ltd. Macmillan® is a registered trademark in the United States, United Kingdom and other countries. Palgrave is a registered trademark in the European Union and other countries.

ISBN-13: 978-1-4039-8430-2
ISBN-10: 1-4039-8430-1

Library of Congress Cataloging-in-Publication Data is available from the Library of Congress.

A catalogue record of the book is available from the British Library.

Design by Scribe Inc.

First edition: December 2007

10 9 8 7 6 5 4 3 2 1

Printed in the United States of America.

Chapter 6, "The Pornographic Barbarism of the Self-Reflecting Sign," by Paul A. Taylor appears with permission from Hampton Press and the *International Journal of Baudrillard Studies*, in which a similarly titled book chapter and article appeared.

Contents

INTRODUCTION

*Anne-Marie Obajtek-Kirkwood
and Ernest A. Hakanen*

Man is but a reed, the weakest in nature; but he is a thinking reed.

—Pascal[1]

Pascal wrote this in the seventeenth century, celebrating man's—and woman's, one would add—capacity of thought. Human beings have always tried to make sense of the universe around them and of past and current events through various means, including "signs." References to signs abound, such as these from the Old Testament: "And this shall be a sign unto thee from the Lord" (Isaiah 38:7); "Say, I am your sign" (Ezekiel 12:11), denoting that "semiotics" have been of use long before they ever constituted themselves as a critical and deciphering approach in the twentieth century.

Trying to understand is always more urgent and necessary when times are hard, troubling, unsettling, and destabilizing as in periods of latent conflict or of declared war. In this collection of essays on signs of war, three major wars are present. One belongs to the past—the war the United States waged in Vietnam—and the other two are still being waged either abroad or both abroad and on American soil. The current war abroad is the Iraq War and occupation that started in March 2003, which is the aftermath of the unsatisfactorily finished Gulf War of the early 1990s. To this current war in the Middle East can be added "the war on terror," a consequence of September 11, 2001, that designates the attack in the United States on deeply symbolic targets to al-Qaeda: the Twin Towers of the World Trade Center, "evocative of America's economic dominance," and the

Pentagon, "representing U.S. military power,"[2] one of the ugliest forms of terrorism ever imagined. The ensuing and ongoing "war on terror" has the United States waging war on its own territory and abroad on mainly two fronts, Afghanistan and Iraq. Iraq did not harbor terrorists before March 2003 but has since become a stronghold for terrorists as a consequence of the initial 2003 onslaught. To these must be added whatever place the United States deems dangerous for their security, like Sudan in 2006.

In this context of war and signs, what is a sign? What can be interpreted as a sign? Dictionaries give us several definitions, like this first one:[3] "an object, quality, or event whose presence or occurrence indicates the probable presence or occurrence of something else." Others include "something regarded as an indication or evidence of what is happening or going to happen"; "a gesture or action used to convey information or instructions"; "a notice that is publicly displayed giving information or instruction in a written or symbolic form"; "an action or reaction that conveys something about someone's state or experiences"; and " a gesture used in a system of sign language." To this can be added the tenth definition of the Webster dictionary online,[4] which directly refers to linguistics and to what would then be imported into semiotics as "a fundamental linguistic unit linking a signifier to that which is signified" with this added indication by Saussure: "The bond between the signifier and the signified is arbitrary."

Signs analyzed in this volume fall into one or more of the definitions listed and can be visual, written, auditory, or a combination of these. They include political cartoons, photographs, car bumper stickers, ribbons, the American flag, Bush's war rhetoric, newspaper editorials, blogs, underground press, prayer, and film. Pertaining to the wars mentioned previously, their origins are diverse in time and place; they are abundantly from the United States but also Canada (Québec), Mexico, Iraq, and several countries around the world in the case of films.

In times of war, sides may be quickly drawn. Supporters want to catch the enemy off guard, while dissenters want to stop aggression. Both sides know the importance of signs that represent their stance. These signs are a rallying point around which quick mobilization of the cause occurs. As a result, groups hasten to adopt a sign. The quick adoption of signs has many effects.

Recent events, especially the Iraq War, have demonstrated the explosion of signs used to represent the sides being taken. People not only draped themselves in the American flag or displayed yellow ribbons and bumper stickers on their cars, they also used a multitude of the same sign or combination of signs to emphasize their position. On another level, editorialists and cartoonists used slogans or stereotypes dug up from years past to depict their stance on the war.

All of these signs of war help people express their views with great simplicity and speed. Many were borrowed from previous conflicts in which a similar meaning was articulated. Others were new signs that were easily understood, for example, "these colors don't run" referring to the colors of the U.S. flag. What was impressive was the speed at which they were chosen and used, sometimes with the help of corporations behind them. Even more puzzling was the fact that, in spite of their polysemic meanings, many signs were unquestioned as to their "real" meaning.

Contributors of this book provide answers to these questions of contradiction. Some signs, especially of the most mercantile and simplistic aspect like car stickers or flag-related paraphernalia, were chosen at times in haste for their simplicity or their vagueness, were adopted from past conflicts in history, or relied on stereotypes. These factors lead to analyses of their significance, purpose, impact, or interpretation at various levels of population, not only in the United States but also abroad in various countries, as one conflict initiated by one country unfortunately has a ripple effect that involves countries for and against the conflict-initiator and countries neighboring the country under siege or occupation. Whether analyses in this book bear on signs of iconic stature or whether they bear on more elaborate products of rhetoric, artistic, or literary design, they are all products of various times and places, created by human beings and perceived by other human beings. Having no intrinsic meaning except the interpretation that is grafted on them, their meaning is not absolute, not fixed in time and space, but changing and evolving as humans are. This is therefore an attempt at deciphering some signs of war in the flow of time and knowledge.

Notes

1. [*L'homme n'est qu'un roseau, le plus faible de la nature; mais c'est un roseau pensant*], Pascal, *Pensées* (1670), fragments 339, 346, 347, and

348, in L. Brunschvicg's edition.
http://www.cyberphilo.com/textes/roseau.html. Retrieved on
March 24, 2007.

2. Lawrence Wright, "Sept 11—Five Years Later," *Washington Post*,
September 11, 2006.

3. This definition and the following one, unless otherwise indicated, are
all from the Apple Mac OSX integrated dictionary.

4. http://www.websters-online-dictionary.org/definition/Sign.

PART I

THE IRAQ WAR: REAL AND VIRTUAL

Yellow Ribbons Everywhere and No Meaning to Be Found

Ernest A. Hakanen

One day shortly following the start of the Iraq War, I was stunned and then numbed by the number of plastic, magnetized, yellow ribbons I was seeing on vehicles that passed me on my way to work. They seemed to have exploded like pollen in the spring, coating every vehicle. Most of the ribbons were yellow with the words "Support Our Troops" printed in black. I immediately began wondering not only where the ribbons came from but also what they meant. I wondered if the people who were displaying the symbol thought about any of the multitude of meanings the ribbons could have.

For me, the ribbons brought back memories of the end of the Gulf War, the taking of hostages in Iran, and, I admit, the popular song by Tony Orlando and Dawn, *Tie a Yellow Ribbon 'Round the Ole Oak Tree*. But the meanings associated with those events or themes did not seem to fit this case.

Fortunately, a group of undergraduate students was waiting for me and, even more fortunately, I was going to lecture on semiotics. I asked my students what the yellow ribbons on the cars meant to them. (None of them knew the song by Tony Orlando and Dawn.) Most of them, to my surprise, said that the ribbons were a fad and were designed to convince people to join the proverbial bandwagon. I reminded them about the war and they responded that the ribbons were a rallying call to other people, a kind of pep rally on wheels. I could not help but think that these were not just another fad, like mood rings or hula hoops.

That evening, my graduate students thought that the ribbons represented hope for the safety of American soldiers. One student went further and said that the ribbons were an absolution of sorts for the troops' actions. In other words, the soldiers were being forgiven in advance. By the end of the day, I had more questions than answers. I decided to look at the history of the yellow ribbon and try to understand the permutations of its meaning.

BACKGROUND

Ribbons have been used to represent different levels of awards at state fairs (blue, red, and yellow) and as sashes worn by beauty queens. But the yellow ribbon enjoys a special history in that it has often been used to represent allegiance to something or someone. For example one of the earliest uses was by the Puritans in England to represent their hope for a protestant country. In the United States the wearing of the yellow ribbon is said to go back to either the War of 1812 or the Civil War in which women wore them as a sign of devotion to their betrothed who had gone to war.

Whether this is fact or fiction hinges on the origins of the classic 1949 movie with John Wayne, *She Wore a Yellow Ribbon*, directed by John Ford in which the female lead wore a yellow ribbon to express her undying love for a cavalry officer. I say "fact or fiction," because the idea for the movie came from either the practice previously mentioned or from the theme song to the movie (which bore the same name) that was the most recent version of a common college song of the 1930s. The song is about a young woman's devotion to a college man. The color of the ribbon change according to the colors of the school, for example, crimson for Harvard or orange for Princeton. Frank Lynn's *Songs for Swingin' Housemothers* (1963, 42) provides a verse typical of the college type:

> Around her knee, she wore a purple garter;
> She wore it in the springtime, and in the month of May,

And if you asked her why the Hell she wore it,
She wore it for her Williams man who's far, far away.

It is also fairly clear that the college song is a rendition of a Cockney classic from the 1830s called *All 'Round My Hat 'Round Her Neck She Wore a Yellow Ribbon*. The original was written by J. Ansell, Esq. (John Hansell) and composed and arranged by John Valentine:

All round my hat, I vears a green villow,
All round my hat, for a twelvemonth and a day;
If hanyone should hax, the reason vy I vears it,
Tell them that my true love is far, far away

So indeed, we do see a roundabout connection with the era extending from the War of 1812 to the Civil War. The producers of *She Wore a Yellow Ribbon* might not have known the original song, but their ideas stem from it. In the 1950s the song reemerged and was codified for the modern era through television's Mitch Miller.

She Wore a Yellow Ribbon
(Written by Russ Morgan, Performed by the
Andrew Sisters and Mitch Miller)

Around her neck
She wore a yellow ribbon,
She wore it in the springtime
And in the month of May.
And if you asked her
Why the heck she wore it,
She'd say "It's for my lover
Who is far, far away."
Refrain:
Far away!
Far away!
She wore it for her lover far away.
Around her neck she wore a yellow ribbon.
She wore it for her lover who is far, far away.
Around the block she pushed a baby carriage . . .
Around her thigh she wore a yellow garter . . .
Behind the door her daddy kept his shotgun . . .
And in the church the preacher kept a license.

In June of 1972, *The Readers Digest* reprinted *Going Home* by Pete Hamill. In it, college students on a bus trip to the beaches of Fort Lauderdale make friends with an ex-convict who is watching for a *yellow* handkerchief on a roadside *oak*.

Later that same year, Irwin Levine and L. Russell Brown registered a copyright for the song *Tie a Yellow Ribbon 'Round the Ole Oak Tree*. The authors reportedly heard the story while serving in the military (Brown 1981). In the Army story, according to Brown, the symbol was a white kerchief, but "white" would not scan in the melody to which Levine and Brown set their lyric.

Tie a Yellow Ribbon 'Round the Ole Oak Tree, recorded by Tony Orlando and Dawn, debuted on *Billboard's* Hot 100 in March 1973 and remained there for seventeen weeks, four of which were spent at number one. *Tie a Yellow Ribbon* sold three million records in its first three weeks. In 1974, the song was recognized by the *Guinness Book of World Records* as the second most recorded song of all time. The lyrics that are engraved in my generation's collective mind follow:

Tie a Yellow Ribbon 'Round the Ole Oak Tree

(L. Russell Brown)

> I'm comin home, I've done my time,
> Now I've got to know what is and isn't mine.
> If you received my letter tellin' you I'd soon be free,
> Then you know just what to do if you still want me,
> If you still want me.
>
> Tie a yellow ribbon 'round the ole oak tree,
> It's been three long years, do ya still want me?
> If I don't see a ribbon 'round the ole oak tree
> I'll stay on the bus, forget about us, put the blame on me,
> If I don't see a yellow ribbon 'round the ole oak tree.
>
> Bus driver please look for me,
> 'Cause I couldn't bear to see what I might see.
> I'm really still in prison and my love she holds the key,
> A simple yellow ribbon's what I need to set me free,
> I wrote and told her please.

Tie a yellow ribbon 'round the ole oak tree,
It's been three long years, do ya still want me?
If I don't see a ribbon 'round the ole oak tree
I'll stay on the bus, forget about us, put the blame on me,
If I don't see a yellow ribbon 'round the ole oak tree.

Now the whole damn bus is cheering and I can't believe I see
A hundred yellow ribbons 'round the ole oak tree.

In January 1975, Gail Magruder, wife of Jeb Stuart Magruder of Watergate fame, covered her front porch with yellow ribbons to welcome her husband home from jail. The event was televised on the evening news. And thus a modern folk legend concerning a newly released prisoner was transformed into a popular song, and the popular song, in turn, transformed into a ritual enactment.

On November 4, 1979, Iranian revolutionaries seized the U.S. embassy in Tehran and held Ambassador Bruce Laingen and the rest of the embassy staff hostage. Six weeks later, on December 10, the *Washington Post* printed two short articles by Barbara Parker: "Coping With 'IRage'"and "Penne Laingen's Wait." The *Post* articles mentioned that Laingen, "tied a yellow ribbon round the old oak tree." The article concludes with Penne Laingen saying, "So I'm standing and waiting and praying . . . and one of these days Bruce is going to untie that yellow ribbon. It's going to be out there until he does" (B2).

The story went national on the CBS Evening News broadcast on January 28, 1980, Penelope Laingen was televised outside her home in Bethesda, Maryland with a yellow ribbon tied around a tree. "It just came to me," she said "to give people something to do, rather than throw dog food at Iranians. I said, 'Why don't they tie a yellow ribbon around an old oak tree.' That's how it started." Mrs. Laingen's reported that her inspiration was the song *Tie a Yellow Ribbon 'Round the Ole Oak Tree.*

METHOD: THE SOCIAL GRID AND MUTATIONS OF THE SIGN

Levi-Strauss (1966) explained social unity in terms of communication. Members of a society are not, in his mind, drawn toward a single belief, as Durkheim might argue. He believed that members are "bonded together by a perpetual weave and shuttle of transactions" (Harland 1987, 25). Exchanges, whether they are exchanges of marriage, kinship, or something else, explain the nature of community. This shift in locus of influence changed social thought in two ways. First, it emphasized the value of communication at the core of social structure. Second, it argued and illustrated that the more important factor in defining community was the relationship between families, not within them.

In other words, communication patterns and rules put down by family-to-family interaction form a social system. These rules then formulate existing actions. This overlay of rules forms a grid. The grid not only classified what is important in a community but it also, and more importantly, makes communication possible. The grid is used to decipher information. The grid also helps one contrast and compare choices and, therefore, make decisions. In this way identity is not that one perceives oneself as a member of a community, but that their membership in a community is interpreted through it. This is a subtle way of saying that communication is membership.

Foucault adopted the idea of grids as a means to describe the power of industrial modern grids to both individuate and totalize. Foucault (1970) saw census enumerations as an individualization technique within a totalization procedure. He believed that "grids" of statistical social analysis created not only a new individual but also the very idea of an individual. There was no individual until the self entered into the larger picture or grid. Conversely, once one begins to think about oneself as an individual, one must think more about the notion of the social. Foucault believed that the grid created by social analysis transforms the individual into a marketable product. And as we individuate our society becomes much more complex. The need for additional grids becomes an invaluable aid.

Further, Foucault believed that as the types of grids increase, we are increasingly pressured to distinguish ourselves with more and more grids. The result is an increasingly fragmented person owing all allegiances to many and none to a few. Foucault argues that the individual now spends most of his time fitting oneself into the market. This action commodifies the self and, to a degree, makes for a fragmented (Foucault 1970), schizophrenic (Baudrillard 1983a), or saturated (Gergen) self.

If the grid is the dominant code upon which we operate daily, then fads may be looked at as a sign of the code and may signal changes in the code. Now, overlying the code is the evolution of the sign. In other words, for a sign to stand out it must evolve in a particular way.

Baudrillard's method in particular addresses the evolution of signs from a cultural point of view. In particular, he believes that signs "mutate" through three phases: counterfeit, production, and simulation (Baudrillard 1983b). All signs begin as direct signifiers (counterfeit) and remain so to some degree throughout their life. However, they mutate to include and simulate more powerful social codes (production and simulation). One stage of mutation does not replace another. The stages represent greater co-optation of the sign into the market and grid of capitalism. That which evolves is a greater commodification of the individual under capitalism. So, by examining a set of signs using this method, one can judge its maturity within the social system. It is not meant to imply maturation or history of that sign. For example, a sign could be introduced with all three stages contained in its code, which is one of the markers of postmodernism, or it could develop the stages over time. The following sections explain the mutations and how yellow ribbons, in particular, operate within each as signs of the dominant code.

Analysis

Yellow Ribbons as Counterfeit

The first order of the sign, the counterfeit, mirrors that which it represents. The counterfeit is clearly understood as a fake. Users are not duped. However, counterfeits are "anything but arbitrary" (Baudrillard 1983b, 84). The primary function of the counterfeit is to pass value from one class to another. To know or own a sign represents an upward transcendence of class. At the same time, counterfeits enforce class structures in their unequivocal reference to status and their production by the bourgeoisie. For example, an advertisement or facsimile copy of a status symbol such as a Rolex watch transmits its class referent. It reminds the wearer that they are not of the class that has the Rolex and of their own class, which prizes fakes.

A yellow ribbon is directly produced and, later, controlled for distribution by the producer. The code shares the wealth of the producers but at the same time controls what and how much the consumer can consume. The ribbon acts as a powerful self-promotional tool for its producers. The irony is that producers are now seen as self-promoting because the yellow ribbons is produced by an objective third party that is free from influence. Such an illusion helps to "double" the size of the business, making it seem as if the industry is larger than it really is. This certainly happened as the song *Tie a Yellow Ribbon* multiplied music across genres. Today's yellow ribbon acts slightly as a counterfeit in that some people purchased ribbons believing that they were physically contributing to the USO or other military related organizations. Therefore, buyers were more likely to overspend on the item.

The consumer, under the illusion of the wealth of the ribbon, gains a social definition of their broad, common tastes—that is, low-taste culture. Being part of low taste culture not only positions one vis-à-vis those who appreciate high culture but also makes one aware of what is unachievable, thereby marginalizing one's tastes despite the fact that they are in the majority. Therefore, ribbons as counterfeits remind us where we fit in the class/culture grid. All of this reminds one of the popular music and movies that represent low culture. The ribbon at this point is well known but mainly as kitsch. In the end, what is important here is that everyone knows the sign of the yellow ribbon regardless of its "real" referent.

Yellow Ribbons as Production

The second order of signs refers to the boundless possibilities of mass production. The "energetic-economic myth proper to modernity" (Baudrillard 1983b, 97) is the sign's Industrial Age purpose. Most signs come to convey the modern myth of production. The value of the industrial sign is no longer only in its referential value but in its commercial value vis-à-vis other signs and is "conceived from the point-of-view of [its] very reproducibility." (Baudrillard 1983b, 100). To buy into the competition of signs and choosing a sign gives a stronger sense of belonging to industrial progress than holding a single counterfeit. For example, the multiplicity of ads or copies of the Rolex reminds us of the gifts of industrialization. In our case, can anyone name the producer of the yellow-ribbon sign?

Under this mutation, yellow ribbons are valued as counterfeits in an additional way. It is no longer just the primary item that is popular, bought or sold. Ribbons negotiate not just the marketplace; they have become more important in the value of the product. What is popular is good; yellow ribbons are popular; therefore, ribbons are good. This tautology makes the value that is inherent in the individual product benign. Yellow ribbons are good and, more importantly, apolitical. What's more is that they are not to be questioned.

To belong to the mass industrial society is increasingly important. Ribbons not only remind the individual of their inclusion but also of their own frail existence. Life expectancy of the frail human form is symbolically emphasized. The ribbons remind the consumer of his own struggle to belong. Ribbons help searchers find and channel themselves into increasingly marginalized and lonelier crowds.

All of the "history" of a sign transforms it into a representation of the industry that produced it to the point that the "map," in our case ribbons, becomes seemingly indistinguishable from the business. The function of this reproductive sign is to define the benefits of mass production and marginalization to willing consumers. By reinforcing the myths of capitalism, especially its inclusiveness, the lists sell the industry; the product becomes immaterial. The purpose of the second order of signs is to promote the very *idea* of the industrial, scientific marketplace or capitalism. The market and capitulation of the market increasingly define the grid.

Lists as Simulation

The third mutation or postindustrial sign is a simulation in spite of the reality. It no longer has to signify class, social reality, or even the market. The sign can stand for itself. It has broken free of its referent and its market and is in the hands of the consumer. The reality in the sign is concocted by the individual(istic) consumer.

Baudrillard calls this societal shift "hyperreality." The hyperreal world emphasizes a cybernetic relationship between the consumer and the product (Baudrillard 1981). The consumer believes that he or she is the sender of a message, ("I get what I want") and the sign represents not a message but feedback (Sarup 1993). Consumers come to believe that the sign is their own creation. The sign must tactfully allow the consumer to believe that he or she is in complete control of the sign. "The receiver/consumer is the god who guarantees that the [media content] 'works' or has 'meaning.' Only the recipient of the message can guarantee that the language . . . is spoken well" (Poster 1990, 67).

The value of the sign lies, therefore, in its emotional interaction with the consumer. I will continue to use the term "consumer" for the sake of convention and organization, although it implies a sense of receiver of messages instead of sender. Poster describes Baudrillard's position on media effects in terms of advertising:

> Baudrillard's argument is not that people "believe" the ad; that itself would assume a representational logic, one subject to cause-effect analysis (how many people bought the product because they saw the ad). Nor is his argument based on irrational manipulation; the ad works on the unconscious of the viewer, subliminally hypnotizing the viewer to buy the product. . . . Instead Baudrillard sets his argument in linguistic terms: the ad shapes a new language, a new set of meanings (floor wax/romance) which everyone speaks or better which speaks everyone. (1990, 58)

What is even more seductive is that knowingly collecting signs gives the consumer more emotional feedback or feeling of belonging to a world of free choices. The new consumer fetishism is the stockpiling of repetitious signs. The consumer "freely" collects signs that signify the self. As they are caught up in a play of repetitive images, the consumer world becomes relative and external to "reality." As in any evolutionary system, sameness and lack of reference points creates a greater level of comfort with day-to-day existence (Baudrillard 1983a). At this point, my original question about the meaning of the yellow ribbon could be answered. There is no meaning beyond the emotional display. It does not matter what the ribbon says or what it has printed on it; the ribbon is depoliticized and inert.

Supporting our troops means only feeling grateful that it is not us doing the fighting. The troops are reduced to unseen men and women destined to become part of an unseen military. The ribbon has absolutely nothing to do with why the troops are in action. Again the sign is completely depoliticized. What is even more interesting is that when the meaning is depoliticized, one cannot discuss the position of the sign. In other words, one cannot argue that supporting the troops is wrong. If the sign were attached to the leadership or reasons for war then one could argue that rallying is wrong. But in this case there is no value that can help us determine truth or falsity.

This behavior is reinforced by the market economy. Since information has become the key to moving product, information has been given precedence over the product. To limit the probable confusion in the market, distinction is given to information, while products are made to fit simple, broad, and arbitrary categories. Once classified, products become more alike. The consumer is not concerned with product limitation, since he or she equates the proliferation of information with the real product choice. Ribbons for POW/MIAs are yellow; Pope John Paul memorial ribbons are yellow; Lance Armstrong ribbons are yellow—they all erase one another.

With the wealth of information, yellow ribbons seemingly allow for *knowing about the product rather than knowing its value*. Here, then, is the creation of a simulacrum of the product. Statistics makes for much easier participation when one does not have to know the original. For example, fantasy sports competitions are based upon statistical information from the real competition. A player does not have to understand the actual game to compile the best statistics and make good predictions from them.

Second, stockpiling contributes to a culture in which overwhelming repetition is accepted as action, especially when there is a sense that nothing else is happening. The longer a favorite ribbon proliferates, the more the people displaying them feel a sense of belonging and contributing to mass society. In this sense, individual contribution to popular culture depends on the ability to put up with more of the same over and over again. The obvious notion, although not so obvious to the consumer, is that as part of the mass culture, the consumer will always have a favorite public and never lose contact with his own popularity. I bought Mitch Albom's *Tuesdays with Morrie* because it was on the *New York Times* Best Seller list for such a long time. How many people bought Stephen Hawking's *A Brief History of Time* for the same reason?

At the social level, stockpiling lends itself to illusions of sociotemporal control. Attali refers to this as the "stockpiling of sociality." People who display the signs no longer stockpile what they want to display but "stockpile what they want to find time to hear," read, view, and write (Attali 1989, 101). Having reserves of "knowledge" gives a sense of future action, which is as important, if not more, as knowing about the moment in our fast-paced information society. By the same token, the stockpiler can pretend to know about the items in the list. Understanding other tastes no longer requires knowing the actual cultural product, only its ranking system. So yellow ribbons might not be a bandwagon effect. Having a ribbon is right because it's recreated on every vehicle that passes.

In the end, product value is measured by its exposure and recognizability, not by its use or exchange value. The actual products themselves can become increasingly similar as long as an illusion of choice is constructed by and for the consumer through the media. This brings us full circle back to a gluttonous consumer who emotionally envisions him or herself as the prime mover in the explosion of information. In such an environment, the consumer wants to express him or herself in the increasingly visible explosion of brand information.

Ultimately, the consumer identifies himself as being as unique as a brand, which is not unique at all. Sarup refers to this production of consumer as the illusion of "privatized individuals" (Sarup, 1993, 165). What the market "does to you is what you do to yourself and the way it does this is by being about itself" (Wagner 1995, 61). "People are about *it* in somewhat the same way as the product is about it and it is the contingency of each to the other that the ad performs or replaces" (Wagner 1995, 60).

A marketer's dream follows: Stockpiling and lack of value explain the proliferation of ribbons for different causes and spin-offs, such as Lance Armstrong. Since there is no meaning in the object, cheap changes can be made to make the consumer believe they have choices. The market evolves toward sameness and extinction can be timed.

CONCLUSION

About a year after the ribbons exploded across the highways of America, they imploded in themselves and their own extinction. Besides the fact that people didn't like the negative bleach marks that they left on their vehicles, the ribbons had run their course. Troops were still in Iraq and would be there a long time and I'm sure that they are still supported. My hope is that Americans started to see the political meaning of the ribbons and question who was the "man behind the curtain." But I know I'm wrong.

Yellow ribbons were all that my students said they were—a fad, bandwagon, hope for a safe return—but in reverse. Because each individual believes the depoliticized sign is their own creation, it is easily disposed of. After all, the consumer had a choice of buying it that comes with the choice to throw it away.

References

Attali, Jacques. 1989. *Noise: The political economy of music.* Minneapolis: University of Minnesota Press.

Baudrillard, Jean. 1983a. *In the shadow of the silent majorities.* New York: Semiotext(e).

———. 1983b. *Simulations.* New York: Semiotext(e).

———. 1981. *For a critique of the political economy of the sign.* St. Louis: Telos Press.

Brown, L. Russell. 1981. *Washington Post.* January 27, p. B2

Foucault, Michel. 1970. *The order of things: An archaeology of the human sciences.* New York: Vintage.

———. 1972. *The archeology of knowledge and the discourse on language.* New York: Vintage.

———. 1982. The subject and power. In *Michel Foucault: Beyond structuralism and hermaneutics,* ed. Paul Rabinow and Hubert Dreyfus, 240–60. Chicago: University of Chicago Press.

Gergen, Kenneth J. 1973. Social psychology as history. *Journal of Personality and Social Psychology 26*:2, 309–20.

Harland, Richard. 1988. *Superstructuralism: The philosophy of structuralism and post-structuralism.* London: Routledge.

Lévi-Strauss, Claude. 1966. *The savage mind.* Chicago: University of Chicago Press.

Poster, Mark. 1990. *The mode of information.* Chicago: University of Chicago Press.

Postman, Neil. 1993. *Technopoly: The surrender of culture to technology.* New York: Vintage.

Sarup, Mahan. 1993. *An introductory guide to post-structuralism and post-modernism.* Athens: University of Georgia Press.

Wagner, R. 1995. If you have the advertisement you don't need the product. In *Rhetorics of self-making,* 59–76. Berkeley: University of California Press.

Chapter 2

Political Bumper Stickers and Vehicle Class: Are SUVs the Enemy?

David J. Koch
Douglas V. Porpora

Sport utility vehicles (SUVs) have acquired an image problem in recent years (Friedman 2006; Mills 2001; Fletcher 2003). Their fuel inefficiency has come to signify drivers without regard for the environment, especially among those on the left politically. SUV drivers came to symbolize a kind of thoughtless consumption combined with an imagined rightist partisanship. We shared the same prejudice. Thus, we had a hunch that SUVs would carry more pro-war bumper stickers than other types of vehicles. We set out to see whether this hypothesis was correct.

A bumper sticker is a kind of badge for a car. The first badges worn by automotive vehicles were license plates, which were used as early as 1890 but were not standardized until the 1950s. Early on, these badges of identification were made mandatory, but motorists in most states were originally forced to fashion their own. When the Ford Motor Company put some fifteen million look-alike Model-T's on the road—the overwhelming majority were colored black—license plates assumed another purpose. They became the means for people to identify which car was their own.

Today, as a plethora of makes, models, and colors have made motor vehicles much more distinguishable from each other, license plates are no longer needed for this purpose. It is rather governmental and insurance agencies that continue to utilize license plates for vehicle identification. Yet even with the ability to purchase unique automobiles, a demand for badges of identity has not only remained but also intensified. Today, car badges have emerged in the form of bumper stickers, displayed not for utilitarian reasons but primarily for self-expression (Case 1992).

Many stickers are immediately telling of the ideology they carry. There is little question, for example, that a sticker saying "Impeach Bush" is against the Iraq War. Conversely, the most prevalent "sticker" is also the most ambiguous—the yellow ribbon urging "Support Our Troops." The ribbons actually were not really stickers but magnets that are easily removable at the owner's convenience.

What exactly, though, is the message of these magnets? Are they issuing a command? An admonition? Other than commending support for the troops, with which few could take issue, what else do they signify? Specifically, do they also signify support for the war? As it turns out, not necessarily. We asked a non-random sample of forty-two people whether someone could simultaneously support our troops and take a position against the war. Almost half said yes, indicating ambiguity as to what these signs are asserting. From a speech act perspective, the "Support Our Troops" insignia might publicly count as support for the war, whatever the intentions are of the drivers who attach them to their cars. Yet, it is quite possible that in displaying ribbons urging support for the troops, many drivers do not understand themselves as simultaneously expressing support for the war. The grandmother of one of the authors, a woman strongly opposed to the war, sported a yellow ribbon on her car in mid-2005. Telling her that "Support Our Troops" ribbons conveyed support for the war came as quite a surprise to her, and she promptly removed it. Sommer (2005) refers to these magnets as "faddish," and it is fairly accurate in that they do not say anything of real ideological value; supporting our troops is not the issue at debate, the issue at debate is whether or not our troops should be overseas.

While all political messages were initially searched out for this study, we became highly interested in "Support Our Troops" ribbons and the cars on which they were displayed. Similar to the first Gulf War, the second war in Iraq prompted a profusion of yellow ribbon bumper stickers. Later, the stickers took on other colors as well and even stood for support of other things besides our troops: cancer patients, POW/MIAs, and even rock and roll.

The symbolic nature of yellow ribbons is likely derivative of the 1940s Russ Morgan military marching song, *She Wore a Yellow Ribbon*, but the symbolism was reified culturally by the 1970s hit, *Tie a Yellow Ribbon 'Round the Ole Oak Tree* performed by Tony Orlando and Dawn, in which the yellow ribbon was a sign for whether or not the singer would be welcomed home by his significant other after being released from prison. During the first Iraq War, it became hugely popular to tie yellow ribbons around trees or to display them prominently in front of one's home. By the second Iraq War, the ribbon had become a commodified symbol that could easily be bound magnetically to one's car, where it now most often appears.

For this study, bumper stickers were sought on roads and in parking lots in the states of Florida and Pennsylvania, looking for correlations between car type and engine size and bumper sticker ideologies. Studies in the past observed fewer bumper stickers on expensive cars (Case 1992), but these studies were conducted before the advent of magnetic stickers. Thus, now even individuals with expensive cars are free to display their ideologies without worry of the damage incurred by adhesive bumper stickers. Whereas irremovable stickers used to express ideological permanence, the utilization of solvent and magnetics make bumper expression much more disposable and impermanent (Salamon 2001).

LITERATURE REVIEW

Although bumper stickers have received some scholarly attention (for example, Case 1992; Newhagen and Ancell 1995), they have not been much studied as a form of political expression (Bloch 2000). There are, however, two studies from Israel that examine the political function of bumper stickers (Bloch 2000; Salamon 2001). One reason Israeli scholars might have paid more attention to the political nature of bumper stickers is that, in contrast with America, in Israel "the vast majority of messages on cars are of a political nature," (Bloch 2000, 50) most often dealing with the Israeli-Palestinian conflict.

Whether or not they are a nontraditional form of communication, bumper stickers are a "structured means of expression with identifiable forms, rules, and usages, affording the person in the street a way of participating in national discourse, bypassing traditional avenues of influence" (Bloch 2000, 48). As Bloch notes, the "creation of such a sphere of communication shows, first and foremost, that there is a need for it" (Bloch 2000, 49). The need is an easy outlet for busy citizens to participate in the public sphere. Newhagen and Ancell concur: "As much as the automobile plays a central role in the lives of many Americans, so has the bumper sticker become a vehicle for such political expression. Perhaps nowhere else in this society can people show their feelings to such a large audience with so little effort" (1995, 312).

While each bumper sticker is an isolated message, as more and more of them appear, they begin to engage in dialogue with each other. Bloch (2000) and Solomon (2001) found that in reference to the 1995 assassination of Israeli Prime Minister Yitzak Rabin, Israeli bumper stickers began to constitute an entire discourse with more and more created to respond to those already on the road. To an extent, a similar phenomenon is observable in this country. Consider, for example, those bumper stickers saying,"Support Our Troops: OUT OF IRAQ!" that are a riff on the ambiguous nature of ribbons telling us to "Support Our Troops." If it is true that bumper stickers get the kind of on-road attention scholars contend, then bumper stickers may be considered part of the public sphere and more an ideal speech situation than many other forms of real discourse because all displayed bumper stickers have equal voice, whether placed on a Rolls Royce, an old Honda, or even a stop sign.

If, however, the bumper sticker offers such a potential for political expression, it is as yet a largely unfulfilled potential in the United States. Whereas in Israel, the majority of bumper stickers are political (Bloch 2000; Salamon 2001), in the United States, political messages constitute a relatively marginal percentage of all bumper stickers (Case 1992; Endersby and Towle 1996).

Bumper stickers of all kinds are displayed by 13 percent of motorists (Newhagen and Ancell, 1995), which is a substantially higher percentage than the 5 percent of individuals participating in more strenuous political action (Putnam 2000, 39). According to Endersby and Towle, American citizens tend to be "free riders-eager to receive the collective benefits of organized political action, yet reluctant to share in the costs of participation and organization" (1996, 309). The disparity between those citizens who are more politically involved and those who just display bumper stickers may be indicative of "free riding." Endersy and Towle further observe that since becoming a political device in the 1956 presidential elections, bumper stickers have gone on to become one of the most prominent forms of political expression in the United States (Endersby and Towle 1996, 310).

It is uncertain whether the form of political expression represented by bumper stickers is employed differentially by social class. Some scholars have found that people are more likely to have bumper stickers if they own less expensive automobiles or live in low-income neighborhoods (Case 1992; Newhagen and Ancell 1995). Case (1992) theorizes that owners of expensive cars have less need of an expressive outlet such as bumper stickers because their ideologies are better represented in the media. Conversely, those with less expensive automobiles are less represented in the media, and so they buy and display more bumper stickers.

While there may be some merit to Case's logic, it is hard to imagine that the more affluent have no desires to express themselves any further. Whether or not one has a representative voice in the media, all humans have basic psychological needs of expression. Even without bumper stickers, cars themselves are a form of self-expression (Case 1992), and are "powerful symbols that express cultural values such as power, freedom, materialism, success, and individualism" (Stern and Solomon 192, 169). If affluent people express themselves through the price of their cars, why do they not also express themselves via bumper stickers? Especially with magnetic technologies allowing for their expression now to be damage-free, the affluent should be expected to display stickers of various kinds.

The need for self-expression is related to the need for identity and group membership. Expressing oneself through a bumper sticker communicates who one is and who one is not and to which group or category one does and does not belong. Thus, a union worker puts a union sticker on his car. Similarly, Democrats distinguish themselves as Democrats by displaying bumper stickers that take potshots at President Bush and the Iraq War. When we display such political bumper stickers, we call out to others in our group or category, signaling our solidarity with them in much the way that owners of Volkswagen Beetles used to honk or wave at each other.

Of course, the same bumper sticker that marks our solidarity with others of our in-group simultaneously makes us a target of opprobrium by members of the out-group. Thus, in Israel, Salamon (2001) found that motorists often deny responsibility for the bumper stickers they display, responding to questions about them by saying, "it was like that when we bought it," or "someone stuck it on." Others put contradictory statements next to each other, possibly to "confuse the enemy" or maybe saying, "Don't put me in a box—look, I've put both these messages on my car!" (Solomon 2001, 285). Such distancing from ownership of the political message conveyed by the bumper stickers reflects a wider fear in Israel that one might face damage to their car—or worse—from those antagonized by one's bumper sticker. For that reason, some motorists report that they are afraid to display political bumper stickers or even remove those they have had.

Thus, whereas for concern for their safety Israelis seek political anonymity, Case suggests that Americans rather are trying to overcome anonymity (1992, 107). Among earlier generations in American society, ideas, values, symbols, and identities were shaped and shared more through personal, face-to-face interactions in families, churches, schools, local political institutions, and neighborhoods. In contrast, the modern urban society is characterized by interactions among anonymous strangers and communications received through mass media sources.

In terms of political campaign stickers, those in the United States have remained relatively simple, carrying the candidates, party, and/or year of the election while Israeli stickers were much more reflective of national ideological values (Bloch 2000). This pattern might have changed with the U.S. presidential election in 2004, during which many complex statements, homemade stickers, and personal ideological values were displayed. Interestingly, Republican stickers remained relatively simple, (such as "Bush 2004," or "'W' for president") while opposition stickers were generally much more creative (e.g., "Bush Lies, People Die" or "War is NOT the Answer").

The focus of this chapter is how bumper stickers can be related to the vehicles on which they are displayed. The motivating idea is similar in origin to one described by Salamon.

> I sometimes play a kind of game with myself, a sort of quiz. While I
> am still quite a long way behind the car, and can't yet see exactly what

stickers they have, I try to guess their political orientation. For example, I go by the type of car, how many people are sitting in it, or whether there are a lot of children. Sometimes—and I can really get mad at myself about this—I even go according to how they are driving: If they are driving badly, I tell myself that they must have a particular political leaning. I know all these generalizations are really dangerous, but unfortunately in most cases, it turns out to be true. (Salamon 2001, 280)

Salamon was attempting to discover "whether the face matches the stereoptypes" (Salamon 2001, 280). We were trying something similar. Our stereotype was that SUV drivers would carry pro-war ideologies (i.e., pro-Bush stickers, "Support Our Troops" ribbons, military affiliation stickers, etc.). Many of the stickers projected messages that made reference to the conflict in Iraq.

The trend of ribbon display flourished when the United States attacked Iraq, and ribbons were "snapped up as quickly as stores [could] roll them out" (Hale2003). Ribbon factories ran low, and stores had trouble keeping magnets on the shelves. As late as 2006, ribbons could be seen on the floor of the NCAA Final Four Tournament; but not all have jumped on this wagon. Sommer (2005) explains that "Support Our Troops" "is neither a request nor a statement; it's a command." Thus, those "who presumably need to be admonished to support the troops are those who oppose the decisions of the administration" (Sommer 2005).

METHODS

The major question of this study was whether the ideology of a vehicle's bumper sticker would correspond in any way with its make and model. It would be difficult to answer this question via a random sample. What would be the sampling frame?

This study being an exploratory one, we used an exploratory method. Essentially, we walked or drove around different neighborhoods and parking lots, observing the vehicles with bumper stickers. Generally, these vehicles were parked, although if one passed by and there was an opportunity to observe its bumper stickers, we recorded that too. What we wrote down in these circumstances were 1) the make and model of the car; 2) whether or not it had a ribbon calling for support of the troops; 3) whether the vehicle was displaying multiple political stickers; and, if so, 4) the nature of at least one of the other political messages.

Although our sampling was certainly not random, we did try to achieve some measure of representativeness. We therefore chose neighborhoods in two different metropolitan areas, one in a blue state and one in a red state. The red metropolitan area was Tampa, and the blue metropolitian area was Philadelphia. In each area, we made observations in both suburban and inner city neighborhoods. The inner city neighborhoods sampled in Philadelphia were South Philadelphia, which is working class and racially mixed, and Center City, which tends to be more gentrified and upscale. The suburban neighborhood sampled in the Philadelphia area was Narberth, which is one of the affluent towns on Philadelphia's "Main Line." In Tampa proper, we sampled Ybor City, which is a popular, inner city nightspot. The suburban neighborhoods we sampled in the Tampa area were Tarpon Springs and Palm Harbor, both are middle to upper class neighborhoods north of Tampa.

In addition to matching the ideology of bumper stickers with car models, we also wanted to get some sense of how many cars display bumper stickers. What is the best way to count bumper stickers on cars? One way might be to position ourselves on a corner and count the number of cars that go by with and without bumper stickers. While this method may be sufficient for counting stickers, it is much less effective for simultaneously identifying specific messages. Cars go by too quickly to observe any bumper sticker messages other than electoral stickers and other short statements (let alone cars with multiple stickers), it was found that counting cars with bumper sticker versus those without was done best in parking lots. Therefore, we counted cars in two parking lots where the cars were stationary. Both parking lots were for shopping centers, one in Tampa and the other in Philadelphia. The one in Florida was a mall, and the one in Philadelphia was the site of several large stores such as Ikea; the lot in Philadelphia was visited twice. Counted in each parking lot was 1) the total number of cars; 2) the total number of cars with politically oriented bumper stickers (including ribbons urging support for the troops); 3) the total number of cars with religious bumper stickers; and 4) the total number of cars with posted messages other than that of religious or political natures.

Vehicles themselves were classified by make and model. Later, these classifications were reduced to two different variables. One variable simply distinguished whether or not a vehicle was an SUV. The other variable identified the engine size of the vehicle, that is, how many cylinders it possessed.

HYPOTHESES

We began with a simple idea, an idea that would occur to anyone more or less on the left. We began with the idea that drivers of SUVs would be much more likely to sport yellow ribbons and other pro-war stickers than drivers of more fuel-efficient, ecologically friendly vehicles. What we were actually looking for were expressions of pure ideology, such as depicted in Figure 2.1. Our view was similar to that of Sommer (2005), whose son was serving in Iraq. Sommer's point was that the trope of supporting our troops too easily conveys support for whatever policy it was that sent the troops into danger in the first place. The ribbons then are less about the troops and more about in-group solidarity. This led to our first three hypotheses:

1. SUVs will be more likely than other passenger vehicles to display ribbons urging support for the troops.
2. SUVs will be more likely than other passenger vehicles to display additional stickers supporting the war or the president.
3. SUVs will be less likely than other passenger vehicles to display stickers opposing the war or the president.

Of course, SUVs are not the only kind of "overly consumptive" vehicle. They have just become culturally most symbolic of profligate American consumption; there is now even an organization to defend SUV owners against defamation. Other cars, however, are also inefficient. What most makes for fuel inefficiency are the size of the engine and the weight of the vehicle. Thus, we expected some relationship between engine size and support for the war. Aside from vehicle type, we did not test for weight. As noted, however, we did test for engine size. Hence our fourth, fifth, and sixth hypotheses:

4. The larger a passenger car's engine size, the more likely it will be to display ribbons urging support for the troops.
5. The larger a passenger car's engine size, the more likely it will be to display additional stickers supporting the war or the president.
6. The larger a passenger car's engine size, the less likely it will be than

Table 2.1 SUVs and Yellow Ribbons

	Car Type		
Count	*Non-SUVs* (N=135)	*SUV* (N=82)	*TOTAL* (N=217)
a. Has Yellow Ribbon			
NO	58.6 %	56.1%	57.6%
YES	41.5%	43.9%	42.4%
TOTAL	100%	100%	100%
b. Has Other Pro-war Display*			
NO	76.3%	57.3%	69.1%
YES	23.7%	42.7%	30.9%
TOTAL	100%	100%	100%
c. Has Anti-War Signs**			
NO	53.3%	67.1%	58.5%
YES	46.7%	32.9%	41.5%
TOTAL	100%	100%	100%

* α = .003
** α = .032

other passenger vehicles to display stickers opposing the war or the president.

RESULTS

All told, we observed 217 cars that had political bumper stickers. We also did a count in two parking lots of the percentage of cars with bumper stickers of any kind. Out of 829 vehicles total, 29 percent (243) displayed some kind of bumper sticker. Only 12 percent (97) displayed political bumper stickers, which actually is less than generally reported in the literature, but our sample was not a random one.

As it turned out, our first hypothesis was not confirmed. As Table 2.1a indicates, the SUVs we observed were no more likely than other passenger vehicles to display ribbons urging support for the troops. On the other hand, our second and third hypotheses were confirmed. As is indicated in Table 2.1b, almost 43 percent of the SUVs we observed displayed some kind of pro-war or pro-administration sticker other than a yellow ribbon. In comparison, other pro-war or pro-administration ribbons were displayed by less than 24 percent of vehicles that were not SUVs (α = .003). Similarly, we see from Table 2.1c that whereas about 47 percent of non-SUVs displayed anti-war stickers, only 33 percent of SUVs did so.

Given the differences observed between SUVs and non-SUVs when it comes to politically unambiguous bumper stickers, perhaps we also have an explanation for the failure to observe a statistically significant difference between SUVs and non-SUVs in the display of "Support Our Troops" ribbons. Quite simply, ribbons calling for support of the troops actually are politically ambiguous. They may be displayed almost as often by those who support the war as by those who oppose it.

That conclusion is reinforced by our further findings, which uniformly indicate a relationship between car type and political ideology. In fact, all our remaining hypotheses (4–6) were confirmed. As Table 2.2a indicates, the greater the number of cylinders possessed by a vehicular engine, the more likely the vehicle is to display a "Support our Troops" ribbon. Specifically, such ribbons were displayed by only 27 percent of cars with four cylinders or less, that is, hybrids. In contrast, ribbons were displayed by 45 percent of vehicles with six cylinder engines and by 61 percent of vehicles with eight or more cylinders (α = .005). The relationship in fact is almost linear.

It is not just ribbons that larger cars are more likely to display. Many, like the six cylinder mini-van pictured in Photo 1 are further

Table 2.2 Bumper Sticker Display by Energy Efficiency of Vehicle

	Energy Efficiency of Vehicle			
	*4 Cylinder or less** (N=62)	*6 Cylinder* (N=124)	*8 Cylinder or more* (N=31)	*TOTAL* (N=217)	
a. Has Yellow Ribbon**					
NO	72.6%	54.8%	38.7%	57.6%
YES	27.4%	45.2%	61.3%	42.4%
TOTAL	100%	100%	100%	100%
b. Has Other Pro-war Display†					
NO	87.1%	62.9%	58.1%	69.1%
YES	12.9%	37.1%	41.9%	30.9%
TOTAL	100%	100%	100%	100%
c. Has Anti-War Signs†					
NO	27.4%	66.9%	87.1%	58.5%
YES	72.6%	33.1%	12.9%	41.5%
TOTAL	100%	100%	100%	100%

* i.e., hybrid vehicles

** α = .005

† α < .001

decked out. That van is actually flanked by two "Support Our Troops" ribbons, one in red, white, and blue, which definitely indicates support as well for the country that sent the troops into battle. Were this driver's "patriotism" not clear enough, additionally displayed is an American flag. There are also three stickers making religious references. One is sticker asserts "God bless America." Another is a man with a halo in front of yet another American flag, saying "American and Proud." Finally, not very visible is a Ichthus (Jesus fish). Aother sun-faded, murky image of the face of Jesus Christ has been placed on the upper right.

This van is emblematic of what we expected, and, again, the hypothesis was confirmed. As Table 2.2b indicates, the greater a vehicle's engine size, the more likely it is to display pro-war or pro-country stickers. Specifically, only 13 percent of cars with engines of four cylinders or less displayed such stickers. In contrast, 37 percent of vehicles with six cylinders did so, as did 42 percent of vehicles with eight cylinders or more (α = .001). Again, the relationship was almost linear as in the case of anti-war stickers as well (see Table 2.2c).

Figure 2.1 Florida. Copyright ® by David J. Koch, 2007.

Whereas 73 percent of the cars with four cylinders or less displayed anti-war signs, less than 13 percent of the cars with eight or more cylinders did.

Conclusion

So are SUVs the enemy? Well, that is putting the point rather strongly and rather facetiously. It does seem, however, that there is a relation between make and model of a car and the ideology of its owner. While this study was an exploratory one, its findings are suggestive. They suggest that people do use their cars for political expression and that the political opinions they express are at least loosely an extension of the meanings symbolized by the cars they buy.

Does the clash of bumper stickers rise to the level of dialogue? It all depends on what one means by dialogue. Certainly, bumper stickers are not conveying the details of any kind of argument. In a sense, they are an exchange of shouts that do more to establish a pattern of in-group allegiances and out-group antagonisms than to contribute reasoned discourse to a public debate. Perhaps in this sense, Sommer (2005) is correct to consider bumper stickers faddish.

At the same time, even an exchange of shouts is dialogue—if by dialogue we mean a symbolic interaction. Meaning is not only conveyed through bumper stickers from one motorist to another, but the bumper stickers themselves react to each other.

It is true that bumper stickers largely convey lines of solidarity and antagonism, but they also convey more than that. Some argumentative points are made. A sticker that reads "Support Our Troops: Out of Iraq!" actually says a number of things. First, it suggests superficiality among those who sport the bumper sticker reading only the first part. Second, it indexes a larger argument—that if we really cared about our troops, we would bring them home. That suggestion also implicitly condemns the stationing of our troops in Iraq.

Even just in identifying lines of solidarity and antagonism, a public argument is unfolding. In a sense, the display of bumper stickers is like a poll—not a scientific one to be sure but one designed to convey where the political momentum lies. They are like a show of hands in favor or opposed to a position. In displaying bumper stickers affirming or opposing a certain position, those doing so hope to show others how much support their position has, causing them, thereby, to stop, think, and reconsider.

In the end, therefore, bumper stickers may not be the most articulated form of political communication, but they nevertheless have their own place in the societal debate that constitutes the public sphere.

REFERENCES

Bloch, Linda-Renee. 2000. Mobile discourse: Political bumper stickers as a communication event in Israel. *Journal of Communication* 50 (2): 48–76.

Block, Melissa. 2005. Trouble with the phrase "Support Our Troops" on yellow ribbon magnets. *All Things Considered*, NPR. February 14.

Case, Charles. 1992. Bumper stickers and car signs: Ideology and identity. *Journal of Popular Culture* Winter:107–19.

Colavecchio-Van Sickler, Shannon. 2005. Bumper sticker evokes road rage. *St. Petersburg Times Online.* March 10. http://sptimes.com/2005/03/10/Hillsborough/Bumper_sticker_evokes.shtml.

Endersby, James, and Michael Towle. 1996. Tailgate partisanship: Political and social expression through bumper stickers. *The Social Science Journal* 33 (3): 307–19.

Fischer, Roger. 1988. *Tippecanoe and trinkets too.* Urbana: University of Illinois Press.

Fletchtner, E. 2003. Letter to editor: SUV tax break just what we don't need. *Chicago-Sun Times.* January 30:36.

Friedman, Thomas. 2006. A quick fix for the gas addicts. *New York Times,* May 31.

———. 2006. GM is still on the wrong road; gas guzzlers' defense has loopholes to drive through. *Pittsburgh Post-Gazette,* June 15.

Hale, Sarah. 2003. Patriotic consumers snap up yellow ribbons as quickly as stores roll them out. *Knight Ridder Tribune Business News.* March 27.

Mills, Donald. 2001. For the war effort, scrap your SUV. *The Boston Globe,* September 28.

Newhagen, J. E., and M. Ancell. 1995. The expression of emotion and social status in the language of bumper stickers. *Journal of Language and Social Psychology* 14:312–23.

Putnam, Robert. 2000. *Bowling Alone.* New York: Simon and Schuster.

Salamon, Hagar. 2001. Political bumper stickers in contemporary Israel: Folklore as an emotional battleground. *Journal of American Folklore* Summer:277–309.

Sommer, Bob. 2005. Cited in news segment by Melissa Block. Trouble with the phrase "Support Our Troops" on yellow ribbon magnets. *All Things Considered*. National Public Radio. February 14.

Stern, B. B., and M. R. Solomon. 1992. Have you kissed your professor today?: Bumper stickers and consumer self-statements. *Advances in Consumer Research* 19:169–73.

Suttles, Gerald. 1984. The cumulative texture of local urban culture. *American Journal of Sociology* 90:283–304.

C H A P T E R 3

The Stars and Stripes in the Year After 9/11: "Rally 'Round the Flag" or "The Flag Is a Rag"

Ronald E. Ostman
Harry Littell

"The American flag is but a piece of cloth decorated with stars and stripes, yet people have loved it, hated it, sworn allegiance to it, fought for it, and died for it."

—Hinrichs and Hirasuna, 2001

In the momentous year after the terrorist attacks on September 11, 2001, that killed thousands, destroyed the World Trade Center's Twin Towers, damaged the Pentagon, and led to the crash of a hijacked commercial airliner in Pennsylvania, we set out to document the public's response focusing primarily on the public's use of the U.S. flag as a visual and symbolic icon of personal feelings.

We made observations in several regions of the country but primarily kept cameras and notebooks handy when going about our business in and around Ithaca, New York. This chapter reviews highlights in the flag's history and etiquette, comments on famous and infamous historical flag photographs, and discusses our own flag photos. Most visual expressions using the flag were of "rally 'round

Figure 3.1
Elmira, New York, 2002. Copyright © by Harry Littell, 2007

the flag" sentiment. Moreover, the creative expression in public displays was often compelling. Minority dissent against George W. Bush and his administration's actions in response to 9/11 echoed earlier protest movements and deeply held anti-authoritarian beliefs that challenged mainstream expectations of proper public display of the stars and stripes.

FLAG HIGHLIGHTS IN AMERICAN HISTORY

Various local and regional flags that denoted the rising spirit of an American public predated the stars and stripes icon that symbolizes the United States in the early twenty-first century (Canby and Balderston 1909; Fow 1908; Guenter 1990; Mastai and Mastai 1973; Quaife, Weig, and Appleman 1961). In October 1917 The *National Geographic* magazine published several pages of famous flags in American history, including colonial flags, continental flags, the Bunker Hill flag, and flags of various military units. Some slogans still current in American idiom come from those early flags, including "Liberty or death," "Don't tread on me," "Join, or die," "An Appeal to Heaven," and "Don't give up the ship." Visual flag symbols included snakes, beavers, ravens, cannons, swords, anchors, and trees.

As the Revolutionary War got underway, several founders asked Philadelphia widow Betsy Ross to sew a symbol of unity for the emerging nation. Many legends have been told about the event. An accepted version is that the seamstress was visited by George Washington, Robert Morris, and George Ross (her late husband's uncle) of the Continental Congress in May 1776. They asked her to sew a prototype flag to match a design they submitted. She asked for one change: that the stars be changed from six-pointed to five-pointed, because she could make the latter with but one snip of her scissors. Why Betsy Ross? First, she was a relative of George Ross. Second, her pew was next to that of George and Martha Washington in Christ Church, Philadelphia. Third, George Washington knew her work from the shirt bosom and cuff ruffles she sewed and embroidered for him. Reportedly, Betsy completed the flag prototype in late May or early June 1776.

George Washington displayed the flag over a battlefield encampment when the Declaration of Independence was signed, establishing an American ritual of "showing the colors." It was both a snub at the Redcoats and a source of unity and pride for the troops. Some Continental Army soldiers began carrying powder horns with the design in scrimshaw. The Second Continental Congress approved the general design in Betsy Ross' flag on June 14, 1777. John Adams pronounced in his resolution to adopt the flag design, "Resolved: that the flag of the thirteen United States be thirteen stripes, alternate red and white; that the union be thirteen stars, white in a blue field, representing a new constellation."[1] Presumably, there were many things that concerned those leaders of a young republic. Apparently, it was not a frivolous waste of their time to talk about a cloth rectangle, its design, and its colors. Obviously, it stood for so much more—the very entity upon which they had staked their lives, their honors, and their sacred fortunes.

That physical flag, as well as iterations to come, was a visual embodiment of what they aspired to, created, and hoped for in their vision for generations of Americans. No painting has expressed this more forcefully than Emanuel Leutze's *Washington Crossing the Delaware*, painted in 1851–52. Washington faces forward, foot on the boat's gunwale as it inched through water with miniature icebergs and Lieutenant James Monroe (another future U.S. president) holds a partially furled flag behind him. The painting has been copied, engraved, and reproduced many times from the nineteenth century to the present. Washington and his variously dressed soldiers, rowed by Gloucester fishermen, were memorialized as they crossed the river to surprise the British on Christmas Eve, 1776. The resulting Battle of Trenton was a first victory for the Continental Army and a vital morale booster for the new nation.

Francis Scott Key composed "The Star-Spangled Banner," a poem that, after being set to music, became the U.S. national anthem in 1931. Key penned his words after witnessing the British bombardment of Fort McHenry near Baltimore during the night of September 13, 1812, and then, thrilled, saw by the dawn's early light September 14 that the star-spangled banner still waved. Later, John Philip Sousa, the "march king," composed "The Stars and Stripes Forever" during his tenure as conductor of the U.S. Marine Corps Band from 1880–92. In 1897, he distributed the song nationally and it was a staple of every concert he conducted thereafter until his death in 1932. Many flag songs, poems, stories, and legends were created during this flag-fevered period (Guenter 1990).

New stars representing new states to the Union were added during the year of admittance to the Union on Independence Day, the last being the fiftieth state of Hawaii in 1960 (Arthur 2002; Kohn 2002). Because of the number of stars they contain, old flags can be dated quite precisely. Very few old flags from 1777–1860 are available, because only wool fabric imported from Britain was used and stars remained difficult to cut, especially for those who had not learned Betsy Ross's trick. The flag achieved some recognition as a respected symbol of America during the Mexican-American War between 1846 and 1848. At that time, some hoteliers incorporated it into advertising by sewing their establishment names on the flag and flying it from their hotel roofs or hanging it over doorways (Guenter 1990).

However, until the onset of the Civil War, flags were flown mostly on military bases, on naval ships, on and in state and federal buildings, and wherever public officials or candidates for public office were found. At the outset of the Civil War, in response to Southern patriotism and the "stars and bars" (Confederate flag), incensed Northern citizens adopted the stars and stripes as their personal expression of belief (Kohn 2002). The trend accelerated after the Civil War, leading to a "cult of the flag" in the preserved Union. According to the July 4, 1992, *Ithaca Journal*, that wave of patriotism peaked in the 1890s. Flags and buntings abounded in response to renewed patriotism and to commercial developments in cheaper fabrics that tolerated advances in textile printing technology ("Glance" 1992).

The pledge of allegiance to the flag was authored by Francis Bellamy (perhaps with the assistance of James B. Upham) and published September 8, 1892, in *The Youth's Companion*. The pledge of allegiance might have been part of that commercial flag boom. The pledge has a controversial history. Bellamy was a socialistic Baptist minister who was asked to leave his Boston church due to his strong points of view. Later, as chairman of a committee of state superintendents of education within the National Education Association, he helped plan the four hundredth anniversary of Columbus Day. The commemoration ritual suggested by the committee and widely followed by many school districts featured a flag raising and a pledge of allegiance (Baer 1992; Ellis 2005; Sonneborn 2004). However, critics suggested that the owners of *The Youth's Companion* were in the business of selling flags to schools and hired Bellamy as part of their advertising campaign.[2]

Millions of new immigrants to the United States could not help but see the huge American flags hanging over the Registry Hall at Ellis Island during its heyday of the early 1900s (Novotny 1975; Quaife et al. 1961). Immigrant children were exposed to smaller flags that they could hold on the playground of the Ellis Island roof garden as they rode in an "Uncle Sam" wagon (Goldberg and Silberman 1999). Their familiarity with the flag increased daily in the schools, where "regardless of the many racial stocks from which these children may have sprung," school children were inculcated with respect for the flag (*National Geographic* 1917, 285). Schools across the country after 1892 routinely sponsored salutes to the flag and recitation of the pledge of allegiance. School children across the country often were taught how to form a huge living flag, patterning their red, white, and blue costumes as they faced large audiences from stadiums and other risers. Their show usually was the culmination of civic pageants. "Americanization Days" led to extravagant displays of flags that schoolchildren waved while forming with their bodies and dress as a collective, living flag for public display (*National Geographic* 1917). Meanwhile, schoolbooks were a common vehicle for displaying the flag in illustrations and infusing patriotism through reading texts. This continued for decades. An "Alice and Jerry" basic reader (1942, 1947, 1954, and 1956), for example, contained excited crowds, parades, and flags galore in Independence Day and first flight stories (O'Donnell 1956).

The Wright brothers' first flight gave way to an historic flight of a different sort in 1969. Astronaut Neil Armstrong placed the U.S. flag on the moon July 20, 1969, during the Apollo 11 voyage. A few years later, Commander David R. Scott photographed lunar module pilot James B. Irwin repeating the feat during Apollo 15 in 1971. This obvious and potent symbol of American pride and power was documented in both photographs, but it is the latter photograph that shows the astronaut saluting the stars and stripes, arranged to appear as if it were unfurled and blowing in the wind, a fantasy that was carefully orchestrated in Earth planning and provisioning (Fulton 1988; Goldberg and Silberman 1999). Not everyone revered the flag thereafter, however.[3] Federal agitation for flag respect led to "The Flag Desecration Constitutional Amendment" that would have made flag burning a punishable crime. It was narrowly defeated after acrimonious Senate debate December 12, 1995.

BEHAVIOR LEADING TO CREATION OF FLAG ETIQUETTE

Throughout its history, the flag has been subject to many creative uses. For example, the flag was incorporated into advertising for all manner of products. By 1880, a House of Representatives bill was introduced "to protect the national flag from desecration" and cited alleged abuses in printing, stamping, and impressing of words and designs in advertisements, on merchandise, or at trade locations. However, the use of flag words and designs continued amidst the give-and-take of national debate. Gambling houses and saloons were among establishments and organizations that adopted the flag as a promotion device. The U.S. Patent Office had issued twenty-five trademark patterns incorporating the flag by 1896. From July to December of that year, six more companies filed for the right to use the flag in trademarks, including producers of bacon, pickled pork, biscuits, and soap (Guenter 1990).

During the Spanish-American War, "Dewey Fever" swept the country after Admiral George Dewey's defeat of the Spanish fleet in the Manila Harbor of the Philippines in May 1898.[4] An ad proclaiming "The Two Best Things That Float" featured Dewey, the American flag, and a bar of Fairbank's Fairy Soap awash in the sea (Hinrichs and Hirasuna 2001; Kohn 2002). At first, traditional and hereditary groups such as the Grand Army of the Republic, the Loyal Legion, Sons of the American Revolution, and Daughters of the American Revolution actively promoted public displays of the flag. The market responded with a cornucopia of flag-emblazoned products, including stationery, greeting cards, calendars, silverware, glassware, furniture, candy molds, game boards, playing cards, dolls, mechanical banks, cigar boxes, and jugs, while homemakers stitched items such as quilts, pillow covers, and samplers (Kohn 2002).

After the trend expanded, further backlash developed. Opposition voices were heard against "inappropriate" commercial uses of the flag motif—excesses such as awnings, handkerchiefs, hammocks, clothing, underwear, equine fly nets, dog blankets, and the like. Those objects in particular were vilified as disrespectful. The American Flag Association was formed in New York in 1898, dedicated to coordinating efforts to pass legislation barring flag desecration, which found success in Illinois, Nebraska, New York, and South Dakota (Guenter 1990). The *Ithaca Journal* noted on July 4, 1992, that flags were "sat on, rained on, thrown away, burned or dragged and stepped on by man or beast" ("Glance" 1992). Qualms about commercialization and disrespect of the flag waxed and waned but were not completely absent from the period between the Spanish-American War and the end of World War I.

In the period immediately before World War I, Americans became more serious in their respect for the flag. War-leaning Americans were incited by the German U-boat sinking of *The Lusitania*, a Cunard steamer en route from New York to Liverpool on May 7, 1915. It sank off the coast of Ireland in 18 minutes, drowning 128 Americans among the 1,198 dead. American flags were used to drape the bodies of retrieved U.S. citizens. As early as 1914, employees in the Manchester, New Hampshire mills of the Amoskeag Manufacturing Company perhaps sensed the mood of the country as the United States edged toward its participation in World War I in April 1917. Prior to America's joining "the war to end all wars," Amoskeag employees made a huge flag that proved perfect for veneration. Each star was a yard wide. It measured fifty-by-ninety-five feet and weighed two hundred pounds. The flag was a tremendous hit in the spring of 1916 as part of a "Preparedness Parade," an 11-hour affair that included hundreds of Amoskeag employees among the 125,000 who participated (Lacayo and Russell 1995; *National Geographic*, 1917, 2002). Women's suffrage marchers proudly carried the American flag in their pursuit of voting rights for women, which they finally earned in 1920 (Lacayo and Russell 1995; Norback and Gray 1980).

Feeding the fever for war once the Americans had joined their allies were posters and song lyric sheets, most of which prominently featured the flag and exhorted potential volunteers for the marines, navy, and army: "First in the Fight—Always Faithful—Be a U.S. Marine," "The Navy Needs You! Don't READ American History—MAKE IT!!," "Let's Keep the Glow in Old Glory and the Free in Freedom Too." War flames were fanned at home by a constant series of orchestrated events promoting sacrifice in food, drink, and fuel. Funds were solicited by reminding the public through Liberty Loan bond posters that the war came with a price tag. One such poster featured a beauty wearing a transparent dress in front of a billowing flag, which might have coupled physical and patriotic desires. Mass rallies, attended by thousands, featured a variety of motion picture film entertainers touting the same causes. Douglas Fairbanks, Charlie Chaplin, and Mary Pickford were among prominent stars that head-lined parades and made speeches that provided mass exhilaration and picture-perfect moments. One of the most stunning propaganda images was a dynamic, seemingly spontaneous photograph of Boy Scouts running down New York City's Fifth Avenue, each carrying a flag. The exuberant youth were flanked at their sides by flags hung from building windows. Yet more flags were ahead, unfurled from building roofs. In 1917, *National Geographic* captioned the image "WAKE UP, AMERICA!" (Josephy 1964).

The parade was typical of attempts engineered by George Creel's Committee of Public Information, a public relations organization, to affect public opinion. Influential print media assisted Creel in orchestrating events that raised and attempted to maintain war fever. However, fatigue did set in. By the conclusion of World War I, Charles Fouqueray's painting of doughboys marching in loose for-mation though the Arc de Triomphe in Paris was aglitter with flags and rifles, but the faces of the weary Yanks were anonymous and obscure. Clearly they suffered battle fatigue and were exhausted in the moment of victory celebration (Josephy 1964).

After World War I, a code of flag etiquette was established in 1923. However, the code did not become law of the land until 1942, after the United States entered World War II ("Passion" 1992; "Grand Old" 1993). Even today, commercial businesses and adver-tising continue to challenge the limits with new and sometimes bizarre adaptations of the flag motif. A pulp murder mystery, for example, featured a blood-drenched flag draped over a corpse, which was certainly of questionable taste (Dam 2000).

America has been reluctant to enter world wars. Prior to World War II, the country was divided on the issue of joining the fighting in Europe. However, the strong isolationist movement eventually dissolved with the Japanese bombing of Pearl Harbor on December 7, 1941. The flag that flew over Pearl Harbor that "Day of Infamy" was the flag that flew over the White House on August 14, 1945, when the Japanese officially surrendered on the *U.S.S. Missouri* in Tokyo Bay.

Curiously, flags are highly visible at the beginning and end of wars; artists' renditions of wars in progress and photographs during the waging of war rarely feature flags. There is one notable exception—flags as a capstone memento of conquest and battle victory. World War II offered just such a supreme visual moment on a "trivial scab barely cresting the infinite Pacific . . . eight square miles," a rotten, formerly obscure bit of volcanic-spewed earth named Iwo Jima (Bradley and Powers 2000, 6). Joe Rosenthal's Associated Press photograph of six Marines raising the flag at the top of Mount Suribachi on February 23, 1945, is said to be "the most recognized, the most reproduced" image in the history of photography (Bradley and Powers 2000, 3; Fulton1988). It was the ultimate "feel good" photograph of World War II. Rosenthal's image won an admiring "Here's one for all time!" from John Bodkin, AP photo editor in Guam (Bradley and Powers 2000, 215) and a Pulitzer Prize for "the most famous of all war photographs . . . that spoke for all America . . . about her pride, her valor, her sacrifice" (Leekley and Leekley 1978, 20). Less remembered, however, is the horrific reality of Iwo Jima—the slaughter of Americans (6,821 dead, 19,217 wounded and maimed) and Japanese (an estimated 20,000 dead). In "To the Finish: A Letter from Iwo Jima" for *The Atlantic Monthly* in 1945, Edgar L. Jones revealed what he saw when he toured the sulfuric island a week after the Marines' landing: "On the afternoon I walked by, there was half an acre of dead Marines stretched out so close together that they blanketed the beach for two hundred yards. The stench was overpowering. . . . The smell of one's countrymen rotting in the sun is a lasting impression" (Jones 1998, 490). In fact, three of the six Marines shown in Rosenthal's photographs died later in combat. The battle of Iwo Jima continued for a month after the iconic image was made (Fulton 1988). The photograph has since been criticized as a staged reenactment (Norback and Gray 1980), which is a claim denied by Rosenthal (Lacayo and Russell 1995).

In celebration of the national symbol, president Harry S. Truman signed a bill on August 3, 1949, that requested U.S. presidents to designate Flag Day by proclamation each year on June 14. After World War II, stimulated by the sense of America's power and the prospect of an economy that was back on track, Americans were to face momentous challenges by groups that traditionally had been marginalized, discriminated against, or taken for granted. Feminists, for example, strove to capitalize on a new role for women in the workplace and a new freedom due to birth control. Minority groups felt the time had come to sit anywhere on the bus they chose. The flag became part of their persuasive repertoire, perhaps inspired by Farm Security Administration photographer Gordon Parks, who took an ironic icon photo in 1942 of Ella Watson, a black cleaning woman of federal buildings in Washington, DC. She holds a mop and a broom and has a defeated look on her face. A flag fills the entire background. It suggests that American had not delivered on the pledge promise of "liberty and justice for *all*" (Goldberg and Silberman 1999). Parks later pictured memorable moments in the civil rights movement and in discrimination against blacks in his work depicting Harlem gangs, ghettos, and introducing the nation to controversial black leaders and groups, such as Malcolm X, Elijah Muhammad, and the Nation of Islam (Lacayo and Russell 1995). More conventionally, Dr. Martin Luther King, Jr., the Southern Christian Leadership Conference, the NAACP, and the many freedom marches in support of civil rights were rarely without a flag (Fulton 1988; Levitas 1969).

However, a flag also could be a weapon against civil rights. During the 1963 school integration struggles at Birmingham High School in Alabama, racist whites prominently displayed confederate flags as a symbol of opposition (Fulton 1988). A well-known photograph shows the flag being used as a spear. The 1977 Pulitzer Prize winner, titled "The Soiling of Old Glory," was a sad abuse of the flag, so many of which had flown proudly the previous year during America's bicentennial. A frenzied white man, participating in an anti-busing demonstration in Boston, prepares to thrust the flag's staff into the head of a black lawyer who was walking near City Hall where the demonstration was centered. Theodore Landsmark was singled out by someone in the crowd, shouting "Get the nigger; kill him." Badly beaten, he later was treated for a broken nose, facial cuts, and body bruises (Leekley and Leekley 1978).

Other cultural shifts were afoot at the same time. The rebellious era of the 1950s and 1960s, exemplified by the beat generation, hippies, anti-war protesters, and the pro-war reaction, also called upon the flag for service to their causes. The beatniks found in the flag a symbol that could be mocked or used as a reminder of the Establishment's shallowness. Swiss-born photographer Robert Frank shocked conventional America with his mid-1950s images that were unsentimental, brutally honest, and unflattering in their depictions of blank, bored, expressionless, bland, captive, and wary citizens (Lacayo and Russell 1995; Tucker 1986). Many viewers of his book

The Americans (1958), including some photography critics, believed it was "sinister" and "perverse" because they saw it as "anti-American" (Frank 1983). Indeed, Frank's photograph of an Independence Day gathering in Jay, New York is dominated by a see-through flag that has been patched and bears a tear at the bottom (Fulton 1988). His photograph of a tuba player wearing an Adlai Stevenson campaign button during a 1956 Chicago political rally seems to put a hollow oompah in the scene characterized by flag bunting on the wall above (Tucker 1986). Frank's 1959 film, *Pull My Daisy*, was made from beat writer Jack Kerouac's script and was narrated by Kerouac. Again, the flag was seen in a scene that depicted Americans as mindless flag-wavers (Frank 1983). Only the young and the hip seemed to understand Frank and Kerouac.

Vietnam engendered fierce pro and con reactions from a population that seemed dichotomized at times. Photographers like Donald McCullin showed the boyish faces of soldiers in turmoil and terror. Many felt they were too young to die for a war whose purpose had not been satisfactorily explained or justified (Levitas 1969). Soldiers' coffins with flags draped on them were common photos in the nation's press and were often shown in a very emotional and moving manner. To counteract the growing national sentiment against the war, pro-war demonstrations were held in the spring of 1967. Diane Arbus, who specialized in photographing topics that most people felt were creepy, freaky, and bizarre, attended one such event and came away with images that did not disappoint those who knew her work. Her images of the pro-war parade held in New York City on May 13, 1967, to "Support Our Men in Vietnam" captured demonstrators in costume, including Revolutionary War uniform, Native American feathered headdress, tall Uncle Sam hats, scout uniforms, and the like. However, one of the most compelling from her contract sheet of that day's work was of a young man with bushy eyebrows and jug ears, wearing a straw hat and a bowtie slightly askew. His sports jacket prominently displayed buttons with slogans ("Bomb Hanoi," "God Bless America") and a small lapel bowtie flag. He clutched a flag. Another of Arbus' flag-carrying images from this period featured a young man with bad teeth, bad complexion, bad hair, an "I'm Proud" lapel button, and an unusual cast in his eyes (Arbus 2003; Arbus and Israel 1972).

The election of 1968, featuring two Minnesotans vying for the nomination, brought anti-war and pro-war confrontations to a violent head, particularly in Chicago during the Democratic National Convention. Vice president Hubert Horatio Humphrey represented the establishment. Senator Eugene McCarthy represented the anti-war perspective. Much went wrong inside the United States. Dr. Martin Luther King, Jr. fell to an assassin's bullet in April 1968, followed by Robert Kennedy on the campaign trail in June. Thousands of protesters agitated in Chicago under the banners of the National Mobilization to End the War in Vietnam, the Students for a Democratic Society, and the Youth International Party ("Yippies"). Radical anti-war protesters abused the flag in powerful and provocative ways. They sewed the flag upside down (a sign of distress in conventional usage) on the seats of their ragged pants. They sometimes soiled it or burned it. Such actions could not have pleased Mayor Richard Daley's city police, members of the Illinois National Guard, and regular Army troops, who lost self-control and brutally beat protesters and bystanders alike in a "police riot." Their savagery was broadcast on television to chants of "The Whole World is Watching." Alabama Governor George C. Wallace mounted a third-party candidacy. Wallace drew many lower and middle class enthusiasts to his cause, pledging to shoot black rioters, run over protesters who blocked his car, and disparaging "pointy-headed college professors." During his appearances, the former Confederate flag made a dramatic reappearance, vouching for the large Southern contingency he attracted. In the end, Republican Richard M. Nixon was elected. He spent much of his Presidency dealing with winding down the war, a process begun by his predecessor, Lyndon Baines Johnson (Levitas 1969), and dealing with the Watergate scandal, which ultimately led to his resignation. Nixon was the ultimate photo op president and the number of American flags in his photographs is truly impressive (Fulton 1988).

A Modest Visual Assessment of the Flag's Use

After 9/11 the flag suddenly appeared everywhere. Some public expressions were the result of simple acts of low-cost consumption as millions purchased bumper stickers and magnetic decals. However, more creative, elaborate, and sincere folk art expressions incorporating the flag appeared. Some communities even painted the center-lines on their roads in red, white, and blue.

On the commercial side, some startling products were displayed and offered for sale. An appointment calendar's cover featured a tongue, stuck out like the Rolling Stones logo. Only this tongue was painted in the colors and motif of the American flag. One questions the purpose. Was it respect? Was it reverent memory? What did the tongue denote? Was it there solely for shock value? Who purchased the calendar?

Popular culture's use of the national symbol amounted to silly inanity akin to the happy face, the syrupy yellow ribbon, the mischievous bad boy decal in the rear pickup window urinating on various car logos, the Mickey Mouse balloon, and *Mad* magazine's leering Alfred E. Neumann "What, me worry?" face. Red, white, and blue colored candy and pretzels was for sale. Birdhouses were painted like flags. There were also flag pillows, bedspreads, swimming suits, ties, shirts, shoes, jewelry, purses, window decals, key chains, car deodorizers, and more. It became impossible to avoid the ubiquity of flag connotations.

The Almighty Dollar

So many of flags and flag spin-offs produced were motivated by commercialism. There were "Stars & Stripes" check blanks featuring the waving American flag. Patriotism each time a check was authored for only $3.99 for 200 checks, with the fourth box FREE! (Second choice, at a slightly higher price—Marvel Comics with Spiderman and THWIPP!—one of four scencs.) JCPenney offered a free sitting for children's portraits and a portrait of the little tyke holding an American flag. Additional portrait sheets were only $4.99 (regularly $12).

Yet another opportunity was to collect twenty-five Old Glory stamps for just two dollars and save 50 percent. Remember that many of the stamps showed national landmarks in the background, such as the White House, Mount Rushmore, Independence Hall, and the Capitol. Consumers needed only to locate their American Flag check blanks. The Mystic Stamp Company in Camden, New York awaited their payment, guaranteed their satisfaction, and delivered free.

Polo Ralph Lauren, long-time leader in creative alterations and adaptations of the American flag, offered a Independence Day special on children's t-shirts with "RL" where the stars normally would be found, accompanied by nine stripes, along with the Ralph Lauren signature over the whole works ($9.99). And there were the Ralph Lauren flag logo throw pillows (13 stars, 13 stripes, $34.99, a $5 savings), the 12-star, 11-stripe women's sweater, designed to sit at a suggestive angle ($39.99–$59.99), and the flag logo beach towels (13 stars, 13 stripes, $14.99). Children's flag sweaters sold for $29.99–$39.99. RL Polo was pleased to answer inquiries concerning telephone numbers, business hours, and directions to the nearest factory store.

Hummel New York Firefighter ceramic figurine hit the market in early June. That darling little guy, wearing appropriate firefighting gear and holding a hose, had a bucket at his feet and a flag behind him. "Just 6 Americans in a million" would possess him. Only 1,911—"the total world production!"—were made available on Independence Day to "savvy collectors." The ad copy reminded potential investors that "[i]n 1973, prominent Ohio collector Robert Miller bought 8 rare Hummels for $900" and "one year later he was offered $250,000.00." How much did 1,911 savvy collectors pay for the rare figurine? An amazingly low $289.50, or $57.90 per month! Good deal! Sadly, however, sales were limited to only two per customer. Truly, as Maden's (America's largest Hummel store in Milwaukee, Wisconsin) opined, this little guy was created to "honor the heroic acts of New York's firemen."[5]

Kay Connors of Shelton, Washington, wrote an Independence Day letter-to-the-editor, printed in the July 6, 2002, *Seattle Post-Intelligencer*. She evidently had been reading too many Ralph Lauren and Maden's ads. She wrote, "The stores have been selling everything you can possibly print a flag on all day, and for that matter ever since the dreadful 9/11 event. . . . How can we refute the image of greedy opportunists if we frantically exploit the deaths of thousands of people by selling everything we can color red, white and blue and use 'security and safety' as issues to persecute the poor and whoever else it suits our purposes to do so? We cannot show our love of our country if we do not care about our fellow Americans" (Connors 2002). Ms. Connors' lament is one instance of what Professor Stewart M. Hoover of the University of Colorado referred to as a sense of shame regarding the excesses of materialism, so much a part of U.S. modernity, in the post mortem of 9/11.[6] The United States dominates the world marketplace and nowhere is our wealth more apparent than in the mass media portrayal of American popular culture. Hoover speculates that this unending spectacle of consumption and greed is at least partially responsible for the distaste and contempt that many outside of America feel toward the "good guys," as most Americans think of themselves. Hoover spoke of the perceived image of America as the land of profane culture, bereft of values. Initially after 9/11, many joined our national leaders in asking, why do they hate us so much? However, a shared sense of victimization and blanket outrage directed at "them" dominated the national psyche and response energy, pushing the root question to the background, hushed by the roar of military jets and various explosions resulting from a wide variety of ordinance and "delivery systems."

THE FLAG IS A RAG

When we started taking photographs in the Ithaca, New York area, 9/11 was several months in the past. We also took photos in Berkeley, California and elsewhere in the vicinity along the coastline north of San Francisco and eastward to Yosemite. We found mostly a right-of-center conventional, heartfelt expression of patriotism in upstate New York and interior California. However, we also found the flavor of the old hippie-like antiestablishmentarianism of the Vietnam era in leftist coastal California. It takes both kinds in a democracy, and it is a healthy expression of honest differences in opinion that is part of the free dialogue that makes the United States a vibrant country, a place where you really can say what you think, if you're brave enough and don't go beyond certain admittedly hazy areas of libel, slander, treason, and the like. Among our photographs was heartfelt folk art that was 100 percent supportive of America, some of which really was heartwarming. We saw similarly creative uses of the flag in California in contexts that questioned the sanity of our national leaders and our collective bellicose behavior. The creators of those expressions were also sincere Americans.

Public opinion during that period was documented in national surveys. The Pew Charitable Trusts reported that Americans were "united in their approval of the nation's leaders, paying rapt attention to news, and (nearly eight in ten) say they are willing to suffer thousands of military casualties in a protracted conflict to retaliate for last week's terrorist attacks." President Bush's approval, as measured by job performance, went from 51 percent a few weeks earlier to 80 percent immediately after the attacks. By October, Pew reported that the American public was "beginning to recover from the shock of the terrorist attacks" and "has little discomfort with the widespread expressions of patriotism and religious expression—just 8 percent say there has been too much showing of the flag, 10 percent believe there has been too much playing of patriotic songs, and 12 percent say the expressions of religious faith and prayer by politicians has been excessive." Republicans and white evangelical Protestants were most in favor of public patriotic and religious displays. At the same time, sizeable majorities felt open-minded about allowing dissidents to express their opposition with 71 percent open to allowing peaceful protests of military action and 75 percent saying the mass media should air views of those who blame U.S. policies for the terrorist attacks. However, the extent of open-mindedness varied by age, political party preference, and education. Older and less educated Republicans were less tolerant. A year later in 2002, Pew reported "many of the dramatic reactions of the public to the events of Sept. 11 have slowly faded" (http://www.pewtrusts.com). President Bush's approval rating had slipped to 60 percent. Only about 30 percent of the public rated military action as the most important response to the attacks, although the public continued to support the use of military action as a weapon in the war against terrorism, and growing criticism of the homeland defense initiative was noticed. In news media and nonpartisan polls conducted from September 2005 to February 2006, President Bush's overall job rating was down markedly. The approval minus the disapproval percentage responses ranged from −2 to −24 for 64 polls, with only one poll giving a positive (+3) difference. The percentage of approval for President Bush ranged from a low of 35 percent to a high of 50 percent, averaging 40.8 percent.[7]

By the end of March and the first part of April 2002 dissidents were among the American minority. The majority was represented by those who sought the 6,000 tickets issued daily by New York City, enabling them to visit a wooden observation platform that overlooked the site of the former World Trade Center Towers, known as "Ground Zero." Available at the South Street Seaport seven blocks away, tickets were free, issued on a "first-come, first-served" basis for half hour intervals. Tickets usually were spoken for by midday on weekends and late afternoon on weekdays. While the experience of being at the site itself was intensely emotional for most, Janice D'Arcy of the *Hartford Courant* found the wait between picking up the ticket and the designated time was often hours long. As a result, D'Arcy said, "What else to do but browse the shops or order a lobster roll at a seafood joint? It all feels too slick, considering the wretched destination."[8] A great color photograph by the *Hartford Courant* accompanied D'Arcy's article. It showed the skyscraper New York City skyline in the distance, lit up in the darkness. In the foreground, Rick Chupp of Bloomington, Indiana, hunches down to write a tribute message on the plywood of the structure, a tradition begun by former Mayor Rudy Giuliani when he was the first official visitor. The weather was cold. Chupp was wrapped in a garment that depicts at least five visible U.S. flags.

THE EVOLUTION OF FLAG DISPLAY ETIQUETTE

Does wrapping oneself in the flag conform to traditional flag etiquette? Those traditions are articulated in a variety of places. On Flag Day, June 14, for example, Ann Landers printed a letter by "Marilyn Rae in Ohio" that boils dos and don'ts of flag etiquette down to six principles (see also Quaife 1961):

> 1. When the flag becomes frayed and worn, replace it with a new flag, and destroy the old one by burning it in a dignified manner. 2. Display the flag only from sunrise to sunset, unless it is properly illuminated. 3. Never let the flag touch the ground. 4. Do not fly the flag in inclement weather, unless it is an all-weather flag. 5. The American flag should fly above any other flag on the staff. 6. When flying the flag at half-staff, first raise the flag quickly to the top, then lower it to the halfway mark. When lowering the flag, reverse this procedure. ("Display," 2002)[9]

Venerable sources of flag lore are in scout handbooks. The *Girl Scout Handbook*,[10] for example, instructed Girl Scouts in the mid-1950s that the flag stood for oneness in the nation. The thirteen stripes stood for the original thirteen states. Each star stood for a state. Red stood for valor, white for purity, and blue for justice. The handbook explained that Public Law 829 had set forth the rules for civilian use and display of the flag, followed by a brief enumeration similar to those repeated in the Ann Landers column. Additions include the stipulation that the flag should be raised rapidly and lowered slowly. When two or more national flags are displayed, they must be flown from separate poles of the same length and the flags should be the same size. If carried with another flag, the U.S. flag must be on the right and it must be the first to be picked up. In the company of three or more flags, the U.S. flag should be in the center. Hung on a wall, "the blue field should be uppermost and to the flag's own right. When it is hung against the wall with another flag, the flag of the United States should be at the spectator's left." Moreover, the flag must never be used as a drapery or cover. Objects should never be placed on the flag.

The gradual relaxation of flag etiquette, along with other prescribed mores in America's past (e.g., sexual modesty, bans on certain drug uses, courteous driving), has not occurred overnight since 9/11. Historic photographs from earlier in the twentieth century depict such flag uses as fabrics for hammocks and underwear. In and of itself, the flag *is* only fabric, of course. But as a symbol, as an icon, it used to mean something else. It was a symbol of pride for all Americans, not just a particular ideological wing. Recently, its depiction as a symbol of disgust for terrorists has given it an ideological slant that probably has alienated a significant portion of the population not subscribing exclusively to right-wing beliefs. Earlier, militant left-wingers accelerated an extreme right-wing interpretation of the flag. In the late 1960s and early 1970s, some rabid anti-war demonstrators chose to badly abuse the flag as a symbol of Establishment "Amerika," their actions duly covered in living color by the mass media. In our own day, the flag increasingly has come to connote a "bomb 'em back to the Stone Age" and a "kill 'em all now and let God sort 'em out" mentality, that is, when it isn't the backdrop for a cute little Hummel figurine with big bucks potential.

Therefore, we must consider more than the fabric flag. Syndicated columnist Cecil Bothwell wrote that the "mercantile aspect of the Bush war on terrorism is impossible to overlook. The local gas station sells patriotic t-shirts and posters with a "bulls-eye" on bin Laden's forehead. Hardware and drug stores have baskets full of lapel pins, key chain dangles, and plastic signs with suction cups for car window display—each bearing flags and slogans and crying eagles."[11] If the Founding Fathers had known how popular and profitable their creation was to become would they have "copyrighted" or "trademarked" their design? (The concept of exclusive rights to and protection of one's creation was not unfamiliar, although copyright and trademark per se did not exist then.) Or did the flag have an entirely different meaning for them? The answer to these questions will suggest how far the American icon has evolved.

We need to think carefully before treating the flag just as so much inventory for Capitalism, just so much pro-us and anti-them, just so much the private property of a certain political point of view. Domestically, the flag stands for all within the geographical boundaries of the United States of America. So the flag represents and celebrates that diversity and decency. Ricky Flores' photograph of three dirty, exhausted firefighters who had just raised the U.S. flag amidst the dirt, dust, rubble, smoke, and twisted steel of the World Trade Center ruins on September 12 (first published in *The Journal News*, Westchester County, New York) echoed the flag's majesty. However, unlike the Iwo Jima image, these men are seen from the photographer's perch above, not below, and they are static, not dynamic. It was not a victory image but a perseverance image, an image that portended many weary months and years ahead before things might be set right (Currie 2001).

In the year after 9/11, a public fatigue already had begun to set in. David Remnick and Hendrik Hertzberg (2002, 31) wrote, "This week, we remember the dead. It will be an overwhelming commemoration. Some of refined sensibility have complained in advance that the media will exploit this anniversary, that television commentators will wax fatuous, that people are tired of it all—tired of the anthems and the flags, tired of the invocations of '9/11,' tired of a certain kitsch, civic and commercial, that has attached itself to the event." They questioned whether a rush to war against terrorism and to neutralize weapons of mass destruction as advocated by president George W. Bush and his advisors represented true patriotism or whether a reasoned, thoughtful, nuanced, and thoroughly debated approach was the mark of real patriots. Now time has passed and the facts are clearer (there were no weapons of mass destruction in Iraq, for example). Since that first anniversary, public sentiment in support of the president and the war has steadily eroded.

How important is the flag? It is extremely important, especially during and immediately after significant events that provoke national and international crisis. Then, passions are emotional and

Figure 3.2

Route 89, Ithaca, New York, 2002. Copyright © by Harry Littell, 2007.

raw. Inflammatory and extreme rhetoric is heard, running rampant and uncensored. Some individuals literally wrap themselves in the flag or garb themselves in clothing bearing flag motifs. Their flag becomes a security blanket. With the passage of time, feelings about the flag generally become more reasoned but nonetheless salient and important. Months after the bombing of Pearl Harbor, leading to the U.S. entry into World War II, nearly three hundred U.S. magazine covers of July 1942 featured the flag in a visual representation (Kohn 2002). This rallying 'round the flag as if it is an almost sacred object is a commonly noted public opinion phenomenon that is early in crises (Baker and Oneal 2001; Edwards and Gallup 1990). In upstate New York shortly after 9/11, we found an automobile painted in a flag motif. The proud owner discussed the fresh paint job. He said he was unable to find a flag after experiencing the trauma of 9/11, so he decided to paint his car red, white, and blue, which took only a couple of hours. The car also sported a bumper sticker that announced to the world "Osama bin Laden can kiss my American ass." We saw a number of vehicles painted in flag motifs.

As seen in this image, the rally phenomenon is psychologically important. The activities involved allow the individual to use the senses—primarily tactile, olfactory, visual, and kinetic—to express powerful emotions and beliefs. Flag displays as symbols of rally also are socially important. Not only do they provide individuals with a personal outlet for patriotism and anger, they collectively signal to peers something about the dominance of those personal feelings. Thus, individual expressions ultimately might help to form public opinion and sentiment. Flags are an immediately recognizable and richly connotative visual sign of unity and identification, often interpreted as "all for one and one for all."

And while many who were opposed to U.S. policies and actions after 9/11 might have been intimidated by the "pro-war, pro-U.S. at all costs" interpretation placed on flag display, with time they seem to understand that the U.S. flag does not belong to one group or to one particular ideology. The *Ithaca Journal* expressed this well in a June 11, 2002, editorial about the flag before the first post-9/11 Flag Day: "We think flying a flag isn't about a lockstep mentality but a love for a nation with vast assets, huge flaws and another chance tomorrow to try and get it right. It's about what America could be, years from now, and where it has been, warts and all" ("New kind," 2002).

Notes

1. Retrieved February 7, 2007, from http://www.ushistory.org/betsy/flagtale.html.
2. See http://www.geocities.com/CapitolHill/4182.html (retrieved June 24, 2002) and http://bensguide.gpo.gov/3-5/symbols/pledgeallegiance.html (retrieved June 24, 2002).
3. Retrieved February 6, 2006, from http://www.esquilax.com/flag/history.html; http://www.flagburning.org.html; http://www.law.umkc.edu/faculty/projects/ftrails/conlaw/flagburning.html; http://www.aclu.org/freespeech/flag/index.html; and http://www.salzi.com/whatever/003585 .html.
4. Retrieved January 18, 2006, from http://www.spanamwar.com/dewey.html.
5. NY FIREFIGHTER SEPTEMBER 11, 2001. Paid advertisement found in the *Ithaca Journal*, *dated* June 6, 2002.

References

Allen, T. B., ed. 1975. *We Americans*. Washington, DC: National Geographic Society.

Arbus, D. 2003. *Diane Arbus revelations*. New York: Random House.

Arbus, D., and M. Israel, eds. 1972. *Diane Arbus*. New York: Aperture Monograph.

Baer, J. 1992. *The pledge of allegiance, a centennial history, 1892–1992*. Annapolis, MD: Free State Press.

Baker, W. D., and J. R. Oneal. 2001. Patriotism or opinion leadership: The nature and origins of the rally 'round the flag effect. *Journal of Conflict Resolution* 45:61–87.

Bradley, J., and R. Powers. 2000. *Flags of our fathers*. New York: Bantam.

Canby, G., and L. Balderston. 1909. *The evolution of the American flag*. Philadelphia: Ferris and Leach.

Currie, P. 2001. *The best of Gannett 2001*. McLean, VA: Gannett.

Dam, J. M. 2000. *Red, white, and blue murder*. New York: Walker and Company.

Display the Old Glory with pride on Flag Day. 2002. *Ithaca Journal*, June 14.

Edwards, III, G. C., and A. M. Gallup. 1990. *Presidential approval: A sourcebook*. Baltimore, MD: Johns Hopkins University Press.

Ellis, R. J. 2005. *To the flag: The unlikely history of the pledge of allegiance*. Lawrence: University Press of Kansas.

Fow, J. H. 1908. *The true story of the American flag*. Philadelphia: J. Campbell.

Frank, R. 1958. *The Americans*. New York: Grove Press.

———. 1983. *Robert Frank*. Paris: Centre National de la Photographie.

Fulton, M. 1988. *Eyes of time: Photojournalism in America*. Boston: Little, Brown.

Glance at the cult of the flag. 1992. *Ithaca Journal*, July 4.

Goldberg, V., and R. Silberman. 1999. *American photography: A century of images*. San Francisco: Chronicle Books.

Grand old flag. 1993. *Ithaca Journal*, June 12.

Guenter, S. M. 1990. *The American flag, 1777–1924: Cultural shifts from creation to codification*. Rutherford, NJ: Fairleigh Dickinson University Press.

Hinrichs, K., and D. Hirasuna. 2001. *Long may she wave: A graphic history of the American flag*. Berkeley, CA: Ten Speed Press.

Jones, E. L. 1998. Iwo Jima. In *Eyewitness to America*. New York: Vintage Books, 489–90.

Josephy, A. M., Jr., ed. 1964. *The American Heritage history of World War I*. New York: American Heritage.

Kohn, J. K. 2002. Stars and stripes. *Country Living* (July): 77–78, 80.

Lacayo, R., and G. Russell. 1995. *Eyewitness: 150 years of photojournalism*. New York: Time Books.

Leekley, S., and J. Leekley. 1978. *Moments: The Pulitzer Prize photographs*. New York: Crown Publishers.

Levitas, M. 1969. *America in crisis*. New York: Ridge Press Book.

Mastai, B., and M. D. Mastai. 1973. *The stars and the stripes*. New York: Knopf.

National Geographic. 1917. October. http://www.nationalgeographic.com/ngm/flashback/9707.html (accessed June 24, 2002).

Flashback. 2002. *National Geographic*. http://www7.nationalgeographic.com/ngm/flashback/0207.html (accessed January 17, 2006).

New kind of Flag Day: Considering what America could be. 2002. *Ithaca Journal*, June 11.

Norback, C. T., and M. Gray. 1980. *The world's great news photos 1840–1980*. New York: Crown Publishers.

Novotny, A. 1975. The world enters America. In *We Americans*. Washington, DC: National Geographic Society, 259–77.

O'Donnell, M. 1956. *The new engine whistles*. Evanston, IL: Row, Peterson, and Company.

Passion of Old Glory. 1992. *Ithaca Journal*, April 24.

Pilgrimage to heal. Genuine sentiment overpowers opportunities at Ground Zero. 2002. *Ithaca Journal*, April 6.

Quaife, M. M., M. J. Weig, and R. E. Appleman, R. E. 1961. *The history of the United States flag, from the revolution to the present, including a guide to its use and display*. New York: Harper and Row.

Remnick, D., and H. Hertzberg. 2002. A year after. *New Yorker*. September 16: 31–33.

Sonneborn, L. 2004. *The pledge of allegiance: The story behind our patriotic promise*. Philadelphia: Chelsea Clubhouse.

Tucker, A. W., ed. 1986. *Robert Frank: New York to Nova Scotia*. Boston: Little, Brown.

CHAPTER 4

A SMALL WORLD—AND ITS FLAGS—IN A MUCH BIGGER ONE

Anne-Marie Obajtek-Kirkwood

THE AMERICAN FLAG, PAST, AND PRESENT

Paraphrasing Gertrude Stein: "a flag is a flag is a flag," or is it? As a rose is not just a flower, the U.S. flag is not just a piece of cloth with fifty white stars in a blue field and thirteen alternate red and white horizontal stripes. The dictionary definition of the object runs thus: "A piece of cloth or similar material, typically oblong or square, attachable by one edge to a pole or rope, and used as the symbol or emblem of a country or institution or as a decoration during public festivities: *the American flag.*" The American flag is a sign that ties the private to the national and collective in a number of ways: it represents the country and its values, it is flown to celebrate its past events and mark patriotic festivities. It occupies a special place in American history and hearts. As such it has been protected by flag desecration statutes, applied in 1897 by the states of Illinois, Pennsylvania, and South Dakota and in 1932 by all the states. As a result, we have a more historic and "legal" definition of the flag, dating from 1897: "Under the model flag desecration law, the term 'flag' was defined to include any flag, standard, ensign, or color, or any representation of such made of any substance whatsoever and of any size that evidently purported to be said flag or a picture or representation thereof, upon which shall be shown the colors, stars and stripes in any number, or by which the person seeing the same without deliberation may believe the same to represent the flag of the United States."[1]

Nowadays, it is still strictly controlled by flag etiquette of which presidents in power are sometimes ignorant,[2] or institutions like the U.S. Postal Service in its issuing of American flag stamps.[3] USHistory.org, the site created and hosted by the Independence Hall Association in Philadelphia, mentions the Flag Code: "The laws relating to the flag of the United States of America are found in detail in the United States Code. Title 4, Chapter 1 pertains to the flag; Title 18, Chapter 33, Section 700 regards criminal penalties for flag desecration; Title 36, Chapter 3 pertains to patriotic customs and observances. These laws were supplemented by Executive Orders and Presidential Proclamations."[4]

USHistory.org also gives an updated definition of the flag: "The flag of the United States is any flag of the United States, or any part thereof, made of any substance of any size, accurate or not, that is recognized as a flag by the reasonable observer[5]." The site proceeds to illustrate this visually by providing examples of what can be considered as a flag, such as the logo of the Bank of America, or, a child's watercolor painting of a rectangular surface with one pale blue star in a darker blue upper left corner surrounded by three horizontal white and red stripes. It also refers the reader to the Library of Congress and the more recent Flag Protection Act of 2005 introduced in Senate by Senators Benett and Clinton, which holds a similar definition of the flag: "In this section, the term 'flag of the United States' means any flag of the United States, or any part thereof, made of any substance, in any size, in a form that is commonly displayed as a flag and that would be taken to be a flag by the reasonable observer" (SEC. 3 Sec. 700 [a]).[6]

SYMBOLIC AND OTHER MEANINGS ATTACHED TO THE AMERICAN FLAG

Section 2 (a)(1) of the SEC also states the symbolic meaning of the flag: "the flag of the United States is a unique symbol of national unity and represents the values of liberty, justice, and equality that make this Nation an example of freedom unmatched throughout the world." As meaning attached to the sign, USHistory.org gives some flag quotes[7] similar to the preceding one, for example, from Robert C. Winthrop (1809–94), Senator from Massachusetts: "Our flag is our national ensign, pure and simple, behold it! Listen to it! Every star has a tongue, every stripe is articulate"; General Colin Powell, May 1999: "Americans revere their flag as a symbol of the Nation"; president Woodrow Wilson, 1917: "The flag, which we honor and under which we serve, is the emblem of our unity, our power, our thought and purpose as a nation. It has no other character than that which we give it from generation to generation. The choices are ours"; echoed by Steve Lonegan, mayor of Bogota, New Jersey: "The true things that bind us together as neighbors and community is our belief in the American flag and our common language."[8]

President Wilson, by stating that the flag "has no other character than that which we give it from generation to generation," also points to meanings that can be attached to the flag other than the widely accepted or traditionally assumed ones and we can illustrate this by other quotations from the very same site:

"We have two American flags always: one for the rich and one for the poor. When the rich fly it, it means that things are under control; when the poor fly it, it means danger, revolution, anarchy" (Henry Miller, *The Air-Conditioned Nightmare*).

"If the flag needs protection at all, it needs protection from members of Congress who value the symbol more than the freedoms that the flag represents" (Rep. Jerrold Nadler, 2005).

"Patriotic societies seem to think that the way to educate school children in a democracy is to stage bigger and better flag-saluting" (S. I. Hayakawa).

"It seems like the less a statesman amounts to, the more he loves the flag" (Frank McKinney Hubbard).

"A person gets from a symbol the meaning he puts into it" (U.S. Supreme Court).

Consent on the meaning of the flag does not therefore exclude some more personal interpretation, criticism, meanings, or uses that are more genuine to a certain time in history, as President Wilson indicated. From all the various quotes, it is obvious that the flag-signified varies, is somewhat floating, and that it never totally corresponds to the signifier in a one on one stable equation. As Blonsky puts it, "we can try to grasp the culture's bloodstream as sign *and* secret practices, as the language of our rationality and also silent, infinitesimal procedures. Semiotics must not weigh on a part (whether literature, politics, commerce, or social life) without awareness of the flow of the process in which that part was immersed and within which it lived."[9]

FLAGS IN SEASIDE PARK, NEW JERSEY, AUGUST 2005

I now turn to a particular place and time, the small world of Seaside Park, New Jersey, the second week of August 2005. This seaside community of Central Ocean County comprises a residential resort and town (of 2,263 residents year-round,[10] mainly white[11]) with a few shops, a beach and a mile and a half ocean front boardwalk. It is home to Island Beach State Park (acquired by the state in 1953), an undeveloped almost ten-mile long beach, bordered by the Atlantic Ocean on the east and Barnegat Bay on the west, one of the thirty-nine New Jersey State Parks. Seaside Park boardwalk seamlessly joins the amusement pier, arcades, and rides of Seaside Heights. Seaside Park advertises itself as a family resort and families do flock there every summer. Politically speaking, for the 2004 presidential elections, according to unofficial vote totals, Bush received 143,797 and Kerry 92,621 votes in Ocean County[12].

Why did I choose Seaside Park? I had spent some vacations there in the past and had decided to retreat to the pleasures of sun and sea again after a year's work in academia, thinking I would enter a totally different world that was cut off from my daily preoccupations and life. The *2005–2006 Visitor's Guide* (to Central Ocean County) available at the local real estate agencies soon dashed this illusion. It was indicative of what bore its distinctive mark all over Seaside Park (and Seaside Heights) then. On the brochure cover, above a landscape of sand and sea with gently breaking waves and two hovering seagulls, the top third of the cover space, showed only a tiny triangle of the sky—the rest was being occupied by the American flag unfurling in the wind. The beach and the whole resort were thus, pictorially and symbolically, protected by the flag and the values attached to it. This actually did not stop with brochures but could be physically perceived all over town and beach. The place was so awash with flags that one might have thought that it was the eve of July 4. The pro-liferation of flags might then be due to some extent to people not having bothered to remove their Independence Day flags and deco-rations, but their prevalence could not be explained away by just this factor, since proliferation there was indeed.

Walking along Central Avenue (the main thoroughfare), one could not fail noticing flags by restaurants, souvenir shops, a general store, and a bakery; flag festoons were all along the front and side streets of a bait-store, which also had a flag pole, public buildings (on a pole near a church entrance, by the police station and flag stickers at the rear of some police cars), at every public entrance of the boardwalk to the beach, flying high above the two biggest park-ing-lots in the State Park, and painted on the municipal water-tank towering over the city and sending its beacon all around. Business or semi-public waste-containers of one particular manufacturer came from the factory with a flag stuck to them. Paper flags were also hanging side-by-side on a string along the inside walls of a super-market. Even in a restaurant, the paper tablecloth had a flag pattern.

Side streets did not lack their portion of flags either, in all pos-tures and positions: at the top of flag poles, several houses in a row at times, American flag alone or adjacent to an Italian flag, on smaller poles fastened to house-fronts, onto the top of stairs, near banis-ters, on deck-fences, growing in flowerpots (when the flag was not recalled by red, white and blue petunias growing in a white pot), held in the hands of dwarf-fishermen, and of standing or perched Uncles Sam on fences as weather-wanes. They also draped deck-rail-ings, hung down on porch-fences, at times towels with flag motifs were drying on deck-railings in lieu of the real object, or on clothes-lines in yards. Flags flew in the wind as wind-socks, appeared in yards as parasols or on ice-buckets. Made out of cloth, or plastic, some would be quite lowly and small, planted at a corner of the front yard, or stuck to windows as stickers, or, if larger, by suction cups inside the house. One house-entrance proudly displayed a thick, semi-cir-cular flag as a doormat, oblivious of the fact that "the flag should never touch anything beneath it, such as the ground."[13]

It was especially impossible not to notice them all the more because many houses had more than one flag displayed, in a com-bination of flags— on poles, smaller flags on balconies, or flags in windows, and on house-doors, or on balconies and flower pots— with great inventiveness and imagination. Sometimes houses already adorned with flags stressed the national symbol also on cars parked in their driveways. Repetition did not exclude variation on the theme: a wooden red, white and blue eagle attached to the house-front substituted for the flag. Redundancy in the theme itself was noticeable: towels had the Statue of Liberty or the eagle again super-imposed on the flag-background; one house flew a small flag on a pole which also had a yellow ribbon imprinted across it, and, further in the driveway, a heart in the shape of a wooden flag plus beneath, fastened to it, a yellow ribbon AND and a white plate with red letters saying: "God bless our troops." Such combinations could also be found as two big magnets stuck to a restaurant cash-desk, a circular one with the flag as a garland around it and the mention at the top of "Support our Our Troops" plus the eagle in the middle, and the other a flag with "God bless America." This redundancy was also found on car-stickers. Strangely enough, two of the marinas appeared "sober" in contrast as they evidenced way fewer flags and flag-insignia: Could this be a sign of class-distinction?

Flag-manufacturers had a field day and so did designers and manufacturers of all the flag-bearing household goods and souvenirs that covered Seaside Park. One souvenir shop displayed flag paper napkins, pot holder gloves, ashtrays, rubber thongs, teddy bears dressed in flag-pattern cloth, porcelain figurines with flags in their attires, towels with in-laid "flag" bikinis, flag knife-handles, flag-painted on wooden toy trucks, a flag design on soft balls the color of the flag, plastic and cloth, small and large flags, American flag kits, flags embroidered above on cap-visors, light-houses with flags, beach canvas-chairs in flag colors with a flag design on their backs, dogs with flag hats, vanity car plates with a flag background and and "Support Our Troops" in yellow at their bottoms, metallic, old-style lunch-boxes with the flag as pattern, wooden coat-hangers with a painted beach scene, and a young girl sitting on a white and red striped towel, wearing a white and blue swimsuit,—in short, there was a sea of blue, white, and red of quite questionable taste, that was bordering on kitsch and trash.

As for Seaside Heights, a souvenir shop on the boardwalk specialized in flags from various countries, of all shapes and sizes. The prevailing one was the American flag, but the old Confederate flag (with or without the eagle) was also for sale, as were the words "Red Neck" in flag colors, in metal or plastic stickers—examples of a particular vein of patriotism, which were not so benign or humorous as the type encountered so far.

Magnetic bows as commonly stuck on cars, SUVs, and pickups, could be purchased at the resort. They ranged from the yellow ribbon to one half yellow-half flag colors, or one entirely in the flag colors, each stating "Support Our Troops." Some yellow bows had the knot of the bow in a heart shape saying: "I ❤ USA" or "Bring 'em home safe!," this heart shape being left in the middle of the bow, or stuck separately from the bow. Other inscriptions on the flag-colored ribbon were: "Proud to be American," "God Bless America," or "Freedom isn't free." There were also black, or half yellow-half black bows with "MIA/POW Never Forgotten" on them. Some rectangular American flag stickers bore phrases such as: "Support America" or "Don't mess with the U.S." Another souvenir shop on the same boardwalk offered different flag-decorated items still: baseballs, scarves, lots of towels, sweat and t-shirts with the above common inscriptions again, or variants such as "Born in the USA," "These colors [those of the flag] do not run," and "All give some/ Some give all."

Car-plates were not only from New Jersey primarily but also from the neighboring states of New York, Pennsylvania, Delaware, Maryland, and occasionally from farther away, like Kansas and Ohio—or abroad: Québec. Cars were adorned with ribbon and flag stickers, stuck to their rears—one or more—profusion there abounding too—very often one yellow "Support Our Troops" ribbon juxtaposed to a flag ribbon. Quite a few vehicles had stickers on their sides as well, or affixed to their radio antennas, and some SUVs had flag pictures imprinted on the cover of their spare-wheels, obviously a single sticker must not have been deemed strong enough to carry the message. Some others must have forgotten that the year was 2005 since they still advertised their choice for the 2004 presidential team, Bush and Cheyney on a flag background, or a "W '0 4" (also with a flag sticker); there were no Democrat past-choice stickers in sight. Others yet made sure everybody would know their progeny's military employment, for example: "My daughter is in the U.S. Air Force" with the official Department of the Air Force logo.

Pickup trucks, SUVs and even Hummers, being of course bigger than sedans and conceived for more "virile" tasks, found it necessary to be overtly redundant in their national emblem and slogan variations and also more aggressive in the size of what they affixed: a black Hummer's owner affixed a big fish-shaped flag sticker; an SUV had a flag metallic frame round its car-plate with: "Proud to be American," another version of this "pride" was noticeable on an SUV with a flag and "Power of Pride" sticker. The most conspicuous signs (in their sheer size) were found on three dark-colored pickups, black or dark-brown, the color of the vehicles making the vivid signs stand out all the more. One had a big flag sticker stuck all across the part of the hood just above the headlights, another had a flag and superimposed eagle stuck to the entire surface of the rear-window as permanent sunscreen, while the third one had a removable sunscreen flag with big letters "United We Stand" in the front window, plus, as if that was not noticeable enough, a flag at the top of the truck radio-antenna. The epitome of flaunting, blatant, aggressive patriotism appeared one evening when a huge black pickup, perched on enormous tires just drove in—as if out of nowhere—across, and out of a big parking-lot in Island Beach State Park, with enormous canvas flags on each side of the cabin and one on the top, horn-hooting, faster than the allowed speed in a parking-lot, and a grin on the driver's face, which seemed to say: "mission accomplished."

In contrast to this collection of signs, only two were ever found presenting an opposite message and paraphrasing two of the above expressions as: "These Colors Do Not Run the World" and "United We Sit / For World Peace."

Sand and sea were not bereft of what was observable on land, though flags and their derivatives were much less prevalent on the beach. Nevertheless towels with flags eagles, Statues of Liberty and other patriotic signs were spread on the ground, folded as markers of territories on a beach chair, drying under parasols, waiting to receive or surround flag-patterned t-shirts, swim-trunks, and swimsuits for children and adults. There was a more provocative turn at times too, like a white bikini worn by a teenage girl who had the "primo" gang hand sign as a flag, on the right-hand breast and left-hand buttock. The whole beach gear was not out of synch, starting with canoes that are usually very bright colors now printed in slices of blue, white, and red. And then there were flags in the shape of kites, boogie boards, beach balls, and adhesive bandages for the little stings and misfortunes. Amidst all this, a parasol stood out that was not harboring the Old Glory colors but sticking out with the Blue Angels'[14] blue and yellow plane logo on a blue wedge of color alternating with

Figure 4.1
Island Beach State Park, 2005. Copyright ® Anne-Marie Obajtek-Kirkwood, 2007

an acidic green wedge that displayed Boeing F/A-18 Hornets darting in their famous four-plane diamond formation.

Behind this U.S. Navy and Marine Corps "goodwill ambassador"[15] and recruiting agent, there was another reality creeping in—not just a benign patriotic celebration and demonstration but also the military reminding of its first and foremost purpose: war-making, incongruous in what was a summer leisure setting.

BEACH ILLUSIONS AND REALITY

By choosing a seaside resort, I had been nurturing the naïve dream of "a counter-world," that is "a world in a state of rupture, explicitly valorizing reversal, and, at least in appearance, the rejection of taboos, inequalities, and other obligatory and coerced behaviors generated by urban society."[16] I wished for a simpler world where my main needs would be swimming, resting, eating, sleeping, and reading for pleasure—a kind of decompression chamber, retreating, as "an émigré from real life,"[17] to an a-historical world, a world preceding any conflict, a kind of Edenic place and state. After all, isn't swimming, diving, floating, or just wading into the sea synonymous with slipping more or less out of the world? Though this dream was to some extent indulged in and lived as reality, I also had to recognize that Seaside Park in August 2005 evidenced this paradox of displaying both the typical features of a seaside-resort and a new historical reality through its prevalent "sea" of red, blue, and white, not noticeable in July 2000. The omnipresence of these signs in a place of relaxation and break from daily routine was all the more striking as current political preoccupations or interests would have been expected to take a little back-step, but it was not so. Vacationers seemed to bring their daily interests and worries to the resort and beach, and I was also critical of it all, because: "the summer vacationer neither changes the world nor changes worlds. He starts the world anew; he reifies it, restoring the infraordinary features of his life for the span of a few weeks, following the rhythm of his desires."[18]

Seaside Park seemed thus to reproduce, through the display and use of various visible signs, the affirmation of patriotism and its values, the pride of being American, and an inherent trust in the well-grounded aims and designs of the U.S. government at home and abroad. On a minor key, it even seemed to mimic the real war raging in the Middle East: every family came and occupied some ground—some plot of sand on the beach—and defined their territory through the ritual of planting "in a foundational gesture . . . [their] umbrella like a flag"[19] or stretching down a big towel or setting some chairs as centerpieces and points of rally for family members and friends. This was their "theater of operations" and their "camp," which would determine relationships with beach-neighbors. "This ritual and tactical dimension of seaside customs."[20] could also be couched in geopolitical, diplomatic, or military terms (trench war or blitzkrieg, strategy of annexation or guerilla tactics, etc.) with its sentinels, guardians, and defenders of the family-determined space that would resist "external aggressions" and keep "vigilant surveillance and maintenance."[21] "Conquest" also seemed to take other forms, like a bather alone on the shore, facing the ocean, a boogie-board decorated with the American flag on his flank, ready to stride the waves and maintain dominance at sea.

These simulacra of conquest and installation at the beach were geared at producing signs and meanings in order to reinstall oneself as an individual, a family, or a group. To define themselves in this resort setting, Seaside Park vacationers not only obeyed beach rituals and practices but also external signs imported there on cars, houses, streets, and smaller and more personal belongings. If war was somewhat parodied by beach rituals, activities, and vocabulary, patriotic signs and slogans alluded to it too, all over the resort but more on land than beach. They echoed the America-at-war spirit of the time by their repetition, variations, size, and connotations, as previously described, through various messages, from the benign and sympathetic understanding of U.S. troops' plight in Iraq or Afghanistan to the conquering assertiveness and aggressiveness of war beyond American borders, to pure chauvinism and self-ascertained superiority. The fact that the overall majority of these signs were pro-nation, pro-president, and pro-war created a community of people who share the same ideals and thus a sense of homogeneity and security among people from various walks of life, most often unknown to each other. If there were dissenters, and in all likelihood there must have been, they were not expressing themselves with overt signs. With only two antiwar stickers spotted throughout the entire week, one would be led to think that antiwar sentiment was expressed at degree zero.

FLAGS AND SOME OF THEIR MEANINGS IN SEASIDE PARK

What to make of all the flags, messages on flags, and flag-imprinted objects found in Seaside Park and Island Beach State Park? What was their meaning? The American flag has visually, aesthetically, a very pleasant design and lively colors. Because of its importance in the history of this country as a national emblem and the values attached to it, it comes as no surprise that it is so cherished and celebrated. All the more the laws of the land make it very accessible and displayable all year round to Americans, which is not the case of national flags in many other countries where they are reserved to public buildings and just displayed on official and commemorative occasions. Joy, celebration, and festive occasions are associated with the American flag, and its presence in Seaside Park under various shapes and guises undoubtedly reflected all these aspects while not discarding the worship for what it stands for.

As could also be observed in public and private places, the flag sells well, just like flag-patterned objects of use (clothing, beachgear) or remembrance (souvenirs). The commodification and marketing of the flag and American patriotism seemed to have reached an apex, but the flag turned commodity was also debased to the rank of disposable goods (adhesive bandages, paper napkins, and so on).[22]

Why did flags suddenly have such an impact on the American landscape, on both public and domestic spaces? To understand the display in Seaside Park in 2005, we need to go back to the past and the horrible tragedy of the collapse of the Twin Towers on September 11, 2001. John Napier[23] gives us the following explanation in context:

> On September 11, 2001, America dusted off its national flag and pressed it into service as an urgent symbol of patriotic solidarity. As the unofficial capital of American skepticism, New York probably had the least number of flags per capita of any city in the United States; the week following September 11, it was impossible to walk a few paces down a Brooklyn side street or Manhattan avenue without encountering Old Glory scotch-taped at half-mast to a car antenna or hastily inserted into a mannequin's hand in a store display . . . In the country at large, red, white, and blue burst forth from townhouses and trailer parks, and with it that most precious of political commodities, national unity.[24]

The flag through that horrific catastrophe, came to symbolize patriotic solidarity and unity, and its presence extended to many quarters, including TV screens and the press, as Catherine S. Manegold noticed at the beginning of 2002:

> In the somber mood of unity that followed the terrorist attacks of last September, Americans took refuge in a grim confetti of red, white, and blue. Even those covering the news caught the spirit. Headlines struck a note of aggressive nationalism not seen since World War II. Flags unexpectedly began to flash on reporters' lapels and on television screens that carried pictures of those two great towers falling. Reporters and editors who did not quickly take the mood sometimes found their jobs in jeopardy. In the first few weeks after the attacks, several journalists were fired from their jobs after questioning the president's first actions or talking of peace when those in power spoke of war.[25]

Manegold anticipated consequences of what she deemed an out-of-place patriotism in journalism and subsequent dire issues that the management of terrorism could raise and that did turn out for the worse:

> Some debates already rage. Should we remake the laws regarding immigration and detention in the aftermath of this tremendous tragedy? Shall we use secret military tribunals to try suspected terrorists, or move them through the existing legal channels that have served us well through history? Is there justification for the use of "unusual means" of getting at the truth from those in prison, or should our standing laws and civil protections hold a greater sway, as they have always done?
>
> There will be more hard choices. If George Bush is right, that we have just begun a war that is likely to take years to win, then we have only started to grapple with all the complicated legal and moral tangles such a war will present. With that in mind, what does it tell our citizens, our visitors, our critics, if those debates take place behind a veil of stars and stripes?[26]

Unfortunately her awareness and worries have not been those of the American population at large. On October 7, 2001, war against al-Qaeda bases in Afghanistan started, and in March 2003 war against the Iraqi regime followed. Americans responded to al-Qaeda's September 11 attack with a proliferation of flags reaffirming national pride and large support for the undertaken warfare as President Bush's reelection in 2004 confirmed. The proliferation of flags at Seaside Park at the beginning of August 2005 is in-line with this overall patriotic, proud, and supportive position.

Deconstructing Some Flag Use and Flagged-Slogans from Seaside Park

Flags and their slogans get the meaning we put into them. As signs they can be considered bearers of accepted, widespread opinion and ideology, even ideological trickery at times, "they can and do deceive us about the world's condition,"[27] and also "lie . . . and *act on people*."[28]

The signs at Seaside Park may be interpreted in the commonly accepted sense, but they can also have a meaning of which their owners are unaware. Signs always escape individual will or collective signification. Saussure insisted on collective signification as their essential feature albeit the one people are least aware of at first sight.[29] Thus when people in Seaside Park in 2005—similar in this to the rest of the country since 2001—painted the seaside resort in blue, red, and white, they meant it as a sign of love for the United States, solidarity, and renewed commitment to democracy. However the volume and presence of the national emblem bordered on frenzy and ignorance. On July 4, 2003, Tony Norman wrote in the Pittsburgh *Post Gazette*: "In the hierarchy of the sacred, nothing enflames the American imagination quite like the flag, the most ubiquitous of our national religious symbols. . . . [T]he star-spangled banner comes saddled with mythologies most Americans feel comfortable pledging undying fealty to, but can't be bothered to familiarize themselves with."[30] Norman here uses some very strong terms relating to the flag, listing it as "one of our national religious symbols." "Religion" in connection with the flag having already been encountered earlier: "The true things that bind us together as neighbors and community is our belief in the American flag."[31] The United States values separation of Church and State but the choice of terms in these instances reveals a slippage—the religious has "contaminated" the secular. This, in a way should come as no surprise, as Marvin states: "Americans traditionally regard the nation-state as the domain of unassailable force and religion, as the domain of unassailable truth. This separation of faith and force is markedly unstable and collapses completely in wartime."[32] She analyzes nationalism as "the most powerful religion in the United States,"[33] its "true God being the nation-state."[34] Drawing on René Girard's *Violence and the Sacred* and expanding on the notion of religious and civil sacrifice, Marvin presents the flag in parallel to the Christian crucifix, to be treated with deference and awe, "as the sacred object of the religion of patriotism," worship is being reinforced by all the rules governing its handling. It follows that "the soldier carries his flag into battle as a sign of his willingness to die, just as Jesus carried his cross to show his willingness to die."[35] Extending the parallel, she terms war as a "large-scale ritual sacrifice" and the military as "the priestly class," which trains the sacrificial lambs. When threat occurs from the outside, there must be ritual victims of the nation threatened who "live apart in monastic orders that discipline and purify themselves for ultimate sacrifice."[36] The sacrifice accomplished then solves the crisis and reconsolidates the group, and thus Marvin adds: "That is why we die for the flag and commit our children to do so."[37] Civil religion thus manages to sanctify killing in the name of state imperatives and cohesion of the nation,[38] which religion per se cannot, according to the tenth commandment: "Thou shalt not kill."

Lila Lipscomb's flag display and veneration illustrate this flag worshipping. Asked by Michael Moore if she considered herself a proud American, she answered: "Absolutely. I'm an extremely proud American. I think I am probably more proud than the average Joe. When I put my flag out, I can't allow it to touch the ground, because I know the lives that were lost and the blood that was shed so that I could be here and have a flag." Asked then how often she displayed the flag, she mentioned she started when her daughter was in Desert Storm (1991 war against Iraq) and has since displayed the same flag and the same yellow ribbons "every single day, every single day."[39]

From this glorified, quasi-religious but also very nationalistic and militaristic dimension of the flag, we now come back to Norman who deploring, in the same article, the lack of true democratic commitment on the part of Americans, especially at the voting booth, added: "The proliferation of flags after the agony of Sept. 11 should've been a sign of our renewed resolve to truly embody the values we've paid so much lip service to over two centuries, but it wasn't. Are there truths we consider self-evident? If so, what are they? Are we using the opportunities provided by this struggle against terrorism and crypto-religious fascism to advance our civilization or are we undermining it in a haze of patriotic fervor meant to mask our fear?"[40]

Viewed in this light, the use of the flag is somewhat less glorious and does not refer to such a genuine patriotic sentiment, rather it refers to one of masking fear, finding strength and security in numbers, in the "we" that somehow automatically opposes "them." The flag in this sense identifies and unites citizens against others. It becomes a sign that both identifies and unites but also antagonizes.

Beyond the obvious September 11 trauma, Angelika Bammer sees in the very compulsion of its repetition, another fear or trauma—that of the American nation not being able perhaps to stand together and united, as it is claims:

> [T] his fear is about our very united-ness itself, a fear not of others and the harm they might inflict on us, but of ourselves and the harm we routinely inflict on one another, particularly on those of us marked as different in some way. . . . Perhaps the flags express the fear that under such pressure, we might just fracture along the fault lines of our differences, not standing united, but facing off.[41]

Samuel Huntington, grappling with the notion of American identity, recalls the central, quasi-religious role of the American flag in nation building: "Since the Civil War, Americans have been a flag-oriented people. The Stars and Stripes has the status of a religious icon and is a more central symbol of national identity for Americans than their flags are for peoples of other nations. "[42] He confirms that never had it been so omnipresent as it has been since September 11. This ubiquity was to him a healthy sign: "The flags were physical evidence of the sudden and dramatic rise in the salience of national identity for Americans compared to their other identities."[43] But the issue raised by Bammer about the cohesion of the American nation or a national American first identity for Huntington does persist. Huntington emphasizes it in the first chapter of *Who are we?* undermining the strength of the American flag as a "central symbol of national identity" he had previously stressed:

> The post-September 11 flags symbolized America, but they did not convey any meaning of America. Some national flags such as the tricolor, the Union Jack, or Pakistan's green flag with its star and crescent,

say something significant about the identity of the country they represent. The explicit visual message of the Stars and Stripes is simply that America is a country that originally had thirteen and currently has fifty states. Beyond that, Americans, and others, can read into the flag any meaning they want. The post-September 11 proliferation of flags may well evidence not only the intensified salience of national identity to Americans but also their uncertainty as to the substance of that identity.[44]

The fact that Huntington assesses the American flag so differently and contradictorily illustrates again how the meaning of the sign can fluctuate.

Flags and their derivatives in stickers and slogans might also be a way of confronting the fear about U.S. loss of safety and its vulnerability fully apparent since September 11, a fear which lingers onto today, "with its ongoing sense of helplessness, humiliation, anger, fear and grief." The disappearance of the myth of American invulnerability "has left us with a sense of how small we really are."[45] Sklarew's psychoanalytical interpretation of the ubiquitous flag is that the "the proliferation of flags and signs asking that 'God Bless America' signifies patriotism, solidarity, and power against this new awareness of fragility. Like the lamb's blood on the doorposts described in Exodus which signaled the angel of death to pass over Jewish homes and spare the firstborn, symbols such as flags are also amulets. The implied message—we have no evil in us; we are the good, holy, loving ones—is an appeal against evil forces, including the projected 'evil' within us that we fear could turn against us."

He thus characterizes American subsequent course of action in the light of "when an individual or a political entity cannot mourn and bear responsibility for failure, it may attempt to inflict guilt, helplessness, and humiliation onto another."[46]

The use of the American flag in Seaside Park conveys conflicting messages not mutually exclusive and often not so conscious in their users' mind. Slogans and catch phrases, most of the time also set against a flag background, bear multiple meanings, too. Though their obvious and less obvious messages are multi-layered, for the sake of clarity, those found in Seaside Park and Island Beach State Park will be summed up into three main categories.

The first one is the "God bless" category, with "God Bless America," and "God Bless Our Troops," which can be interpreted as "amulets" warding off evil or helping to cope with fear. This constant obsession on a God showering its blessings on America or its military can be also be viewed as Americans claiming monopoly on God's blessings, annexing Him as an all American deity—in short, making Him a nationalistic God.[47]

The second is the "Support" category with "Support America," "Support Our Troops," and kindred injunctions about the troops: "Bring 'em home safe," "MIA/POW Never Forgotten," or displays of patriotic duty and sacrifice: "My daughter is in the US Air Force" and, "All give some/Some give all." Here again, the "Support Our Troops" sign does not lead itself to a single interpretation. Any human being can support the troops from a basic humanitarian approach. In the case of families, support can mean sending their sons or some of their family members in Iraq, messages of love and, comfort, and parcels, but also, alas, for an army that is the first in the world, buying for and sending its insufficiently equipped soldiers adequate anti-bullet vests, or GPS units, which should not be a family task. Support can equate feeling for all these youths and what they go through, in their daily physical exposure and witnessing of horror, but this support should not stop with those on the battlefield. Sympathy should also include soldiers who return, burnt, maimed, with limbs missing, maimed in their flesh for the rest of their days, with all the consequences that this entails, or psychologically damaged, sometimes beyond probable recovery (some thus commit suicide—another form of war-casualty). Wars never are as the glorious as the pictures and movies portray, especially those pictures and movies aimed at catching new recruits or used for propaganda aims. They have severe damaging effect, which does not stop once conflicts are over,[48] as a soldier, Sean Huze, Corporal, U.S. Marine Corps, in the documentary *The Ground Truth* puts it: " Who we are when we leave is not who we are when and if we're lucky to return."[49]

"Support Our Troops" could also mean, then, for the government to allocate enough funds to take care of these men[50]—unfortunately the contrary trend is happening—and better help army widows, widowers, and orphans in their daily lives. All this is meaningful support and not the easy patriotism of "slapping a magnet with a slogan on your car, so glib, so self-righteous," as Bob Sommer, who had a son in Iraq, knows only too well.[51] Besides, this "glib" support often increases in size and multiples, the bigger the car.

The "Support Our Troops" phrase is, grammatically speaking, in the imperative, thus a command. One might feel somewhat irritated by this command, especially when, quite often, this yellow ribbon sign transforms itself into a half yellow, half American-flag ribbon or an altogether whole flag-ribbon. The visual metaphor is then clear: support our troops and support our government, and its policy. If the message were not clear enough yet, some signs in the ribbon shape do say: "Support America." When the message is not thus reinforced but just on a yellow ribbon, it is often alongside a flag sticker, a "God Bless America" sticker, or an eagle/flag sticker, which all deliver the same point: support the administration's policy as well as the troops. Actually, the yellow ribbon sticker and the flag sticker frequently appear at opposite ends on the back of the car, to attract full and better attention this way and oblige the viewer to gaze at one and the other, and in this sweeping movement, to assimilate them mentally in a close relationship, in a kind of metonymic process.

Car owners who affix this "Support Our Troops" sticker must not often think of another ramification of the sticker meaning: if you support the army and the government policy enacted by this army, you must totally accept and approve of what is going on in Iraq to be logical with yourself. However, if you watch the news, read multiple sources on the events and daily life in Iraq, can you easily do so, all the more as you hear the ever-changing and untruthful administration rationale for its Middle East course of action?

The third category of slogan-stickers is of a more openly aggressive, patriotic, and nationalistic vein: "Proud to be American," "Power of Pride,"[52] "These Colors Don't Run," and "Don't Mess with the US." What about "pride"? What is it? As a feeling it can oscillate from deep satisfaction and pleasure in one's achievements or from whom one is, to conceit, vanity, vainglory, egotism, or and arrogance. "Pride" is one of the seven deadly sins, according to Catholic dogma; maybe other stickers should be added to this "power" line, such as "Power of Gluttony," or "Power of Laziness," and more.[53] Might "Power of Pride" really mean "Proud of Power"? When one affixes these power stickers such as "Power of Pride" and "Proud to be American," unless one does it without thinking, one must not be embarrassed by all these nuances but be really proud to be American in the here and now and a staunch defender of who governs this country and how, and the world in good measure, as another sticker "Don't mess with the US" infers, recalling yet another U.S. reality: its huge military industrial complex, embedded all over the country, and in many countries abroad.

It is ironical that many of those bearers of pro-government/ pro-war signs display them so light-heartedly, especially since they will never be confronted with the harsh reality of war. To them it will be reality mediated by a small screen, the "glorious" saga of "our troops abroad,"[54] since this country has not known many wars on its territory (apart from the many reprisals and repressions against its Native American tribes to the very second half of the twentieth century). It does not so fully understand the cruelty and reality of war as the signs indirectly advocate. War for Americans means waging— that is, exporting it outside American borders—and this has occurred so often that the United States seems to have been at war unceasingly since 1945.[55] This fiercely aggressive attitude displayed on stickers like "Don't mess with the US" tends to prove right General William Tecumseh Sherman's statement: "It is only those who neither fired a shot nor heard the shrieks and groans of the wounded who cry aloud for blood. . . . War is hell."[56] Then again these pro-war patriots in favor of "a brutal war that lack[s] all international legitimacy"[57] might not even know where Iraq is, as CNN revealed on May 4, 2006: "After more than three years of combat and nearly 2,400 U.S. military deaths in Iraq, nearly two-thirds of Americans aged 18 to 24 still cannot find Iraq on a map, a study released Tuesday showed."[58]

Such then was the "small world" of Seaside Park and Island Beach State Park in early August 2005, similar to the rest of the country with its flags and signs and all the more striking since a *Newsweek* poll from August 7, 2005, which is from the very same time-frame, stated that 64 percent of those polled did not think that war in Iraq had made Americans safer, and 61 percent disapproved of the way the president was handling the war.[59]

Just as the messages the signs delivered, consciously or unconsciously, do not have a single interpretation, their deciphering added together still does not render a complete assessment of those days, in the United States or elsewhere. Yet it is true that "all signs are related to what individuals and their leaders want, rather than to the referents these signs appear to designate: words, images, *signs*-things which appear but are not; and secrets-things which are but do not appear."[60]

Seaside Park and Its Flags within the Bigger World of the United States

The analysis of Seaside Park flags and signs so far does not take into account Americans at large who did not affix these signs or who were critical of them and the ideology they convey. It is true that signs critical of the pervading ones were far and few between, such as the only two noticed then: "These Colors Do Not Run The World" or "United We Sit/For World Peace." Was it due to a lack of popularity, to scarcity of resources for finding or buying them since they might not have been such a lucrative business, or fear of going against the grain and being considered antipatriotic? Or did people who thought otherwise not need that type of sign to utter their opinion, which they vented by other means?[61]

Blonsky again writes that " preparing the scattered pleasure bits of life, most people live 'mouse lives', unable ever to see systems, general social plans or the ideological or political laws revealed by the scattered fragments that make up their land and lives."[62] Would that mean that people who posted the Seaside Park signs fall into this category and that those who are critical of these signs see systems and ideological or political laws? Though there are always exceptions to the rule, there is quite a bit of truth in this, since "the US is an image country in which image is much more important than social or economic facts."[63] Images are pleasant, they send back a pleasant view of how a person is or would like to be, they dull intelligence and thought, they divert from real facts and truth seeking, they lie and perpetrate lies—theirs is a shallow approach full of illusions, as they can tell the "story" one wants to graft on them. As was seen in Seaside Park, they also "unify, make avid consumers, form a substitute for history and family."[64] It is no wonder then that this encountered perception of a thoroughly good, innocent people and the bewildered question that came up again and again after September 11: Why do they hate us so much? from ordinary people,[65] when they did not remain just confused or apathetic. Langston Hughes knew better when he addressed his country as Columbia:

Columbia,
My dear girl.
You really haven't been a virgin for so long

> It's ludicrous to keep up the pretext.
> You're terribly involved in word assignations
> And everybody knows it.
> You've slept with all the big powers
> In military uniforms,
>
>   . . .
>
> Really,
> you're getting a little too old,
> Columbia,
> To be so naive, and so coy.
> Being one of the world's big vampires,
> Why don't you come on out and say so
> Like Japan, and England, and France,
> And all the other nymphomaniacs of power . . . ?[66]

In quoting him, Howard Zinn reminded his fellow citizens of the duty of honesty not just in examining the evil things done elsewhere by other countries but also by their own government and in so doing, losing some of their arrogance:

> One of the boundaries set for us is the idea of our national power, and of our national goodness, that we are the superpower in the world and we deserve to be superpower because we are the best and the greatest and we have the most democracy and the most freedom and that's why terrible things are done to us because we're the best. That's kind of arrogant and that also is a sign of the loss of history and we need to be taken down a peg and taken down at the level of other nations in the world and other peoples of the world and we need some history to be able to come down to earth, and to see that the United States has behaved in the world like other imperial nations in the world. It is not surprising. We have to be honest about our country if we want to be anything.[67]

Eve Ensler's address to "Dear America" bears a title reminiscent of Blonsky's critique of "most people"[68]: *Open Letter to the Apathetic, the Brain-Washed, The Prescription Drug-Dazed and Brain-Dead, The American Patriots and Pseudo-Patriots,* whom she further in the letter also sees as remote and shielded by their "sealed wrapping, [their] self-obsession, their TVheadphonedDVDcell pod."[69] Written on July 1, 2005, this letter aims at driving home some truths not distributed on stickers or slogans and tells about Americans surrounded by a "river of indifference and consumption and denial," who are prey to a "rhetoric of terror and God" whom Ensler wants to wake up. She continues the simile, warning them that "the house is on fire," "the fire is spreading, consuming the world." The worst factor is that "[they] are the arsonists" who, as a result, have grown more and more "isolated, despised and alone." No mention of pride here, but she is using very forceful language to really jolt "American Patriots" into awakening. She produces a dire list of evils at home and abroad, hoping that the "unconscious" will thus regain their touch with reality. Out of her list, the second point is bad enough: "the strategic planning of such atrocities in the boardrooms, the backrooms, the back seats of limos, the organized take over and looting of Iraq right out from under the terrorized, hungry, thirsty Iraqi people," but there is more. She mentions the government having "changed and ended law," "the massive black holes, called prisons we have dug to hold thousands without charging them, without trials or the torture, the meanness, the cruelty we are inflicting upon them," the soldiers as victims "trying to kill themselves now, longing to escape the madness of murdering and maiming for no reason," the illegal weapons used (napalm like-substance, cluster bombs, depleted uranium), all evils befalling the Iraqi people: at the time, "the one hundred thousand dead Iraqi people" and "the cries of children in the exploding houses of Falluja."

Writing shortly after the Abu Ghraib perpetuated torture, and photos discovery, Barbara Ehrenreich shares similar and complementary pronouncements on the policy toward Iraq. She was hoping women in the military would make the army "more respectful of other people and their cultures, more capable of genuine peace keeping," but with the photos discovery, this hope died, and lots of other things with it:

> As recently as April 30, George Bush exulted that the torture chambers of Iraq were no longer operating. Well, it turns out they were just operating under different management. We didn't displace Saddam Hussein; we replaced him. And when you throw in the similar abuses in Afghanistan and Guantanamo, in immigrant detention centers and US prisons, you see that we have created a spreading regime of torture—an empire of pain.[70]

All this and more, the disillusioned patriots[71]—those who believed in their president and his designs and thought them to be sincere—know only too well in their heart, mind, and flesh: the Gold Star Families[72] or Cindy Sheehan who, that very same week of August 2005, started camping a month-long outside of Crawford, Texas to talk to the president,[73] "just park[ing] herself near Bush and becom[ing] the center of national attention, of gravity, around which people gathered, hundreds and hundreds of people."[74] All these informed, wide-awake people form what was quickly termed the "other" America,[75] acting against the war, its lies, and all the propaganda that led to the Iraq War. These are not so prone to flag-worshipping or sign-affixing and all their "story-telling."

Seaside Park and Its Flags in the World at Large

A study of Seaside Park flags and their meaning in the resort and within the United States should include their meaning outside of the United States, since this "global village" displays these signs in its media and analyzes them, too. Paradoxically, in our troubled times, the Americans who quickly come to mind abroad are not often those of "the other America" previously mentioned, though they are noticed as part of American society in Arhundati Roy's tribute:

> That absurd inability to separate governments from people. . . . More than one third of America's citizens have survived the relentless propaganda they've been subjected to, and many thousands are actively fighting their own government. In the ultra-patriotic climate that prevails in the US, that's as brave as any Iraqi fighting for his or her homeland. . . . Most courageous of all, are the hundreds of thousands of American people on the streets of great cities—Washington, New York, Chicago, San Francisco. The fact is that the only institution in the world today that is more powerful than the American government is American civil society. American citizens have a huge responsibility riding on their shoulders. How can we not salute and support those who not only acknowledge but act upon that responsibility? They are our allies, our friends.[76]

The cliché view of Americans held by people abroad conforms to the depiction of the small world of Seaside Park: average American citizens with their patriotism and flags, or flag-related stickers and objects, verging onto chauvinism at times, their arrogance, their lack of information of the world outside of their borders, and their support for the president. Since the War in Iraq has been extraordinarily unpopular from the start outside the United States, except for leaders who backed Bush in sending troops (though their citizens often dissociated themselves from them, such as Italians from then Berlusconi or Spaniards from then Aznar), Americans are often considered abroad in the image of their president and his overall policy, regardless of how all-encompassing, unfair, and biased this judgment is.

Yet it was not always so. Americans enjoyed an immense capital of world sympathy and support after the World Trade Center tragedy, but their positive "image" has been badly damaged with the Bush administration's actions and decisions since September 11, and it deservedly gets, therefore, the greatest blame, in Arundhati's words: "The real and pressing danger, the greatest threat of all is the locomotive force that drives the political and economic engine of the US government, currently piloted by George Bush. . . . It's true that he is a dangerous, almost suicidal pilot, but the machine he handles is far more dangerous than the man himself." And she concludes by stating that through his lack of finesse, Bush "has placed on full public view the working parts, the nuts and bolts of the apocalyptic apparatus of the American empire."

The reasons America has become so unpopular go beyond this very latest conflict and add to it. They can be classified into four causes as Ziauddin Sardar and Merryl Wyn Davies list them. The first is existential: "The US has simply made it too difficult for other people to exist," economically, politically, or culturally.[77] The second is cosmological. "In today's globalised world, America is seen as the prime cause of everything,"[78] an empire with hubris felt on every front: "American empire is a colonization of the future that becomes a total consumption of space and time—rewriting history, changing the very stuff of life in our genetics structure, shifting weather patterns, colonizing outer space and time, indeed, changing the course of evolution itself!" The third cause is ontological, relating to the very nature of being. "America relates to the world through . . . circular, ontological logic: because 'terrorists' are evil, America is good and virtuous . . . [and] the ontological element, the nature of American being, makes America *only* good and virtuous."[79] The coexistence of this claim to overall goodness while doing evil smacks of hypocrisy to non-Americans. The fourth and last cause is related to definitions, that is, how America defines democracy, freedom, justice, human rights, and so on, "[i]n short, what it means to be human,"[80] and imposes it to the rest of the world in terms of American self-identity, experience, culture, and self-interest. Another analysis of anti-Americanism, similar in content, proves by its conclusion how much "signs" do matter, at home in the United States and abroad, and how their perceptions do feed on one another:

"Like people in many other societies, we look outside, as if into a mirror, in order to see our own reflections with a better perspective than we can provide on our own. Anti-Americanism is important for what it tells us about U.S. foreign policy and America's impact on the world. It is also important for what it tells us about ourselves."[81]

Many countries beg to differ with American perspectives or rules, and one of their most visible, physical signs of protest then is often related to burning the American flag, or an Uncle Sam effigy. This confirms once more that the meaning of the "sign"—the American flag in this case—strongly depends on time and place.

TO FLAG OR NOT TO FLAG?

Flags and flag-related signs have their supporters and their critics both within the United States and outside of it, as has been analyzed in these pages. Signs always escape their meaning, shared or contrived, or the story that is meant through them. Polysemic by nature, flags as signs are indicative but unsure, depending on certain time and space configurations though they never tell the whole story. Yet they are very powerful nonverbal communication in spite of their limits, and they also lie, "make no responsible pronouncements," acting on people.[82]

The small world of Seaside Park with its irruption of the real in early August 2005 can be seen as a metaphor or a derisory mimicry of the United States, isolated and isolating, friendly and antagonizing. As Seaside Park evidenced various symbols, slogans, and imagery, in a kind of tri-part slogan, "Beach, Family, Fatherland,"[83] so did America after September 11, enfolding itself in national symbolism and its sustaining myths. But to the rest of the world the picture appeared and appears different: "Americans are perpetually wrapping themselves in the flag, the symbol of their ontological goodness. Since the flag represents everything that is good, it must, in American eyes, attract reverence from all quarters. But to the rest of the world it's just a piece of cloth, wrapped around delusionary ideas of innocence and goodness."[84] Goodwill and goodness do exist in people all over the globe, no nationality has a monopoly on them, as James Lawrence Harrington, Gulf War resister, evidences in his letter of resignation and plea to his U.S. Navy commander and in conclusion to this flag-analysis:

> Our nation suffers from a deep malady in its consciousness that leads it down the path of continual violence and strife. . . . War is but a symptom of a greater concern. I prescribe the treatment of a radical revolution within our nation from that of a "thing"-oriented society to a "person"-oriented community. We must learn to love and respect all people for the sake of divinity and basic goodness that dwells within them. . . . When we deny people the right to exist and to self-determination, we are assuring our own self-destruction.[85]

Notes

1. http://www.ushistory.org/betsy/flagfact.html (accessed September 10, 2006).
2. "Flag Code Violations in the News." http://ushistory.org/betsy/flagetiq.html (accessed September 10, 2006).
3. http://www.ushistory.org/betsy/faqs/q31.htm (accessed September 10, 2006).
4. http://www.ushistory.org/betsy/flagetiq.html#5 (accessed September 10, 2006).
5. http://www.ushistory.org/betsy/flagetiq.html#6 (accessed September 10, 2006).
6. http://thomas.loc.gov/cgi-bin/query/D?c109:3:./temp/~c109TpW69u (accessed September 10, 2006).
7. http://www.ushistory.org/betsy/flagquot.html (accessed September 10, 2006).
8. S. F., What Linguists Talk about When They Talk about Language, *The Pennsylvania Gazette*, September–October, 29, 2006.
9. Marshall Blonsky, ed., *On Signs* (Baltimore: Johns Hopkins University Press 1986), xix.
10. Seaside Park, New Jersey, Official Site, http://www.seasideparknj.org (accessed September 15, 2006); according to the U.S. 2000 Census Bureau and Wikipedia, http://en.wikipedia.org/wiki/Seaside_Park,_New_Jersey (accessed September 15, 2006).
11. White non-Hispanic: 96.2 percent; Hispanic: 2.3 percent; American-Indian: 0.7 percent.

12. In the 2006 legislative elections, Democrat Bob Menendez was re-elected over Thomas Kean, Jr., with 53 percent of the ballot. Podunk, "Political Info of Seaside Park, New Jersey," http://www.epodunk.com/cgi-bin/politicalInfo.php?locIndex=18203 (accessed December 8, 2006).
13. Section 8b of the Flag Code.
14. "The Blue Angels' mission is to enhance Navy and Marine Corps recruiting efforts and to represent the naval service to the United States, its elected leadership and foreign nations. The Blue Angels serve as positive role models and goodwill ambassadors for the U. S. Navy and Marine Corps," Blue Angels Official Web Site, http://www.blueangels.navy.mil/index.htm (accessed September 28, 2006).
15. Labeled as such on the Blue Angels Web site.
16. Jean-Didier Urbain, *At the Beach*, trans. From the French by Catherine Porter (Minneapolis: University of Minnesota, 2003), 113.
17. Ibid., 149.
18. Ibid., 190.
19. Urbain describes, with great humor and in military similes, this gesture which could often be observed at Seaside Park: "Here is a man arriving on the beach, armed with a folded umbrella in his right hand, an ice bucket in the other: the booty. This man is a scout leading a commando that follows close on its heels. He advances among the group that has settled in, inspects the site; he evaluates the situation, spies on the enemy, and collects data. Suddenly, in a foundational gesture, he plants his umbrella like a flag in conquered territory and thereby establishes a center. He unfurls the umbrella, and his territory now extends to the length of its shadow. The rest of the troop arrive, armed with beach towels and mats that are quickly positioned all around the standards, broadening the extent of the bastion and giving its boundaries material form," ibid., 215.
20. Ibid.
21. Ibid., 218.
22. Switzerland, which has the policy of setting its national flag as seal of quality on manufactured goods, recently called for more control over this practice so that abuses in commercialization could be stopped and also quality respected; Denis Masmejan, "Une loi pour mieux protéger le 'Swiss made' des usurpations," *Le Temps*, November 16, 2006, http://www.letemps.ch/ (accessed November 16, 2006).
23. An artist commissioned by the Guggenheim Museum to create net.flag, that is, "an emblem for the Internet as a new territory, one composed of people from various geographical regions and ideologies. Its design changes constantly, manipulated by users who make selections from menus of familiar flag motifs: stars, fields of color, bold patterns, insignia, and stripes. As net.flag's viewers add their contributions to the palimpsest, the cumulative identity of the flag changes as one country's

insignia or symbols temporarily overlap those of another. Expanding upon the model of non-geographic nationalities such as *Roma*, net.flag permits viewers to customize and save personal flags for their own virtual domains" http://www.guggenheim.org/internetart/welcome.html (accessed September 28, 2006).

24. Mark Napier, "A New Relevance," guggenheim.org, 2002, http://www.guggenheim.org/internetart/welcome.html (accessed September 28, 2006).

25. See Catherine S. Manegold, "September 11: Scholarly Responses. Patriotism and the Press, When the News Comes Veiled in Stars and Stripes, Something Powerful Is Lost," *The Academic Exchange* (February–March 2002), http://www.emory.edu/ACAD_EXCHANGE/2002/febmar/manegold.html (accessed October 4, 2006).

26. Ibid.

27. Blonsky, ed., *On Signs*, vii.

28. Ibid., xxi; emphasis original.

29. Ferdinand de Saussure, *Cours de linguistique générale* (Paris: Payot, 1986), 34.

30. See Tony Norman, "Oh, Say, Can You See What Is Happening to Our Liberties?" *Post Gazette*, July 4, 2003, http://www.post-gazette.com/columnists/20030704tony107col2p2.asp (accessed October 8, 2006).

31. Steve Lonegan, Mayor of Bogota, New Jersey, *The Pennsylvania Gazette*, September–October, 29, 2006.

32. Carolyn Marvin, and David W. Ingle, "Blood Sacrifice and the Nation: Revisiting Civil Religion." *Journal of American Academy of Religion* 64, no. 4 (Winter 1996): 769.

33. Ibid., 767.

34. Ibid., 769.

35. Ibid., 770. This quasi mystical/mythical dimension of the flag is also reinforced by the numerous anti-desecration decrees and constitutional amendments, the latest of which dates back to July 26, 2006, sponsored by Senator Hatch from Utah and backed by fifty-nine cosponsors, which says: "The Administration applauds Congress's efforts to protect the flag, a cherished symbol of national unity and of the sacrifices so many Americans have made in defending the Nation. The Administration supports S. J. Res. 12, which would propose to amend the United States Constitution to authorize Congress to prohibit the physical desecration of the United States flag," http://www.whitehouse.gov/omb/legislative/sap/109-2/sjres12sap-s.pdf (accessed October 8, 2006). This move was later criticized as a "tertiary consideration," not worth debating at a time when the country is at war. See Major General (Ret.) Robert Scales, "Forget Flag Burning. Debating a Ban during War Is a Waste of Time and Sends Troops the Wrong Message," *Time* (July 3, 2006): 100.

36. Marvin and Ingle, "Blood Sacrifice and the Nation," 775.

37. Ibid., 774.

38. At the end of *Fahrenheit 9/11*, war is also considered necessary for the cohesion of the nation be it from a slightly different angle: "George Orwell once wrote that it's not a matter of whether the war is not real or if it is. Victory is not possible. The war is not meant to be won, it is meant to be continuous. A hierarchical society is only possible on the basis of poverty and ignorance. . . . .The war is waged by the ruling group against its own subjects and its object is not the victory over either Eurasia or East Asia, but to keep the very structure of society intact."

39. She is filmed and interviewed in *Fahrenheit 9/11* and her words here are transcribed from Michael Moore's, *Fahrenheit 9/11 Reader*.

40. Norman, "Oh, Say, Can You See."

41. Angelika Bammer, "September 11: Scholarly Responses. Flags and Fears. Compulsive Repetition and National Identity," *The Academic Exchange* (April–May 2002), http://www.emory.edu/ACAD_EXCHANGE/ 2002/aprmay/bammer.html (accessed October 30, 2006).

42. Samuel P. Huntington, *Who Are We? The Challenges to American's National Identity* (New York: Simon and Schuster, 2004), 3.

43. Ibid., 4.

44. Ibid., 8–9.

45. Bruce Sklarew, M.D, "Reflections on September 11th and Its Aftermath," *Journal of Applied Psychoanalytic Studies* 4, no. 4 (October 2002): 469.

46. Ibid., 470.

47. A spoof of the "God Bless America" sticker has "America" crossed out and instead "Everyone," http://maikimo.net/radio/2002/11/21.html (accessed October 30, 2006).

48. "In the past five years, the number of veterans receiving compensation for the disorder commonly called PTSD has grown nearly seven times as fast as the number receiving benefits for disabilities in general, according to a report this year by the inspector general of the Department of Veterans Affairs. A total of 215,871 veterans received PTSD benefit payments last year at a cost of $4.3 billion, up from $1.7 billion in 1999—a jump of more than 150 percent"; Shankar Vedantam, "A Political Debate on Stress Disorder. As Claims Rise, VA Takes Stock," *The Washington Post*, December 27, 2005, p. A01.

49. *The Ground Truth*, http://www.thegroundtruth.net (accessed October 30, 2006).

50. A July 2004 report in the *New England Journal of Medicine* indicated that 17 percent of Iraq veterans suffered from PSTD or depression (only 6 percent of soldiers suffered from those illnesses in the first Gulf War).

51. See Bob Sommer, "What Is the Real Message of Yellow Ribbons on Cars?" *All Things Considered*, National Public Radio, February 14, 2005, http://www.npr.org/templates/story/story.php?storyId=4498757 (accessed October 30, 2006).

52. "These bumper stickers are quite common because they've been distributed for free by large businesses to customers of all kinds" (G. I. Joe in Ontario). Another Internet blogger adds: "The 'Power of Pride' bumper stickers are a product of Lowe's, which is promoting a USO tour to entertain our soldiers."

53. Whole sticker parody of "Power of Pride" on the seven deadly sins, http://www.cafepress.com/buy/Power%20of%20pride/cfpt2_/copt_/cfpt_368:______F______P___b7_a2/source_searchBox/x_17/y_5, together with "Power of Hubris," "Power of our Nukes," "Power of Lies," "Do You Take Pride in Power," "Power Goeth Before the Fall," and "Speak Truth to Power" (accessed November 4, 2006).

54. As Susan Sontag puts it: "Wars are now also living room sights and sound"; Susan Sontag, *Regarding the Pain of Others* (New York: Farrar, Straus, and Giroux, 2003), 18.

55. List of wars and conflicts, http://www.zmag.org/CrisesCurEvts/Interventions.htm (accessed November 4, 2006).

56. http://antiwar.com/quotes.php (accessed November 4, 2006).

57. See Robert Fisk, "The Real War Is Just Beginning," *The Independent* (UK), April 17, 2003, http://www.independent.co.uk (accessed November 4, 2006).

58. CNN.com, "Study: Geography Greek to Young Americans," *CNN.com* (May 4), http://www.cnn.com/2006/EDUCATION/05/02/geog.test/index.html (accessed November 4, 2006).

59. See Elaine Quijano, "Soldier's Mum Digs in near Bush Ranch," CNN.com (August 7, 2005), http://www.cnn.com/2005/POLITICS/08/07/mom.protest (accessed November 10, 2006).

60. Blonsky, ed., *On Signs*, xxxiv.

61. Talks, conferences, demonstrations, petitions, blogs, articles in various local or national newspapers, magazines, alternative press, books, movies, documentaries, Web sites, artistic expression—such as paintings, photos, plays, personal testimonies—and some Internet sites with anti-Bush and anti-war stickers for sale.

62. Blonsky, ed., *On Signs*, xxxiv.

63. Ibid., xl.

64. Ibid., xliv.

65. This rhetoric of hate has also been used by the Bush administration in its Manichean opposition of good versus evil, as for example in President Bush's radio address to the nation on September 15, 2001: "this is who we are, this is what our enemy hate and have attacked and this is why we will prevail."

66. See Arnold Rampersad, ed., *Collected Poems of Langston Hughes* (New York: Alfred A. Knopf, 1994), 168.
67. "Langston Hughes, The U.S., and Imperialism" (Track 9), in Howard Zinn, *Artists in a Time of War*, Compact Disc, Virus Records (USA), Lumberjack-Mordam Music G, 2001.
68. Blonsky, ed., *On Signs*, xxxiv.
69. This phrasing is her own. Eve Ensler wrote this text immediately after The World Tribunal on Iraq in Istanbul, where she was one of thirteen jury chaired by Arundhati Roy. The Tribunal consisted of three days of hearings investigating various issues related to the war on Iraq, such as the legality of the war, the role of the United Nations, war crimes, and the role of the media, as well as the destruction of the cultural sites and the environment, http://www.envirosagainstwar.org/know/read.php? itemid=2949 (accessed November 10, 2006).
70. This passage is an excerpt from her 2004 commencement address at Barnard College. To her indignation could be added Susan Sontag's, particularly in her article "Regarding the Torture of Others," following her book *Regarding the Pain of Others*, http://southerncrossreview .org/35/sontag.htm.
71. There are examples of this in Michael Moore's documentary, *Fahrenheit 9/11*, also in the documentary *Why We Fight*, where a retired police officer having lost his son immediately after 9/11 says: "Somebody has to pay for this. Somebody has to pay for 9/11. . . . I wanna see their bodies stacked up for what they did. For taking my son." And later on hearing his President say: "We've had no evidence that Saddam Hussein was involved" in these attacks, the retired police-man bursts out: "What the hell did we go in there for?" and added: "The government exploited my feelings of patriotism, of a deep desire for revenge for what happened to my son. But I was so insane with wanting to get even, I was willing to believe anything."
72. Their Web site, http://www.gsfp.org/, is replete with testimonies of soldiers and anti-war documents.
73. This is similar to what used to take place during the Vietnam War. "'I want to ask the president why he killed my son?' Sheehan told reporters. 'He said my son died for a noble cause, and I want to ask him what that noble cause is'" (Quijano "Soldier's Mum Digs in near Bush Ranch"). Cindy Sheehan's blog URL is: http://cindy-sheehan.org/. She is the founder of the anti-war group Gold Star Families for Peace.
74. See Tom Dispatch, "The Outer Limits of Empire. An Interview with Howard Zinn," *Peuples et Monde*, September 14, 2005, http://www .peuplesmonde.com/article.php3?id_article=328 (accessed November 10, 2006).

75. Collectif, *L'autre Amérique. Des Américains contre l'état de guerre*, is a collection of essays against the "state of war" by Judith Butler, Noam Chomsky, A. Davis, R. Dworkin, I. Wallerstein, H. Zinn, and others. To this book-critical stance can be added a newly published crop assessing the occupation of Iraq and its fiasco, in Mark Leonard's, "Drinking the Kool-Aid: An Anatomy of the Iraq Debacle," *The Chronicle of Higher Education* 52 (19): B6.

76. See Arhundati Roy, "Mesopotamia. Babylon. The Tigris and Euphrates," *The Guardian*, April 2, 2003, http://www.zmag.org/content/showarticle.cfm?ItemID=3368 (accessed November 10, 2006). That appeal to American citizens and change which can only come from them is echoed by Zyad Liman's "Américains, réveillez-vous!" [Americans, wake up!], which can be also found on his *Jeune Afrique* blog at: http://www.afriquemagazine.com/blog/blog_commento.asp?blog_id=200&month=11&year=2006&giorno=&archivio= (accessed November 15, 2006).

77. See Ziauddin Sardar and Merryl Wyn Davies, *Why Do People Hate America?* (New York: Disinformation Company, 2002), 195–97.

78. Ibid., 197.

79. Ibid., 198.

80. Ibid., 201.

81. Katzenstein and Keohane put forth a similar analysis under *Anti-Americanisms* and ponder on social, sovereign-nationalist, radical, and elitist anti-Americanisms (2006), http://www.policyreview.org/139/katz.html (accessed December 10, 2006).

82. Blonsky, ed., *On Signs*, xxi.

83. Reminiscent of World War II Pétain's motto "Travail, Famille, Patrie" [Work, Family, Fatherland], which had replaced the Republican motto: "Liberty, Equality, Fraternity."

84. Sardar and Davies, *Why Do People Hate America?*, 201.

85. See Howard Zinn, *The People Speak. American Voices, Some Famous, Some Little Known. Dramatic Readings Celebrating the Enduring Spirit of Dissent* (New York: Perennial, 2004).

References

Anti-war quotes. n.d. http://antiwar.com/quotes.php (accessed November 4, 2006).

Bammer, Angelika. 2002. September 11: Scholarly responses. Flags and fears. Compulsive repetition and national identity. *The Academic Exchange*. April–May. http://www.emory.edu/ACAD_EXCHANGE/2002/aprmay/bammer.html (accessed October 30, 2006).

Blonsky, Marshall, ed. 1986. *On signs*. Baltimore: Johns Hopkins University Press.

The Blue Angels Official Web site. http://www.blueangels.navy.mil/ index .htm (accessed September 28, 2006).

Boobooday.com. n.d. Power of pride. http://www.boobooday.com/ powerofpride.html (accessed November 4, 2006).

CNN.com. 2006. Study: Geography Greek to young Americans. *CNN.com*. May 4. http://www.cnn.com/2006/EDUCATION/05/02/geog .test/index.html (accessed November 4, 2006).

Dispatch, Tom. 2005. The outer limits of empire. An interview with Howard Zinn. *Peuples et Monde*, September 14. http://www.peuplesmonde .com/article.php3?id_article=328 (accessed November 10, 2006).

Ehrenreich, Barbara. 2004 Commencement address at Barnard College. Retrieved from Susan Sontag. Regarding the torture of others. http:// southerncrossreview.org/35/sontag.htm (accessed November 10, 2006).

Ensler, Eve. 2005. Dear America: The fire is spreading and we are the arsonists. In Environmentalists against War. July 1. http://www.envirosagainstwar .org/know/read.php?itemid=2949 (accessed November 10, 2006).

F., S. 2006. What linguists talk about when they talk about language. *The Pennsylvania Gazette* September–October, p. 29.

Fisk, Robert. 2003. The real war is just beginning. *The Independent* (UK). April 17. http://www.independent.co.uk (accessed November 4, 2006).

Foulkrod, Patricia. 2006. *The ground truth*. Universal Studios Home Entertainment. Focus features. DVD. http://www.thegroundtruth.net.

Gold Star Families for Peace. http://www.gsfp.org.

G.I. Joe in Ontario. n.d. The puzzling power of pride. http://www.irregulartimes .com/powerpride.html. (accessed November 4, 2006).

Hatch, O. Senate constitutional amendment prohibiting flag desecration. http://www.whitehouse.gov/omb/legislative/sap/109-2/sjres12sap-s .pdf (accessed October 8, 2006).

Huntington, Samuel P. 2004. *Who are we? The challenges to American's national identity*. New York: Simon and Schuster.

Jarecki, Eugene. 2005. *Why we fight*. A Sony Pictures Classics Release. DVD.

Katzenstein, Peter, and Robert O. Keohane. 2006. Anti-Americanisms. Biases as diverse as the country itself. *Policy Review*, no. 139 (October–November). http://www.hoover.org/publications/policyreview/4823856.html *(accessed* December 10, 2006).

Kouvelakis, S., D. Bensaid, and S. Budgen. 2002. *L'autre Amérique. Des Américains contre l'état de guerre*. Paris: Coll. la Discorde.

Leonard, Mark. 2006. Drinking the Kool-Aid: An anatomy of the Iraq debacle. *The Chronicle of Higher Education* 52 (19): B6.

The Library of Congress. Thomas. http://thomas.loc.gov/cgi-bin/query/D?c109:3:./temp/~c109TpW69u (accessed September 10, 2006).

Liman, Zyad. 2006. Post-scriptum. Américains, réveillez-vous! (Americans, wake up!). *Jeune Afrique*, October 12.

———. *Jeune Afrique* blog. http://www.afriquemagazine.com/blog/blog_commento.asp?blog_id=200&month=11&year=2006&giorno=&archivio= (accessed November 15, 2006).

List of wars and conflicts. http://www.zmag.org/CrisesCurEvts/Interventions.htm (accessed November 4, 2006).

Manegold, Catherine S. 2002. September 11: Scholarly responses. Patriotism and the Press, when the news comes veiled in stars and stripes, something powerful is lost. *The Academic Exchange*. February–March. http://www.emory.edu/ACAD_EXCHANGE/2002/febmar/manegold.html (accessed October 4, 2006).

Marvin, C., and D. W. Ingle. 1996. Blood sacrifice and the nation: Revisiting civil religion. *Journal of American Academy of Religion* 64, no. 4 (Winter): 767–80.

Masmejan, Denis. 2006. Une loi pour mieux protéger le "Swiss made" des usurpations. *Le Temps*. November 16. http://www.letemps.ch (accessed November 16, 2006).

Moore, Michael. 2004. *Fahrenheit 9/11 reader*. New York: Simon and Schuster Paperbacks.

Napier, Mark. net.flag. http://www.guggenheim.org/internetart/welcome.html (accesssed September 28, 2006).

Napier, Mark, 2002. A new relevance. http://www.guggenheim.org/internetart/welcome.html (accessed September 28, 2006).

Norman, Tony. 2003. Oh, say, can you see what is happening to our liberties? *Post Gazette*. July 4. http://www.post-gazette.com/columnists/20030704tony107col2p2.asp (accessed October 8, 2006).

Podunk, political info Seaside Park, New Jersey. n.d. http://www.epodunk.com/cgi-bin/politicalInfo.php?locIndex=18203 (accessed December 8, 2006).

Quijano, Elaine. 2005. Soldier's mum digs in near Bush ranch. CNN.com. August 7. http://www.cnn.com/2005/POLITICS/08/07/mom.protest (accessed November 10, 2006).

Rampersad, Arnold, ed. 1994. *Collected poems of Langston Hughes*. New York: Alfred A. Knopf.

Roy, Arhundati. 2003. Mesopotamia. Babylon. The Tigris and Euphrates. *The Guardian*, April 2. http://www.zmag.org/content/showarticle.cfm?ItemID=3368 (accessed November 10, 2006).

Sardar, Z., and M. Wyn Davies. 2002. *Why do people hate America?* New York: Disinformation Company.

Saussure, Ferdinand de. 1986. *Cours de linguistique générale.* Paris: Payot.

Scales, Robert, Major General (Ret.). 2006. Forget flag burning. Debating a ban during war is a waste of time and sends troops the wrong message. *Time* (July 3): 100.

Seaside Park, New Jersey, Official Site. http://www.seasideparknj.org (accessed *September 15, 2006).*

Sheehan, Cindy. n.d. Blog. http://cindy-sheehan.org.

Sklarew, Bruce, M.D. 2002. Reflections on September 11th and its aftermath. *Journal of Applied Psychoanalytic Studies* 4, no. 4 (October): 469–72.

Sommer, Bob. 2005. What is the real message of yellow ribbons on cars? *All Things Considered.* February 14. http://www.npr.org/templates/ story/story.php?storyId=4498757 (accessed October 30, 2006).

Sontag, Susan. 2003. *Regarding the pain of others.* New York: Farrar, Straus, and Giroux.

A spoof of the "God Bless America" sticker. n.d. http://maikimo.net/ radio/2002/11/21.html (accessed October 30, 2006).

Sticker parody on the seven deadly sins. n.d. http://www.cafepress .com/buy/Power%20of%20pride/-/cfpt2_/copt_/cfpt_368: _______F_____P___ b7_a2/source_searchBox/x_17/y_5 (accessed November 4, 2006).

Urbain, Jean-Didier. 2003. *At the beach.* Translated from the French by Catherine Porter. Minneapolis: University of Minnesota.

Vedantam, Shankar. 2005. A political debate on stress disorder. As claims rise, VA takes stock. *The Washington Post*, December 27.

Zinn, Howard. 2001. *Artists in a time of war.* CD. Label: Virus (USA). Distributor: Lumberjack-Mordam Music G. Recorded in Boston.

———, ed. 2004. *The people speak. American voices, some famous, some little known. Dramatic readings celebrating the enduring spirit of dissent.* New York: Perennial.

CHAPTER 5

SEARCHING FOR *COMMON SENSE*: THE ROOTS OF GEORGE W. BUSH'S WAR RHETORIC

Michael J. Butler

The profound reliance on rhetorical appeals by political leaders in the articulation and prosecution of U.S. foreign policy initiatives, particularly those involving the use of military force, is a phenomenon both long-studied and widely chronicled. This phenomenon appears to be an especially favored tactic of the current Bush administration. This characterization seems most apt with respect to the Bush administration's framing of the military components of its larger counterterrorism efforts. This chapter seeks to probe more deeply into the use of moralizing rhetoric by political elites with respect to war within the American historical and political context.

While the use of moralizing rhetoric by the Bush administration in the aftermath of 9/11 is the catalyst for this research, I am chiefly concerned with examining the origins of this tactic as a favored tool utilized by political elites for the purpose of framing social views of war. In particular, this research explores the construction of a dominant discourse on the prosecution of "just" wars within the American context, finding the famous *Common Sense* pamphlet authored by Thomas Paine at the source of this construction.

Such an examination allows both for reflection on the utility of moralistic rhetoric on war-making and military intervention decisions within the American polity throughout U.S. history, and for projections of the impact of that particular brand of rhetoric on contemporary U.S. foreign and security policy, particularly with respect to the "global war on terror."

9/11 AND THE "MORALIST TURN" IN U.S. FOREIGN POLICY

A cursory glance at the reaction of Western political leaders to the events of September 11, 2001, seemingly supports the notion of 9/11 as the catalyzing event prompting an unprecedented moralist turn in the international political environment.[1] In his televised address to the public on the evening of September 11, 2001, George W. Bush quoted directly from Psalm 23 of the New Testament while stressing that "America was targeted for attack because we're the brightest beacon for freedom and opportunity in the world. And no one will keep that light from shining. Today, our nation saw evil, the very worst of human nature." British Prime Minister Tony Blair offered with conviction that "we, the democracies of this world, are going to have to come together to fight [fanaticism] and eradicate this evil completely from our world." French president Jacques Chirac depicted the attacks as the work of "monsters" and promised "all French people stand by the American people and . . . express our friendship and solidarity in this tragedy." Canadian Prime Minister Jean Chrétien famously characterized the attacks as "a cowardly act of unspeakable violence," in the process opining "it is impossible to fully comprehend the evil that would have conjured up such a cowardly and depraved assault."

Not surprisingly, 9/11 inspired flourishes of moralistic rhetoric have enjoyed the greatest shelf-life in the United States, particularly with respect to the foreign policy course charted by the Bush administration (as well as within the debates surrounding that course). The collective lament, how could this happen to us? encapsulated public reaction throughout the United States in the immediate aftermath of the terrorist attacks of September 11, 2001. In the ensuing years, Americans have grappled with the difficult dilemmas spawned by this question, such as why religious *fatwas* calling for *jihad* against

America and the West exist and whether, when, and particularly *how* to respond to carefully coordinated past and future attacks motivated and shaped by "evildoers" seeking to perpetrate injustices against Americans and their way of life.

Such questions and debates will undoubtedly persist without adequate resolution for the foreseeable future, given the common tendency within American political discourse to characterize the perpetrators of these actions (and, in some cases, their supporters) as being consumed by such unconscionable hatred and brutality as to place them beyond the bounds of "civilization" and, thus, beyond the bounds of moral consideration. Indeed, this assertion has become the ideological centerpiece of the Bush administration's justification for its military response(s) to transnational terrorism.[2] As a result the course of contemporary international politics has been cast in the American polity as a monumental struggle between the forces of darkness and light, good and evil, right and wrong, or by one scholar's critical reading, "civilization" and "barbarism" (Salter 2002).

Regardless of one's own political or philosophical viewpoint about the causes or extent of the problem of transnational terrorism or the appropriate response, a concern with exacting justice seems to have assumed a larger and more significant role in U.S. foreign and national security policy circles today than ever before. In turn, this conventional wisdom tempts us to conclude that moral conviction (however well or ill-informed) has singularly animated the George W. Bush administration's public definition of the "global war on terrorism" (GWOT) and in particular the rhetorical justifications for military interventions in Afghanistan and Iraq initiated under the guise of that campaign. This realization in turn spawns the question precipitating this research: Is there anything new about this apparent moralist turn?

Assertions as to the emergence of a "moralist turn" rest on the unexamined assumption previously articulated: namely, the crisis spawned by 9/11 represents a watershed moment with respect to the infiltration of morality into the social construction of war within the U.S. experience. Yet in the absence of a detailed enquiry as to whether and how morality has been applied to the construction of social views at other pivotal points throughout U.S. history, such a premise is flimsy at best. Certainly anecdotal observation of the moral rhetoric employed by the Bush administration since 9/11 lends more than a modicum of support to assertions of a "moralist turn." Still, the notion that moralistic rhetoric has taken on unprecedented importance in the framing of U.S. military operations since 9/11 should not be accepted without first tracing the evolution and impact of such rhetoric at other pivotal junctures in U.S. history.

A Note on Rhetorical and Discursive Analysis

Effectively conducting such an enquiry necessitates a foray into the realm of rhetorical analysis. A longstanding tool of the humanities, the careful study of rhetoric—including the close reading of style, form, and content—is a somewhat recent introduction to the social sciences and, in particular, to political science and international relations. Its emergence in that application is undoubtedly reflective of the growing recognition of the importance of discourse to the political process. This recognition is itself a reflection of the rise of constructivist, feminist, postmodern, and other critical theoretical approaches within the study of political phenomena, themselves inspired in part by the contributions of critical theorists such as Jacques Derrida (1976, 1983), Michel Foucault (1976), Fredric Jameson (1992), and the like.

It is difficult and self-defeating to provide a uniform standard for the conduct of rhetorical analysis or discourse analysis with which the study of rhetoric is closely related. Rhetorical analysis is neither quantitative nor qualitative in nature; it can employ either or both tools, but in its essence it is not concerned with measurement and the production of "hard" or measurable outcomes but with deconstructing language in order to identify the ontological and epistemological assumptions behind a statement, text, decision, behavior, and so forth. As such it is itself as much a way of thinking as it is a method. Its own chief operating assumption is that "objective realities" are in fact subjectively constructed and fallacious; stemming from this assumption, rhetorical as well as discourse analysis each view the object of analysis (the aforementioned statement, text, decision, behavior, etc.) to be conditioned by and subsumed within a particular discourse. Thus the main output of this form of analysis is not an absolute answer but rather a deeper understanding of the context underlying the rhetorical specification of both a particular "problem" and its identified to "solution" (Dickens and Fontana 1994).

Given the emphasis that rhetorical and discursive analyses place on examining the context (beliefs, assumptions, norms, values, and so forth) that defines the discourse surrounding a "problem" and its "solution," it is hardly surprising that such approaches focus on the larger historical and social environment from which the discourse emanates (Frohmann 1994). As such, rhetorical analysis invites careful consideration of the following basic elements of any examined discourse:

__What is the rhetorical situation?
__Who is the speaker-author?
__Who is the intended audience?
__What is the content of the author-speaker's message?
__What is the author-speaker's intent in issuing the rhetoric?
__What does the nature of the rhetoric reveal about the society that produced it?

There are, of course, other focal points for rhetorical and discourse analysis; moreover, each of these can be (and typically are) further specified. Still, in any analysis of the evolution of the rhetoric of war in the American context, these questions would seem natural points of departure.

A hatred so vexing that it can only be explained as emanating from a place of inherent evil; policy priorities and security strategies publicly associated with moral conviction; political observers (including, yes, political scientists!) parroting the conventional wisdom that, at least for the short-term, a particular elaboration of "evil" (and by extension, "good") does and will dominate American foreign policy. This, in a nutshell, is the view depicted by those describing the existence of a "moralist turn" as previously described. How can we hope to gain perspective on this current state of affairs and ascertain the accuracy of these claims? The answer lies in a fuller understanding of the past, particularly concerning the rhetorical context surrounding elite discourse concerning the morality of war at critical junctures in U.S. history. In this analysis I adopt a comparative approach in examining elite discourse pertaining to that subject at two discrete points in the "lifespan" of the American nation: the revolutionary era of Thomas Paine and the post-9/11 landscape of George W. Bush.

Liberal democracies such as the United States have always felt some compulsion to seek a reconciliation between their frequent uses of military force and their professed commitments to the promotion of a peaceful and just world order. This much sought after reconciliation has been prompted by the incompatibility between a Clausewitzian view of the military option as a legitimate policy instrument and a Kantian faith in the gradual evolution of societies (particularly those governed by republican institutions) away from conflict as a function of social learning and the appreciation of the costs (human and otherwise) associated with war (Clausewitz 1984; Covell 1998; Kant 1905). Howard (1978), Doyle (1983a, 1983b), Cohen (1984), and numerous others have argued rather persuasively that the incompatibility of these two fundamental visions of the place of military force in the conduct of statecraft is, in fact, the main contradiction faced by contemporary liberal societies. It is the attempts to reconcile this main contradiction through the employment of a moralizing public rhetoric that is the main focal point of this research.

PRESENT AT THE CREATION:
THE *COMMON SENSE* DISCOURSE

Clearly the contradiction between *realpolitik* and idealism has been front and center in the U.S. foreign policy-making process ever since the country's inception. One can find its roots in colonial times by turning to the paramount figure in the establishment of an American ideology and worldview well-disposed to the possibilities of military power as a tool of and for the conduct of an American statecraft steeped in virtue: none other than Thomas Paine. The leading questions introduced help us to systematically evaluate the *Common Sense* discourse. [3]

To begin, it is important to consider the speaker-author as well as the situation and audience; in other words, examine who Paine was as well as the larger context in which his discourse defining contribution of the popular pamphlet *Common Sense* (first published February 14, 1776) was introduced. With respect to the *speaker-author*, Paine himself (as has been well documented) was a personification of two important perspectives: liberalism and deism (Keane, 1995). Like other Enlightenment-inflected liberals, Paine was a

profound believer in the power of individual reason yet simultaneously viewed the ultimate end of one's rational faculties to be the
recognition and glorification of the deity. Thus Paine was an important figure in the cultivation of a radical individualism in colonial and
post-colonial America and of its fusion with a desire for the millenarian transformation to which the individual and his or her
rational faculties should be devoted (Keane 1995). These threads,
converging in Paine's thought and personage, and synthesized by
his works, would have great and lasting resonance in the American
experience in general and with respect to America's foreign relations in particular.

As for the *situation*, rhetorical appeals to national greatness and
millennial destiny were hardly uncommon in the colonial society in
which the *Common Sense* discourse was birthed. Indeed, such
notions form the very basis of American exceptionalism (Hartz
1955; Lerner 1957; Davis and Lynn-Jones 1987). Appeals of this
sort were articulated by nearly all the leading secular and religious
authorities in the colonies (Benjamin Franklin, John Winthrop,
Jonathan Mayhew, and Peter Muhlenberg, among others) and were
ubiquitous prior to and during the Revolution. In part these appeals
were intended to provide moral justification for resistance against a
divinely sanctioned King George III. However, Paine was unique
among his contemporaries for the *audience* to which his efforts were
directed. Paine possessed a singular ability to distill abstract principles into a populist message and used his acumen in this regard to
fashion American exceptionalism into an outward-looking vision for
both the domestic and foreign policies of the new nation (Bloch
1985). For that, and because this vision was packaged in pamphlet
form for the masses rather than his compatriots among the colonial
elite (though it is said that Washington's attitudes toward the British
hardened after reading it), Paine is arguably the single figure most
important to the establishment of the dominant discourse on the
foreign relations (including the appropriate role for the use of force)
of the fledgling republic (Bloch 1985).

With respect to the *intent* and *content* of Paine's message, a close
reading of Paine's thinking and oratory on this subject as contained
in the pamphlet itself shows a singular concern with establishing the
parameters defining the appropriate exercise of state power.[4] Though
typically this concern is characterized in relation to the pamphlet's
denunciation of British rule over the colonies, it has additional

added dimensions of importance for the establishment of a dominant discourse concerning not only the national image of the American nation but also the appropriate use of power (including the use of military force) from the perspective of the new United States itself. Sections III and IV of the pamphlet are particularly instructive on this score. For Paine, this debate springs forth from an observation of the propensity of purportedly liberal states in the Old World to exercise their power through war. Paine viewed this as a singular and repulsive form of exploitation and oppression, which an emerging United States should stand against not only through words but also in example and action through whatever means necessary (Fitzsimons 1995, 578).

The depth and sincerity of this concern would prove to be an important strand in the *Common Sense* discourse as would Paine's intent in articulating it: the rousting of his colonial compatriots from complacency to the embrace of national greatness. For example, in Section III Paine admonishes his future country-men and women to recognize and stand against the tendency of the Old World in general, and Britain in particular, to enmesh all in its constant quest for advantage in the exercise of power politics:

> I challenge the warmest advocate for reconciliation, to shew, a single advantage that this continent can reap, by being connected with Great Britain. I repeat the challenge, not a single advantage is derived . . . but the injuries and disadvantages we sustain by that connection, are without number; and our duty to mankind at large, as well as to ourselves, instruct us to renounce the alliance: Because, any submission to, or dependence on Great-Britain, tends directly to involve this continent in European wars and quarrels; and sets us at variance with nations, who would otherwise seek our friendship, and against whom, we have neither anger nor complaint. . . . Europe is too thickly planted with kingdoms to be long at peace, and whenever a war breaks out between England and any foreign power, the trade of America goes to ruin, because of her connection with Britain. (Paine 1776)

Thus not only does Paine identify the rationale for American independence from Britain, he also establishes the broader purpose for that separation: the moral obligation to avoid partaking in the endless suffering and dislocation caused by the endless pursuit of interest via the means of war by all of the monarchies of Europe (not just the British throne). Indeed, he continues on to state that "[e]very thing that is right or natural pleads for separation" (Paine 1776, sec. III, para. 19). That this separation is presented not only as an act that is in the material interests of the colonies but also as a wider moral duty is made abundantly clear through Paine's own words and is undoubtedly one of the earliest and most effective efforts to publicly equate American national interests with the interests of (in Paine's words) "mankind-at-large." His closing words in Section III underscore the ease with which he linked the spatially and temporally bound concerns of his nation with the concern for promoting universal and eternal justice among all peoples and in the process rendering the American nation the last hope for humanity: "O ye that love mankind! Ye that dare oppose, not only the tyranny, but the tyrant, stand forth! Every spot of the old world is overrun with oppression. Freedom hath been hunted round the globe. Asia, and Africa, have long expelled her. Europe regards her like a stranger, and England hath given her warning to depart. O! receive the fugitive, and prepare in time an asylum for mankind."

Chief among the legitimate concerns for America or any fully credentialed liberal republic, Paine argued, was the liberation of the nations of the world from oppression at the hands of statesmen who lord over the conquered and amass wealth and influence through the military capacities of the state. In constructing the dominant discourse for the foreign relations of the new republic, Paine clearly holds out that the use of organized violence was only relevant as a means toward the former and not the latter end. The perceived need to counter Machiavellian machinations on the international stage would therefore prove to be a major foundation of Paine's thinking as to what might render acts of war acceptable, and even legitimate, for the new United States. Most immediately justified, of course, were acts of war directed at the British Empire, whose dominance and exploitation of the colonies in Paine's view obviated any future possibility of compromise or reconciliation. To wit, "Men of passive tempers look somewhat lightly over the offences of Britain, and, still hoping for the best, are apt to call out, '*Come, come, we shall be friends again, for all this.*' But examine the passions and feelings of mankind, Bring the doctrine of reconciliation to the touchstone of nature, and then tell me, whether you can hereafter love, honour, and faithfully serve the power that hath carried fire and sword into your land?" (Paine 1776, sec. III, para. 19)

Such it is that the ideas of the ancient theory of the just war were first infused into the American discourse on war—through a partial and selective application of that theory's notion of "just causes." In Paine's (flawed) interpretation and application of that concept, once a just cause is established to exist, the possibilities for employing measures of redress short of war are effectively eliminated. In other words, once transgressed against, it is the obligation of the 'just" or morally correct agent to forcefully punish the transgressor without delay. In articulating what would become a particularly American view of the obligations attached to war, Paine quotes Milton's *Paradise Lost*—"never can true reconcilement grow where wounds of deadly hate have pierced so deep" (Milton 2003, book IV, line 98)—articulating this sentiment within the context of the prevailing state of Continental affairs.

This is not inflaming or exaggerating matters but trying them by those feelings and affections which nature justifies and without which we should be incapable of discharging the social duties of life or enjoying the felicities of it. I mean not to exhibit horror for the purpose of provoking revenge but to awaken us from fatal and unmanly slumbers that we might pursue determinately some fixed object. It is not in the power of Britain or of Europe to conquer America if she does not conquer herself by *delay* and *timidity.*

Of course, one might be tempted to interpret Paine's views, both on the excesses of state power and on the duty to oppose it even through forceful means. as a singular outgrowth of the very real and extensive list of grievances between the emerging American nation and their British overseers. By this reading, the exhortations contained within *Common Sense* would hardly be said to constitute the basis of a dominant and lasting discourse on the topic of war within the new United States. Yet there is more to the content of, and intention behind, Paine's rhetoric than merely a desire to cajole his compatriots out of complacency in order to sever relations with George III. The pamphlet, as the bedrock of an entire discourse on the subject, was itself a treatise on the conduct of a just and virtuous foreign policy for a new (just and virtuous) nation and in that vein characterizes the exercise of power by that nation (up to and including the resort to war) as a cleansing act to thwart and even eradicate the unrepentant and un-Enlightened *realpolitik* of the Old World. The *Common Sense* discourse can therefore be summarized as the first major public articulation of what would become an essential part of the American creed: the self-imposed duty to lead the community of nations in the quest for justice through the employment of (divinely sanctioned) warfare.

So what does Paine's pamphlet, and the larger discourse it helped fashion, *reveal about the society* from which it emanated? Though critical of the generally "vile" institution of war, Paine held out a key exception: sanctioning wars of national liberation against repressive governments. Citing in essence an expanded notion of self-defense as well as making an explicit appeal to natural law, the *Common Sense* discourse claimed for the emerging republic the reserved right to act in the common interest of humanity to help threatened nations repel invasion and throw off the yoke of invasive colonial rule. Such actions, in accordance with this discourse, were the right and expected conduct of any society truly faithful to the liberal ideal. In reserving this right, and defining the public discourse around it, the *Common Sense* discourse gave voice to and legitimated the millenarian and missionary impulses that would dominate America's foreign military engagements in the centuries to come.

In sum, Paine's pamphlet established the parameters of a public discourse on the exercise of American military force that would evolve to a position of dominance alongside the evolution of American power and influence. This discourse was fueled by a dualistic attachment to both God and the individual and was directed at rousting a popular audience from complacency. Prominent within this discourse was a clear loathing of the exercise of state power for the end of imperial domination and an appreciation of same as a useful means for promoting the causes of liberal expansion and the promotion of universal justice. Indeed this discourse viewed these causes as the foremost, if not only, moral considerations for Americans to attend to with respect to the decision to employ military force; furthermore, they were causes valued equally by all nations, thus rendering the United States duty-bound to their advancement. Not surprisingly, then, transgressors against these ends were considered irredeemable, and reconciliation with them was a sign of weakness to be avoided at all costs.

It is important to stress that Paine himself never openly sanctioned liberal expansionism, but he argued in a more purely idealist vein that the inherently just and moral nature of the liberal social order could very well achieve the same end through the attractiveness of its ideas rather than the force of its arms (Fitzsimons 1995).

But as is typically the case with the power of a framing discourse, it was not so much what Paine didn't say as what he did that was important. While the *Common Sense* discourse did not openly advocate reckless military adventurism in the promotion of liberal principles, its establishment of a belief in the inherent goodness of the grand American experiment would provide the ideological firmament not only for the expansion of the nation but also for changing perceptions of power and interest as a function of that expansion.[5]

COMMON SENSE AND . . . GEORGE W. BUSH? REALIZATION OF A DISCOURSE

The previous section presents an abbreviated treatment of the historical relationship between moralistic rhetoric and military force as a policy instrument and chronicles the persistence and maturation of the *Common Sense* discourse in that vein. Such a treatment tempts one to expect that the George W. Bush administration would be no different than its forebears in this regard. Thus it should come as no surprise that this president, like those that have come before him, draws heavily upon moralistic rhetoric as a means of framing and justifying his foreign policy agenda. However, critics of the administration (on both the right and left) contend that the current president far outstrips his recent predecessors in this regard, particularly regarding the appropriate use of military force in conjunction with the "global war on terrorism" or GWOT (Zarefsky, 2002). Rather than using moralistic rhetoric as a political tool to legitimize policy goals and the means to obtain them, this line of reasoning contends that such rhetoric provides the George W. Bush administration with its very *raison d'être* (Bovard 2004; Singer 2004).

Observations such as these seem plausible and deserving of further examination when one considers the extent to which contemporary international politics have been cast as a struggle between good and evil within the American policy since 9/11 (Salter 2002). Indeed it has become commonplace in American political discourse to assert that the perpetrators of terrorist attacks (and, in some cases, their sympathizers) are consumed by such unconscionable hatred and brutality as to place them beyond the bounds of "civilization" and thus beyond the bounds of moral consideration. The construction of this stark duality (a process of construction in which Bush

himself has played the lead role) has had significant policy implications, clearly influencing the administration's continued use of torture, extraordinary rendition, and illegal methods of domestic
surveillance (Zarefsky 2004; Beatty 2003). It is also logical that this
construction has contributed at some level to the increasing number
of well-documented atrocities committed by U.S. military forces
against civilians in the Iraqi theater.

Still, before direct connections such as these can be made, assertions as to the unprecedented and excessive nature of the moralizing
rhetoric employed by the Bush administration in the aftermath of
9/11 must be more systematically examined. It seems imperative
that we transcend the realm of blog speak and the vacuum of the
punditry, and we more closely scrutinize Bush's rhetorical record
with respect to its response to global terrorism since 9/11. Certainly
Bush's initial public statements provide at least anecdotal confirma-
tion of the view that 9/11 prompted a moralist turn of extraordinary
magnitude. In his televised address to the public on the evening of
September 11, 2001, Bush quoted directly from Psalm 23 while
stressing that "America was targeted for attack because we're the
brightest beacon for freedom and opportunity in the world. And no
one will keep that light from shining. Today, our nation saw evil, the
very worst of human nature" (Bush 2001a).

Bush followed this address with a public admonition aimed at
convincing Americans to return to their daily life and work routines,
delivered on September 16. He both vowed to "rid the world of evil-
doers" and warned that "this crusade, this war on terrorism, is gonna
take awhile (*sic*)" (CNN.com, September 16, 2001). Bush continued
to tailor his remarks to a similar theme, culminating a week later with
the presentation of a very simplistic dichotomy, seemingly for domestic consumption: "I see things this way: The people who did this act
on America are evil people. As a nation of good folk, we're going to
hunt them down . . . and we will bring them to justice." (George W.
Bush, September 25, 2001, in Bush 2003, 22)

Finally, in a televised address to the nation announcing the commencement of combat operations (and the highly moralistic
moniker affixed to those operations) in Afghanistan on October 7,
2001, Bush framed the purpose of the first major response to 9/11
in similarly grandiose terms: "We're a peaceful nation. Yet, as we
have learned, so suddenly and so tragically, there can be no peace in
a world of sudden terror. In the face of today's new threat, the only

way to pursue peace is to pursue those who threaten it. We did not ask for this mission, but we will fulfill it. The name of today's military operation is Enduring Freedom. We defend not only our precious freedoms, but also the freedom of people everywhere to live and raise their children free from fear" (Bush 2001b).

As even this small sampling of public rhetoric used by George W. Bush in the immediate aftermath of the 9/11 attacks demonstrates, the president's public remarks were steeped in the language of virtue and in the concepts of retributive justice. In most cases, as is evident here, the president's public discourse was also linked to a wider belief in the relationship of the attacks to a larger millenarian struggle between cosmic forces of good and evil and, in doing so, attempts to equate America's interests and objectives with those of the rest of the world. Yet a plausible case could be made that rhetoric such as this would be expected from any president, at least in the short run, given the heinous and unprecedented nature of the atrocities committed against American citizens on U.S. soil. Despite the arresting nature of that rhetoric, we are still left wanting to confirm that the George W. Bush administration has indeed orchestrated and overseen a profound "moralist turn."

In order to address that question, a more systematic and contextually sensitive examination of Bush's rhetoric with regard to the moral basis of a military response to 9/11 is needed. Is the Bush rhetoric truly representative of a grand departure (that is, a "moralist turn"), or is it a continuation and extension of the dominant discourse on the intersection of morality and warfare in the American tradition (e.g., the *Common Sense* discourse)? To conduct a careful examination requires greater separation from the events of 9/11. With that need for distance in mind, I have elected to direct the bulk of the analytical focus to the now-famous January 29, 2002, State of the Union address.

This speech appears to be a logical starting point for any attempt to critically examine the public framing of a military component to the "global war on terrorism" by the administration. First, it was developed and delivered several months after September 11, 2001, allowing for some passage of time; the rhetorical component of the speech cannot be attributed chiefly to emotion. Second, the address occurred well after the undertaking of the first policy responses to the attacks, including the assault in Afghanistan; as a result, the address can better be interpreted in light of its relationship to a larger prevailing discourse than to a concrete policy decision. Third, given the level of care and attention paid to the construction of any State of the Union address (and this monumental one in particular), it is very likely that the authorship and delivery of the address was consciously undertaken with the notion of issue-framing in mind. Given these considerations, then, it seems as if the January 2002 State of the Union address is a logical point of departure in attempting to situate the Bush rhetoric on the justification for war in relation to the *Common Sense* discourse.

In applying the same questions used to structure the earlier analysis of the *Common Sense* pamphlet to the 2002 State of the Union address, a number of important similarities in the employment of the discourse by Paine and Bush are evident. While at first glance the rhetorical situation appears profoundly different, in actuality the contextual environment in which both Paine and Bush were operating met the operational assumptions of "crisis" as defined by most of the leading scholars of that phenomenon (Brecher and Wilkenfeld 2000; Lebow 1981; Snyder and Diesing 1977). That is to say, each faced a situation in which the nation that was the chief audience for the rhetoric they employed faced a significant threat to its basic core values and interests. Moreover, Bush (like Paine) was bound by time constraints, encountered a high degree of uncertainty and imperfect information, and faced a scenario in which the future likelihood for violence was high. In seeking to articulate for the public a broader vision for an apparently limitless campaign against a worthy adversary that would rely heavily on military action, Bush encountered many of the same obstacles (and seized upon many of the same opportunities, at least in terms of discourse framing) facing Paine 225 years prior. Although without further exploration into other discourses (or other articulators of *this* discourse) it is difficult to say whether crisis settings themselves prompt a high level of moralistic rhetoric from the framers of public discourse, it does seem safe to conclude that both Paine and Bush employed such rhetoric when facing what they (and numerous others around them) perceived to be major crises to the future of the nation.

As was the case with Paine and *Common Sense*, it is also necessary to consider the *speaker-author* and, in particular, to evaluate what facets of George W. Bush's personal profile are germane to the rhetoric employed in the 2002 State of the Union address. As is almost universally known, G. W. Bush descends from one of the most prominent elite families in America, one that has taken on something of the character of a multi-generational political dynasty. This dynasty has, with each successive generation, become more closely aligned to the conservative wing of the Republican Party and its support for the individual and private sector and its public embrace of a politically active Christianity. Bush's formative experiences betray the privilege that one would expect from such lineage, and Bush himself was (by his own admission) an unremarkable and relatively directionless student, a pattern that defined Bush the business entrepreneur well into adulthood.

While the reality of Bush's social position as scion of an elite dynasty is markedly different from that of Paine (who was the child of poor and uneducated parents and left school at age twelve), some important biographical similarities do exist. Paine's adult experiences, particularly before emigrating to the colonies, bear two of the major hallmarks of Bush's adulthood prior to entering politics: namely, rootlessness and tumult in both work and family life and an increasing and public adherence to religious faith as a source of comfort and reassurance in times of turmoil (Kaye 2005). While a more systematic comparison of their biographies would seem in order, it would seem as if Bush's policies and rhetoric indicate that he shares with Paine (and countless other Americans, of course) a belief that the nation is best served by the promotion and close marriage of individual liberty with religious conviction and devotion. Furthermore, despite his upbringing (or perhaps because of it), the success story that is Bush's own political career (first as Texas governor, then as two-term U.S. president) has been attributed in large part to his effective use of populist and moralistic rhetoric, especially at critical turning points of perceived political crisis. This tack has been well-chronicled by journalists and pundits and suggest that, like Paine in 1776, Bush would be especially prone to rely on populist appeals laced with moralistic language in the months after the 9/11 attacks.[6]

So what, then, were the *intent* as well as the *content* of the rhetoric employed in the landmark State of the Union address delivered in January 2002? How does it compare to Paine's own discourse defining efforts? It is on this score that the address bears all of the hallmarks of the *Common Sense* discourse dissected earlier. In turning to the elements of the speech most relevant to the subject of intent, it is apparent that the intention of the speaker-author is not just to mobilize the public for the already initiated and ongoing *Operation*

Enduring Freedom (itself a telling, if anecdotal, observation as to the deeply embedded nature of the *Common Sense* discourse), but also to put the nation on a long-term war-footing. In seeking this objective, however, it is made clear in the address itself that the nation must gird itself against the dangers of complacency. This note is sounded early and often in the address; glib admonitions such as "the price of indifference would be catastrophic" give way to a more systematic articulation of the need to mitigate against indifference and to commit to a major war mobilization effort:

> We'll be deliberate, yet time is not on our side. I will not wait on events, while dangers gather. I will not stand by, as peril draws closer and closer . . . our war on terror is well begun, but it is only begun. . . .
>
> We can't stop short. If we stop now—leaving terror camps intact and terror states unchecked—our sense of security would be false and temporary. . . .
>
> It costs a lot to fight this war. We have spent more than a billion dollars a month—over $30 million a day—and we must be prepared for future operations. Afghanistan proved that expensive precision weapons defeat the enemy and spare innocent lives, and we need more of them. We need to replace the aging aircraft and make our military more agile, to put our troops anywhere in the world quickly and safely . . . my budget includes the largest increase in defense spending in two decades—because while the price of freedom and security is high, it is never too high. Whatever it costs to defend our country, we will pay.

In this regard Bush's State of the Union address very much channels Paine's *Common Sense*, which famously (and in highly gendered language) challenged the citizens of the colonies to avoid "fatal and unmanly slumbers" and to "pursue determinately some fixed object," namely, severance of colonial dependency on Britain. Yet the similarity in intent does not end there; both author-speakers bolster their admonitions against complacency with the looming specter of a daunting campaign against a dangerous adversary. The task facing Paine in this regard was relatively simple; *Common Sense* was, after all, attempting to foment insurrection against the world's foremost economic and military superpower within a loose confederation of colonies lacking any significant military assets and constrained by economic dependency. Conversely, Bush's efforts toward the same end were necessarily far more difficult in that the terms of the campaign as well as the nature of the adversary were much less familiar to the intended audience. In addition, rather than occupying the ultimate "underdog" role, the United States was now itself the world's foremost economic and military superpower, and the American public's perception of U.S. supremacy as incontestable and unprecedented presented serious obstacles. Bush's address accordingly took explicit aim at Americans' own sense of invincibility, largely by highlighting the omnipresence, and limitlessness of the terrorist threat[7]:

> Our discoveries in Afghanistan confirmed our worst fears, and showed us the true scope of the task ahead . . . we have found diagrams of American nuclear power plants and public water facilities, detailed instructions for making chemical weapons, surveillance maps of American cities, and thorough descriptions of landmarks in America and throughout the world. What we have found in Afghanistan confirms that, far from ending there, our war against terror is only beginning. . . .
>
> Time and distance from the events of September 11 will not make us safer unless we act on its lessons. America is no longer protected by vast oceans. We are protected from attack only by vigorous action abroad, and increased vigilance at home.

If the overriding intent of the 2002 State of the Union address was similar to the *Common Sense* pamphlet—that is, to protect against complacency by training the collective focus of the nation on the presence of a major threat—it is perhaps not surprising that the two historical bookends of the *Common Sense* discourse also mirror one another in terms of *content*. Paine's vision of the legitimate and morally permissible place for military force in the American experiment (as a just means to counter oppression and domination and promote liberal ideals) is front and center in Bush's address. For instance, with respect to the moral basis or "just cause" of the military dimension of a broader "war against terror," illustrations within the text of the speech abound. The words "just" or "justice" in conjunction with the U.S. military role in that war are used eight times; likewise, with respect to the defined enemy of terrorists and their sponsors, "evil" is used six times. More instructive is the context in which these assertions are situated:

When I called our troops into action, I did so with complete confidence in their courage and skill. And tonight, thanks to them, we are winning the war on terror. The men and women of our Armed Forces have delivered a message now clear to every enemy of the United States: even 7,000 miles away, across oceans and continents, on mountaintops and in caves—you will not escape the justice of this nation. . . .

I assure you and all who have lost a loved one that our cause is just, and our country will never forget the debt we owe . . . and all who gave their lives for freedom. Our cause is just, and it continues. . . .

States like these [e.g., North Korea, Iran, and Iraq], and their terrorist allies, constitute an axis of evil, arming to threaten the peace of the world.

While this proclamation of an "axis of evil" has become the most infamous turn of phrase in this address (and arguably of Bush's entire Presidency, given its instrumental value in linking the 9/11 attacks to Saddam Hussein's Iraq), the excerpts cited as well as others embedded within the speech convey the degree to which the *Common Sense* discourse, which relies heavily on the idea that the United States has a duty to (and naturally does) employ its military force in pursuit of virtuous ends, is reflected in Bush's rhetoric.

Those virtuous ends, as the speech makes clear in repeated instances, are two sides of one coin: the promotion of liberal ideals such as "freedom" and "justice" and the defeat of oppression. On the duty to uphold and promote those liberal ideals long ago articulated by people like Paine, Bush is unequivocal: "America will always stand firm for the non-negotiable demands of human dignity: the rule of law; limits on the power of the state; respect for women; private property; free speech; equal justice; and religious tolerance. . . . History has called America and our allies to action. And it is our responsibility and our privilege to fight freedom's fight."

Of course most, if not all, of these concepts are nebulous and subject to differing interpretations; furthermore, most, if not all, are only entrenched both culturally and institutionally in a small number of nation-states in the contemporary international system. These nettlesome "facts" are hardly troubling for purveyors of the *Common Sense* discourse; in fact, they demonstrate the extent to which that discourse, like any dominant discourse, defines and redefines what "reality" is. And "reality" as created by the *Common Sense* discourse dictates that the use of American military might in defense of the ideals themselves wherever they are deemed to be under threat is legitimate.

With respect to the defeat of "oppression," Bush took occasion to celebrate what appeared to some at the time to be a resounding military victory in Afghanistan. He congratulated the nation for its successful use of military force in this pursuit: "In four short months, our nation has . . . destroyed Afghanistan's terrorist training camps, saved a people from starvation, and freed a country from brutal oppression."

The dubious veracity of these claims notwithstanding, the larger point is that they signify the presence of a *casus belli* consistent with the *Common Sense* discourse; for example, the defeat of oppression, wherever it presents itself, by all means necessary. In this vein, Bush continues in the Address to elaborate on the incontestable barbarity of "the terrorist enemy," which in accordance with the moral logic of the dominant discourse obligates the United States to go to war and, importantly, to engage in a war without limits or restraints:

> We have seen the depth of our enemies' hatred in videos, where they laugh about the loss of innocent life. And the depth of their hatred is equaled by the madness of the destruction they design.
>
> These enemies view the entire world as a battlefield, and we must pursue them wherever they are. So long as training camps operate, so long as nations harbor terrorists, freedom is at risk. And America and our allies must not, and will not, allow it.
>
> My hope is that all nations will heed our call, and eliminate the terrorist parasites who threaten their countries and our own. Many nations are acting forcefully . . . but some governments will be timid in the face of terror. And make no mistake about it: if they do not act, America will.

Having established the striking degree to which the *Common Sense* discourse permeated the intent and content of the 2002 State of the Union address, one must also consider the *intended audience* of the speech. On this score Bush's address is very much similar to Paine's pamphlet and the discourse that it spawned in its reliance on populist-moralist language in making the case for war directly to the public (in a way that only the "bully pulpit" of a State of the Union address can). However, Bush's address was also very much a product of its time and for that reason differs significantly from Paine's initial articulation of the *Common Sense* discourse. The main axis on which this difference turns is in the unqualified equation of American interests with the interests of the world at large. Whereas Paine set the wheels of this equation in motion, the audience for which he intended this message was a purely domestic one; his goal was to bolster anti-British sentiment in the colonies by convincing the citizens of an emerging and vulnerable nation-state that their cause was also the worlds' (or, at least, the world excluding Britain, France, Spain, and the other major powers). By virtue of his role as the role of head-of-state of a global superpower in an era of twenty-four hour news cycles and global media, Bush's audience was both domestic and international. That Bush seized upon this and intentionally delivered his message to both audiences simultaneously is reflected in the manner in which he underscored the constructed overlap of national and global interest, a long-standing tenet of the *Common Sense* discourse:

> I know we can overcome evil with greater good. And we have a great opportunity during this time of war to lead the world toward the values that will bring lasting peace. All fathers and mothers, in all societies, want their children to be educated, and live free from poverty and violence. No people on Earth yearn to be oppressed, or aspire to servitude, or eagerly await the midnight knock of the secret police. If anyone doubts this, let them look to Afghanistan, where the Islamic "street" greeted the fall of tyranny with song and celebration . . . America will lead by defending liberty and justice because they are right and true and unchanging for all people everywhere. . . .
>
> America will take the side of brave men and women who advocate these values around the world, including the Islamic world, because we have a greater objective than eliminating threats and containing resentment. We seek a just and peaceful world beyond the war on terror.

What does the rhetoric contained in the 2002 State of the Union address (much of which was excerpted and deconstructed here) *reveal about society at large*? Clearly it suggests that the concern with framing the use of military force as "just" is a singular preoccupation of American elites, and convincingly establishing a "just cause" that is consistent with the *Common Sense* discourse (e.g., one that turns on the promotion of liberal ideals) seems sufficient to set the country on the course to war. This dynamic seems strongly confirmed by considering the period after the address in which very few voices were raised (in Congress, the media, or the public) in opposition to a looming invasion of Iraq. This analysis also suggests a normative basis for America's war-making in which the use of force is clearly and closely associated with exacting retribution. In turn this is reflective of the particularly (and perhaps peculiarly) American equation of justice with exacting punishment in contrast with other conceptions of justice defined around notions of fairness, restoration, and remediation.

Conclusion

The findings of this comparative discourse analysis suggest that characterizations of a "moralist turn" with respect to the current Bush administration profoundly miss the mark. As is evident here, the rhetoric employed by President Bush with respect to the morality of the military dimension of the "global war on terrorism" is hardly new, either in terms of basic content or frequency of use. Indeed, as this analysis shows, it bears a striking and consistent similarity to the rhetoric of the dominant discourse on that subject: the *Common Sense* discourse first authored by Thomas Paine. As this research shows, Paine was the first major public figure to link the overriding belief in American exceptionalism with the moral obligation to use military force in defense of idealist interests. Potential contradictions within this linkage were then summarily dismissed as that discourse evolved alongside the nation itself. Chiefly this dismissal has occurred through the assertion (sustained and reified by this discourse) that America's interests and the world's interests are indistinguishable, and they are mutually and equally propelled by exacting justice on the global stage.

In this light, the Bush administration's foreign policy rhetoric can be interpreted as the full realization of the *Common Sense* discourse rather than a radical departure in moralism.[8] In the content and intent of the message, the motivations and beliefs of the messenger, the audience(s) to which the message is directed, and in what the message reveals about the larger society that consumes it, Bush's public rhetoric with respect to the moral basis for war is thoroughly reflective of the exceptionalism, idealism, and moral reasoning at the heart of that dominant discourse. Yet there is, in fact, a unique dimension to the manner in which this discourse has been employed by Bush and other foreign policy principals within his administration. Given not only the frequency but also the intensity with which the Bush administration in general, and George W. Bush in particular, resorts to moralistic appeals in framing the question of war in a social context, it can be said that the evolution of that discourse has reached a point of no return. In other words, not only has the Bush administration orchestrated the full realization of the dominant discourse initiated by Paine so long ago, it has also overseen its final stage; that is, the discourse has reached the point when its authors serve it rather than the discourse serving the authors.

These characterizations, all evident in the moral rhetoric analyzed in this chapter, should hardly seem novel, particularly as the world continues to come to grips with the aftermath of the invasion of Iraq. But what is new is the strength and consistency with which these sentiments are found to apply in a study of greater breadth. There is more to representations of the United States as a "global supercop" than mere perception; the *casus belli* (case of war) prominently on display within the rhetorical justifications for the use of military force reinforces this role and thus supports this representation. What emerges in the end is a symbiosis of moral rhetoric and material interests; the "righteous realism" of a superpower bent on projecting its own interests as the interests of all and legitimating its forceful pursuit of those interests through selective appeals to morality.

NOTES

1. See http://www.september11news.com/InternationalReaction.htm, a Web site maintained as a pilot project of the U.S. Library of Congress, which contains these as well as other similar statements and reactions, for further evidence supporting this claim.
2. See The National Security Strategy of the United States of America, September 2002, for copious supporting evidence.
3. It is important to note that "discourses" are broadly defined entities. A few caveats are therefore in order. Though there may be particular windows for dissemination and articulation of a discourse that are especially pivotal in the construction of that discourse, discourses should not be equated with a certain speech, publication, event, etc. Furthermore, discourses are rarely (if ever) constructed by one particular individual;

even when they are predominantly influenced by the contributions of an individual, discourses should not be characterized as "belonging" to that individual. Similarly, while discursive studies by definition explore the interface between dominant discourses and purveyors of political and social power, it is not the case that such purveyors necessarily be office-holders or individuals holding official institutional rank (such as Thomas Paine).

4. That the pamphlet was intended for, and eagerly consumed by, a mass popular audience (it has been characterized as the most widely read publication in eighteenth-century America) only further establishes its importance as a nearly textbook example of a discourse-defining social product.

5. Indeed, this ideological firmament might in some cases have even led the United States to outstrip this maturation process, as in the bold but unenforceable proclamation of exclusivity in the Western Hemisphere in the Monroe Doctrine (1823).

6. Analysis of Bush's populist rhetoric—and the genesis, purpose, and careful construction of it—has become something of a cottage industry of late. See the many analyses by William Schneider in the *National Journal*, or James Fallows in *The Atlantic Monthly*, for examples..

7. While it do not fit neatly within this analysis, it is also instructive to note the degree to which Bush's address uses the stories of the victims of the 9/11 attacks to make the case for vigilance and against complacency and invincibility. Bush's address begins (as have all recent State of the Union speeches) with a public acknowledgement and/or brief intro-duction of individuals deemed deserving of mention by the White House. In the 2002 address, recognized parties included not only Afghan political leaders such as Hamid Karzai and Dr. Sima Samar but also a number of individuals whose sons, fathers, or husbands died in the World Trade Center and Afghanistan. The speech then abruptly departs from this public mourning to the discussion of "discoveries in Afghanistan" that "confirmed our worst fears."

8. The early twentieth-century philosopher Leonard Nelson offers an important distinction between morality and moralism, suggesting that the latter is the more accurate term here. In his *System of Ethics* (1956) he notes: "I call 'moralism' a system of normative moral principles sufficient for the positive regulation of life. In other words, moralism excludes the possibility of morally indifferent actions. According to it, every action must be characterized as either fulfillment or violation of duty."

References

Althus, Scott L., and Devon M. Largio. 2004. When Osama became Saddam: Origins and consequences of the change in America's public enemy #1. *PS: Political Science & Politics* 37(4): 795–99.

Beatty, J. 2003. In the name of God. *The Atlantic Monthly* (March 2003).

Berelson, Bernard, Paul F. Lazarsfeld, and W. N. McPhee. 1954. *Voting: A study of opinion formation in a presidential campaign.* Chicago: University of Chicago Press.

Bloch, R. H. 1985. *Visionary republic: Millennial themes in American thought, 1756–1800.* New York: Cambridge University Press.

Bovard, J. 2004. *The Bush betrayal.* New York: Palgrave Macmillan.

Brecher, M., and J. Wilkenfeld. 2000. *A study of crisis.* Ann Arbor: University of Michigan Press.

Bush, George W. 2001a. Statement by the president in his *Address to the Nation.* Office of the White House. September 11. http://www.whitehouse.gov/news/releases/2001/09/20010911-16.html (accessed May 5, 2006).

———. 2001b. *Presidential address to the nation.* Office of the White House. October 7. http://www.whitehouse.gov/news/releases/2001/10/20011007-8.html (accessed May 5, 2006).

———. 2003. *We will prevail: President George W. Bush on war, terrorism, and freedom.* New York: Continuum.

CNN.com. 2001. *Bush vows to rid the world of evil-doers.* CNN.com September 16. http://archives.cnn.com/2001/US/09/16/gen.bush.terrorism (accessed December 29, 2005).

Clausewitz, C. von. 1984. *On war.* Eds. and trans. Michael Howard and Peter Paret. Princeton, NJ: Princeton University Press.

Cohen, M. 1984. Moral skepticism and international relations. *Philosophy and Public Affairs* 13(4): 299–346.

Covell, C. 1998. *Kant and the law of peace: A study in the philosophy of international law and international relations.* London: Macmillan.

Davis, T. R., and S. M. Lynn-Jones. 1987. Citty on a Hill. *Foreign Policy* 66:20–38.

Derrida, J. 1976. *Of grammatology.* Trans. Gayatri Chakravorty Spivak. Baltimore: Johns Hopkins University Press.

———. 1983. *Dissemination.* Trans. Barbara Johnson. Chicago: University of Chicago Press.

Dickens, D. R., and A. Fontana, *eds.* 1994. *Postmodernism and social inquiry.* New York: Guilford.

Doyle, M. W. 1983a. Kant, liberal legacies, and foreign affairs. Part 1. *Philosophy and Public Affairs* 12(3): 205–35.

———. 1983b. Kant, liberal legacies, and foreign affairs. Part 2. *Philosophy and Public Affairs* 12(4): 323–53.

Fitzsimmons, D. M. 1995. Tom Paine's new world order: Idealistic internationalism in the ideology of early American foreign relations. *Diplomatic History* 19:569–82.

Foucault, M. 1976. *The archaeology of knowledge and the discourse on language*. New York: Harper and Row.

Frohmann, B. 1994. Communication technologies and the politics of postmodern information science. *Canadian Journal of Information and Library Science* 19 (2): 1–22.

Hartz, L. 1955. *The liberal tradition in America: An interpretation of American political thought since the revolution*. New York: Harcourt, Brace, and World.

Howard, M. 1978. *War and the liberal conscience*. New Brunswick, NJ: Rutgers University Press.

Kant, I. 1905. *Perpetual peace: A philosophical essay, 1795*. Translated with introduction and notes by M. Campbell Smith. London: S. Sonnenschein.

Kaye, Harvey J. 2005. *Thomas Paine and the promise of America*. New York: Hill and Wang.

Keane, John. 1995. *Tom Paine: A political life*. London: Bloomsbury.

Jameson, Fredric. 1992. *Postmodernism, or, the cultural logic of late capitalism*. Durham, NC: Duke University Press.

Lebow, Richard Ned. 1981. *Between peace and war: The nature of international crisis*. Baltimore: Johns Hopkins University Press.

Lerner, Max. 1957. *America as a civilization*. New York: Simon and Schuster.

Michels, Robert. 1949. *Political parties: A sociological study of the oligarchical tendencies of modern democracy*. Glencoe, IL: Free Press.

Milton, John. 2003. *Paradise lost*. New ed., ed. Merritt Y. Hughes. Indianapolis: Hackett.

Nelson, Leonard. 1956. *System of ethics*. New Haven, CT: Yale University Press.

Paine, Thomas. 1776. *Common sense*. Philadelphia: W. and T. Bradford. http://www.bartleby.com/133/ (accessed August 8, 2006).

Pew Research Center for the People and the Press. 2001. *Economy, education, social security dominate public's policy agenda*. Pew Research Center for the People and the Press. September 6. http://people-press.org/reports/display.php3?ReportID=4 (accessed February 2, 2006).

———. 2002. *Americans thinking about Iraq, but focused on the economy*. Pew Research Center for the People and the Press. October 10, 2002, http://people-press.org/reports/display.php3?ReportID=162. (accessed February 2, 2006).

Schneider, William. 2005. About that cowboy rhetoric. . . . *The Atlantic* (January 25).

Singer, Peter. 2004. *The president of good and evil: The ethics of George W. Bush.* New York: Dutton.

Snyder, Glenn H., and Paul Diesing. 1977. *Conflict among nations: Bargaining, decision making, and system structure in international crises.* Princeton, NJ: Princeton University Press.

The White House. 2002. President delivers State of the Union address. January 29. http://www.whitehouse.gov/news/releases/2002/01/20020129-11.html (accessed December 18, 2005).

Weimann, Gabriel. 1991. The influentials: Back to the concept of opinion leaders? *Public Opinion Quarterly* 55:267–79.

Zarefsky, David. 2002. The presidency has always been a place for rhetorical leadership. In *The presidency and rhetorical leadership.* College Station: Texas A & M University Press.

———. 2004. George W. Bush discovers rhetoric: September 20, 2001 and the U.S. response to terrorism. In *The ethos of rhetoric.* Columbia: University of South Carolina Press.

C H A P T E R   6

THE PORNOGRAPHIC BARBARISM OF THE SELF-REFLECTING SIGN[1]

Paul A. Taylor

INTRODUCTION

"Fundamentally, such violence is not so much an event as the explosive form assumed by an absence of events. Or rather the *implosive* form: and what implodes here is the political void . . . the silence of history which has been repressed at the level of individual psychology, and the indifference and silence of everyone. We are dealing, therefore, not with irrational episodes in the life of our society, but instead with something that is completely in accord with that society's accelerating plunge into the void."[2] Despite the heated debates and huge mass public demonstrations about the rights and wrongs of Iraq War in 2003, the biggest shifts in the British and American publics' perception of the conflict occurred through a series of vivid, defining images at various crucial stages. Thus what proved to be undue optimism was at its peak during the fall of Baghdad and the Ozymandias-like toppling of Saddam Hussein's statue, complete with a forewarning of the cultural misunderstandings to come when a U.S. soldier momentarily draped the U.S. flag around the statue's face. Further grounds for Western triumphalism were provided with the images of a disorientated and disheveled

Saddam shortly after his capture on December 13, 2003, with the bathos of his last underground hiding-place that contrasted markedly with the pictures of abandoned palaces. In early May 2004, the flip side of this ability of images to dictate the political climate became apparent when President Bush and Prime Minister Blair came under sustained pressure because photographs of prisoner abuse in Baghdad's Abu Ghraib jail appeared in the world's media. There are two key aspects to the subsequent furor that are illuminated by Baudrillard's notion of the *ob-scene* and the consistent attention he pays throughout his work to the excessively explicit, desymbolized nature of the contemporary mediascape.

1. The unequal relationship between the effect the pictures had compared to the words of previously unheeded imageless reports. Amnesty International, for example, had reported months earlier, in February 2004, allegations of torture and serious human rights violations without any impact.
2. The question arises as to why these images made so much more of an impact compared to the large number of previously witnessed scenes of more conventional military violence and its civilian victims.

The thesis offered here as an answer to this question is that, even if only for a short while and for reasons perhaps still not adequately articulated or fully recognized, the "Pornographic" nature of the Abu Ghraib photographs spoke to a strong sense of unease in the public. Despite politicians' protestations about a few bad apples spoiling the barrel, the Western public had an intuitive sense that the photographs represented something deeper about the society that sent out such troops. It is this "something" this chapter seeks to explore.

Perhaps the most iconic and evocative of all the abuse photographs was that of an Iraqi man being subjected to the faked threat of electrocution. The prisoner is perched atop a box in a makeshift shroud, covered with a hood reminiscent of the Ku Klux Klan with pretend electrodes attached to his hands. The image is particularly evocative for Christian viewers. It resonates with connotations of the crucifixion and the representation of Christ the Redeemer with welcoming hands outstretched at his side. This chapter explores the profound implications such a poignant tableau has for our conceptualization of political violence and what it says about the nature of a society that could create the image of an abused, Christ-like figure standing on a box. For those who remain relatively impervious to any unusual level of moral disquiet over the Abu Ghraib pictures, the chapter also raises a pragmatic political issue for consideration. This is the extent to which there is a link between the social processes that constructed the prisoner abuse scandal and the wider political environment of the international coalition's "war against terror."

The chapter concludes by arguing that a keen understanding of the West's unhealthy relationship to the mediated image might lie behind the malevolent orchestration of such heavily mediated events as the 9/11 tragedy. Marshall McLuhan[3] offers the myth of Narcissus as a defining metaphor for the West's problematic relationship to the screen. Following McLuhan and Baudrillard, it is argued that the failure of military intelligence that led to 9/11 is at least partially due to a myopic perspective upon our own culture. Dealing with international terrorism might be a lot easier if we stopped waging a very real and bloody war on an abstract noun ("terror") and instead sought to emulate the malevolently keen media savvy of such figures as Osama bin Laden. Although it is obvious that the West desperately needs to develop a more sophisticated and less reified understanding of the Islamic Other, this would actually be much easier if we were more sensitive to the processes of meaning-construction within our own heavily mediated culture. This culture is increasingly pornographic in a manner both reflected in the Abu Ghraib photographs but also perhaps somewhat obscured by the misleadingly exceptional status claimed for them by our politicians.

THE SELF-REFLECTING SIGN

"From the mutation and conflation of confessional culture and mediated 'real life' had emerged the broader trend of the barbarism of the self-reflecting sign."[4] In this quote, Bracewell refers to the "self-reflecting sign" as a defining feature of the contemporary mediascape. It is not the *self-reflexive sign*, which would involve a sense of reflection upon an image's substantive meaning—rather, this chapter uses the conventional concept of pornography and Baudrillard's concept of *the ob-scene* to explore how the self-reflecting sign refers to the image that has no meaning beyond its own tautological facticity. We shall see how literal Pornography—[upper case

"P"]—acts as a trope for the dominant social values of self-reflecting signs and their visual excess—pornography [lower case "p"]. I examine the present-day manifestations of this extenuated *social porn*, and its profound political consequences, evident across a spectrum of confessional, confrontational, and violent media formats. Just as the obsessively repetitive attention paid by the media to the terrible images of the 9/11 tragedy occluded more substantive considerations of the event's significance, so too do debates about the Abu Ghraib images threaten to obscure the deep social causes and consequences of the symptoms they reflect.

The images of abuse caused widespread shock in the West (interestingly, in the Arab world, instead of shock, the pictures tended to be met with a mixture of anger and a resigned sense of déjà vu).[5] There might also, however, be an element of denial in the Western response. Thus even some U.S. Senators and Congressional Representatives, highly critical of Donald Rumsfeld during his evidence to both Houses, took the opportunity to emphasize how this behavior was not representative of U.S. forces in general (see, for example, Senator Joseph Lieberman's comments[6]). Similarly, speaking to the media while standing alongside King Abdullah II of Jordan in the White House garden on May 6, 2004, President Bush said "sorry for the humiliation suffered by the Iraqi prisoners." He then went on to say that he was "as equally sorry that people seeing these pictures didn't understand the true nature and heart of America."[7] Although these assertions may be true, they still distract from a key element of the disgust the images produced, which is the central focus of this chapter: their pornographic rather than Pornographic nature.

In Britain, the distraction from the deeper significance of the Abu Ghraib photographs came in the form of a debate over whether similar pictures of British troops abusing Iraqi prisoners elsewhere were fake or not. In May 2004, Piers Morgan, editor of the United Kingdom's *Daily Mirror* tabloid newspaper, was fired when the photographs he printed were proved to be false. It is interesting to note that when doubts were raised as to their veracity some debate took place as to whether they were still accurate representations of actual events not originally photographed. In this particular instance, although the issue of authenticity dominated proceedings, possibly fake pictures nevertheless did allow more substantive discussion about actual abuse that had taken place. The debate over *the Daily*

Mirror pictures provided an interesting example of Bracewell's assessment of the contemporary status of the image where: "'authenticity' is the hallmark of truth, and hence the gauge of social value . . . *there is now the sense that authenticity itself can be sculpted to suggest veracity as an image, in which truth remains ambiguous.*"[8] Whilst the fact remains that both the U.S. and British images of prisoner abuse had a disproportionately powerful political impact, the pictures also illustrate the ambivalent political power of images.

Normally the postmodern concept of the *hyperreal* (typically in Baudrillard's *Simulations* and Eco's *Travels in Hyperreality*[9]) the paradoxical notion of a mediated phenomenon that is more real than the real itself has negative connotations. Baudrillard argues that the hyperreal often detracts attention from the real issues. For example, in *Simulations* he suggests that the public investigation that followed the Watergate scandal merely hid the innate corruptness of U.S. politics, and Disneyland's main purpose is to disguise the fact that American society at large is really modeled on a Disney-like ethos of commodified fantasia. In the particular instance of the British photographs, however, fake pictures provoked a valuable self-examination of the coalition's practices and values. Unfortunately, more often the process tends to be reversed: *real images often produce inauthentic discourse.* Images determine politics largely irrespective of their truth or objective significance.

REDEFINING VIOLENCE

"But why should we hear about body bags, and deaths, and how many, what day it's gonna happen, and how many this or what do you suppose? Or, I mean, it's, it's not relevant. So why should I waste my beautiful mind on something like that? And watch him suffer."[10] Notwithstanding his mother's reluctance to confront the full implications of the war in Iraq, the president's concern about the effect of the pictures upon people's perception of the United States is an indication of the need to broaden our understanding of the concept of political violence and the media's role in its portrayal. Political violence can be reinterpreted by concentrating upon the connotations that lie beyond its primary definition of the exertion of physical force. In addition to great physical harm suffered by the prisoners, the word violence also denotes the following:

1. a powerful, untamed, or devastating force;
2. great strength of feeling, as in language;
3. an unjust, unwarranted, or unlawful display of force, esp. such as tends to overawe or intimidate;
4. "do violence to," as in:
     a. to inflict harm upon; damage or violate: they did violence to the prisoners.
     b. to distort or twist the sense or intention of: the reporters did violence to my speech.[11]

Contra President Bush, I argue that the true nature and heart of America is in fact revealed by those photographs, and the media does violence to the fundamental nature of our political discourse. The Abu Ghraib images effected a response that mere words had failed to unblock: "It was the photographs that made all this 'real' to President Bush and his associates. Up to then, there had been only words which are a lot easier to cover up in our age of infinite digital self-reproduction and self-dissemination."[12]

The violence Western reporters do to political speech occurs when, for example, the term "abuse" is used rather than "torture," or the prevailing use of the euphemistic term "contractors" is used to describe, in postwar Iraq, what were previously conventionally referred to as "mercenaries."

We will see in the following sections that definitions one, two, and three are each directly relevant to the media's images from Iraq. However, I will predominantly focus upon definition four and will use the term "violence" to explore the harm done to the body politic by a societal excess of images of which the Abu Ghraib pictures are a particularly offensive and malign example. The impact of the prison photographs brings together all the different definitions of violence. Their effects on public opinion were untamed and produced a great strength of feeling (definitions one and two) and the activities they recorded involved an unjust and intimidating display of force (definition three). Definition five, however, encapsulates the wider social harm of the image.

"THEY DID VIOLENCE TO THE PRISONERS"—THE PORNOGRAPHIC SOCIETY AND RITUAL HUMILIATION

- Pornography is far bigger than rock music and far bigger than Hollywood movies.
- Americans spend more money on strip clubs than they spend on theatre, opera, ballet, jazz, and classical concerts combined.
- In 1975 the total retail value of all the hard-core pornography in America was estimated at five to ten million dollars. Last year Americans spent eight billion dollars on mediated sex.[13]

The Abu Ghraib photographs are Pornographic because of their explicit sexual content, but they are also pornographic in a more attenuated and abstract manner. The pornographic nature of the abuse was part of *a ritual humiliation* of the Iraqi prisoners. Such ritual abuse is an extreme example of a ubiquitous, voyeuristic aesthetic that now pervades wider Western society. It is increasingly Pornographic in the obvious literal and quantitative sense that Pornography is much more socially acceptable and widely available. In addition, more qualitatively, according to Amis, Porn, "is much, much dirtier than it used to be, but Gonzo porno is gonzo: way out there. The new element is violence."[14] "*Gonzo*" refers to wild, eccentric, or bizarre behavior and was first used to describe the almost ethnographic, drug-fuelled, direct-experience journalism of the American reporter Hunter S. Thompson, who rose to prominence with *Hell's Angels* (1966)—a vivid account of his travels with the infamous motorcycling gang.

In more recent years "*gonzo*" is a label applied to a genre of Pornography. The advent of increasingly sophisticated hand-held cameras has added a new amateur look (and indeed amateur involvement) to the more glossy Hollywood-influenced aesthetic that previously dominated the U.S. Porn industry. The Abu Ghraib pictures can be read in the light of this recent evolution in both Porn and its mirroring in the wider trend of social porn. More than this, the permeation of the gonzo aesthetic is evident in the reality TV formats that have evolved to produce increasingly extreme forms of ritualized humiliation. The retrospectively benign formats of such shows *as Candid Camera*[15] have been replaced by a harsher range of programs.

In the hubris-generating, puncturing celebrity-obsessed genre, we have recently witnessed the conspicuous consumption and defecation of *MTV Cribs*, *Celebrity Detox*, and MTV's *Jackass*.[16] A much darker but at first glance semantically related format to both *JackAss* and *Celebrity Detox* is the recent best-selling gonzo-violence video *Bumfights*. This is a U.S.-produced underground video that has recently gained mainstream notoriety for showing homeless people bare-knuckle fighting in return for food, money, and alcohol.[17] In May 2004, British Channel 5 used a "documentary" entitled *Bumfights: A Video Too Far* as a vehicle for showing footage from the video.

The sociological thesis that a general cultural climate is the underlying cause of the Abu Ghraib symptoms has recently received support from an unusual source. Rush Limbaugh, the U.S. right-wing radio shock-jock, said that too much was being made of the Abu Ghraib pictures. He claimed obtusely that they were very similar to the hazing ritual common in U.S. fraternities: "This is no different than what happens at the Skull and Bones initiation and we're going to ruin people's lives over it, and we're going to hamper our military effort, and then we are going to really hammer them because they had a good time."[18] We can now examine in more detail the exact nature of that "good time" by exploring the roots of social porn.

The Pornographic Zeitgeist

I have seen in the windows the pale blue glow of at least one television in every home. And I am told that many family meals are eaten in front of that screen as well. And perhaps this explains the face of Americans, the eyes that never appear satisfied, at peace with their work, or the day God has given them; these people have the eyes of very small children who are forever looking for their next source of distraction, entertainment, or a sweet taste in their mouth.[19]

[W]e need tits and arse because they have got to be available to us; to be pawed, fucked, wanked over. Because we're men? No. Because we're consumers. Because those are things we like, things we intrinsically feel or have been conned into believing will give us value, release satisfaction. We value them so we need to at least have the illusion of their availability. For tits and arse read coke, crisps, speedboats, cars, houses, computers, designer labels, replica shirts. That's why advertising and pornography are similar; they sell the illusion of availability and the non-consequence of consumption.[20]

[W]e were just that bit too old to buy into the rumble of a world described by advertising and products. . . . That was the world where everything had turned into an idea of itself, where life no longer had an inner life. . . . It's a process which just seems to have built up, like an accumulation of fat around the heart's weary muscle.[21]

I have argued elsewhere[22] for the importance of fiction as a useful resource with which to understand the social zeitgeist better. The effect of the Abu Ghraib pictures has been so shocking because, whether explicitly acknowledged or not, they evoke in the viewer recognition of a disturbing Western cultural trend that is only belatedly and involuntarily being faced. The symptoms have been previously acknowledged within contemporary zeitgeist-capturing novels such as those previously quoted. The first quotation is particularly apposite to our purposes given that it presents a Middle Eastern perspective on U.S. culture. In *The House of Sand and Fog*, through the voice of an exiled Iranian army officer, Andre Dubus highlights the childlike dependence upon distraction and entertainment that he perceives to be deep at the heart of U.S. culture. The second quotation is taken from Irvine Welsh's *Porno*, a novel he wrote in response to the growth of gonzo-style, do-it-yourself porn he had observed in Britain. Given the sexual element to the events at Abu Ghraib, the key point to be taken from Welsh is the link between Porn and the essential values of a consumer society. Welsh's claim that commodities provide "things we intrinsically feel or have been conned into believing will give us value, release satisfaction" resonates closely with Rush Limbaugh's exculpatory rationale for the abuse: "You know, these people are being fired at every day. I'm talking about people having a good time, these people. You ever heard of emotional release?"[23] The third quotation, from Bracewell's *Perfect Tense*, gives an office worker's account of metropolitan ennui, and his expression of "the insistence of image over substance" provides a fictional variation of Baudrillard and Eco's concept of the hyperreal. Bracewell's phrase, "the rumble of a world described by advertising and products" speaks directly to how the U.S. government's explicit couching of America's overseas image functions in terms of a consumer brand.

Branding or Branded?

> [T]here is a fundamental flaw in the American view of "perception management" on an international stage. . . . It emanates from a Harvard MBA type of mentality that if you get the marketing right, anything will sell. One of the case studies on that MBA programme was . . . Charlotte Beers, formerly of Madison Avenue (she once led J. Walter Thompson Worldwide and Ogilvy and Mather), and until last year under secretary of state for public affairs and public diplomacy. Colin Powell is famously on record as saying "Well, guess what? She got me to buy Uncle Ben's rice, and so there's nothing wrong with getting somebody who knows how to sell something." Well, Uncle Sam isn't Uncle Ben and you can't sell something to people who have no water to boil it with. But now they do have oil on which to pour yet another troublesome example that Uncle Sam might not be who Uncle Sam says he is. Uncle Sam is looking more and more like the Ugly American . . . the soldiers who were photographed in these "trophy" pictures are of a different breed of Americans. *They are the Jerry Springer elements of American society*, and they are not pretty. . . . Seeing is believing, whether it's on the Jerry Springer show or in this week's newspapers.[24]

There is a certain morbid symmetry in the fact that, in addition to the literal imprisonment they depict, the controversy caused by the Abu Ghraib pictures reflect how U.S. society is confined by its excessive reliance upon the image. The visceral disgust they caused can, however, be seen as the flip side of the image-driven boosterism that is an intrinsic part of America's self-presentation. Its political use of images is violent in the sense of the definitions one, two, and three, and a failure to adequately understand the negative consequences of this is at the core of the United States's poor "image" within international public opinion. Ironically, this image is so poor because of its desire to excessively micromanage the process of image-creation (definition three). The concept of *ideology* is doubtless for some a quaint relic of Marxist theory and media effects are notoriously difficult to irrefutably "prove" to the satisfaction of all. Perhaps a fresh perspective upon both, however, can be gained by looking at the intimate relationship the concept of ideology has with the production of images and how the single most important contemporary ideology is an image-driven discourse of which Jerry Springer is but the (il)logical conclusion.

Mitchell emphasizes the iconic basis of ideology, arguing that the concept is etymologically grounded "in the notion of mental entities or 'ideas' that provide the materials of thought. Insofar as these ideas are understood as images—as pictorial, graphic signs imprinted or projected on the medium of consciousness—then ideology . . . is really an iconology, a theory of imagery."[25] For Burke, ideology is thus related not to truthful images, "but of falsely reductive images that could only lead to political tyranny."[26] For Coleridge: "Any 'idea' worthy of the name . . . is distinguished precisely by its inability to be rendered in pictorial or material form: it is a 'living educt' of the imagination, a 'power' that can be rendered only by the translucence of a symbolic form, never by a 'mere' image."[27]
An idiosyncratically expressed preference for the cultural richness of the symbolic over the essential emptiness of the overloaded, hyper-realistic, and technologically mediated images forms the basis of Jean Baudrillard's theory of the ideology of media images and is explored through his concept of the *obscene*.

THE OBSCENE IMAGE

> [T]his is the enterprise of our entire culture, whose natural condition is obscene: a culture of monstration, of demonstration, of productive monstrosity.[28]

> [T]his viral contamination of things by images, which are the fatal characteristics of our culture.[29]

Jean Baudrillard has compared the West's relationship to images in terms of obscenity. In the light of events in Iraq, frequent accusations that his work is willfully abstruse should be reconsidered. Baudrillard takes the notion of the *obscene* literally. An etymological analysis of the word gives us "ob"—a prefix meaning hindering—and "scene"—from the Latin and Greek words for "stage." Ignoring its conventional connotation of depravity, his reread of the term *obscene* gives us the notion that Western media-dominated society is *ob-scene*, because its proliferation of images has imploded the traditional, symbolically coded distance between the image and viewer that is implied with a stage. Baudrillard's writing contains the repeated theme that in the West we suffer from a virus-like proliferation of immediate images that replace the distance needed for either considered reflection or a developed sensitivity to the ambiguities of cultural meanings.

Baudrillard's analysis illuminates the present mediascape. For example, he argues that " we shouldn't underestimate the power of the obscene, its power to exterminate all ambiguity and all seduction and deliver to us the definitive fascination of bodies without faces, faces without eyes, and eyes that don't look."[30] This has chilling pertinence to the dehumanized images of Iraqi prisoners in which their faces are hooded, deliberately pixilated, or only appear as minor details within a broader tableau (e.g., the naked man cowering in front of snarling guard dogs). Originally used in a different context, Baudrillard also provides an unwittingly prescient description of the furor over the *Daily Mirror* pictures' authenticity: "we don't look for definition or richness of imagination in these images; we look for the giddiness of their superficiality, for the artifice of detail, the intimacy of their technique. What we truly desire is their technical artificiality, and nothing more."[31]

Beyond the manifest obscenity of the Pornography of the Abu Ghraib photographs, Baudrillard's broader theoretical point relates to how their *staging* paradoxically relies upon the actual absence of a *stage*. A surfeit of images is presented to us so that "[o]bscenity takes on all the semblances of modernity. We are used to seeing it, first of all, in the perpetration of sex, but it extends to everything that can be perpetrated in the visible—it becomes the perpetration of the visible itself."[32] In a form of semiotic potlatch, images become their own justification for the decontextualized consumption for its own sake of such formats as *MTV Cribs* and *Bumfights*. Everything becomes a potential image for the voyeuristic gaze and less and less is ruled out on grounds of taste or any other consideration. The pornography of the image lies here in its explicitness. Nothing is left to the imagination and all is revealed to the passive viewer. An apparently overwhelming sexual will-to-reveal that Welsh identified in the rise of gonzo porn might at least partially explain the sexual aspect of the Abu Ghraib pictures. As Sontag recently argued, we live in a world where, increasingly, "[a]n erotic life is for more and more people what can be captured on video. To live is to be photographed, to have a record of one's life, oblivious or claiming to be oblivious to the camera's non-stop attentions. . . . Ours is a society in which secrets of private life that, formerly, you would have given nearly anything to conceal, you now clamor to get on a television show to reveal."[33]

MEDIA TAUTOLOGY: REALITY TV AND THE DEMOCRATIZATION OF CELEBRITY

Today this critical energy of the stage . . . is in the process of being swept away. All that theatrical energy goes into the denial of the scenic illusion and into anti-theater in all its various forms . . . illusion is proscribed; the scission between stage and audience is abolished; theater goes down into the street and everydayness. . . . This is no longer the famous Aristotelian catharsis of the passions. . . . Illusion is no longer valid here: it is truth which bursts into free expression. We are all actors and spectators; there is no more stage: the stage is everywhere; no more rules: everyone plays out his own drama, improvising on his own fantasies. The obscene form of anti-theater, present everywhere.[34]

In the *Ecstasy of Communication* among other works, Baudrillard develops the theme of modern communication's tendency toward uncontrollable circulation (definition one). The roots of this uncontrollable circulation can be found in Sontag's earlier examination of photography's defining status as the groundbreaking technology of the image where she asserts that "[p]hotographs document sequences of consumption carried on outside the view of family, friends, neighbors."[35] This resonates with Welsh's previously cited linking of pornography with consumerism and is poignantly prescient in terms of the distress caused to the families of such U.S. soldiers as the Porn-star sounding Lynndie England. The lack of values with which to judge the appropriateness of the image is for Sontag an intrinsic part of the conceptually reductive nature of the technology. She argues that "there is an aggression implicit in every use of the camera," and that it is responsible for "an ever increasing spread of that mentality which looks at the world as a set of potential photographs."[36]

Specifically in the light of Abu Ghraib, Sontag points out that, although "trophy" pictures have been taken in many previous military and social conflicts, these particular photographs "reflect a shift in the use of pictures—less objects to be saved than evanescent messages to be disseminated, circulated . . . now the soldiers themselves are all photographers—recording their war, their fun, their observations of what they find picturesque, their atrocities—and swapping images among themselves, and emailing them around the globe . . . since the pictures were meant to be circulated and seen by many people, it was all fun. And this idea of fun is, alas, more and more—contrary to what Mr Bush is telling the world—part of the "true nature and heart of America."[37]

Again, the link between fiction and reality is instructive here. In Italo Calvino's short story about the increasingly obsessive mentality of a photographer in Trieste entitled *The Adventure of a Photographer*, for example, he portrays the tautological self-generating tendencies of the need to photograph. The person who feels the urge to photograph, he argues, is "already close to the view of the person who thinks that everything that is not photographed is lost, as if it had never existed, and that therefore in order really to live you must photograph as much as you can, you must either live in the most photographable way possible or else consider photographable every moment of your life. The first course leads to stupidity; the second, to madness."[38]

Calvino compares Trieste's photographers to game hunters, describing in a relatively benign form the innately aggressive and violent nature of the photographic act identified by Sontag: "When Spring comes, the city's inhabitants, by the hundreds of thousands, go out on Sundays with a leather case over their shoulder. And they photograph one another. They come back happy as hunters with bulging game-bags."[39]

Particularly apposite to the case of the Iraqi photographs, Oliver Wendell Holmes predicted that "every conceivable object of Nature and Art will soon scale off its surface for us. Men will hunt all curious, beautiful, grand objects, as they hunt for cattle in South America, for their *skins*, and leave the carcasses as of little worth."[40]

Although they would seem unlikely bedfellows, Baudrillard's notion of the ecstasy of communication was implicitly acknowledged by Donald Rumsfeld who complained that it was much harder nowadays to control the information sent back home by soldiers serving overseas. Unlike conventional letters in which the censors can black out the offending parts, Rumsfeld bemoans the fact that U.S. soldiers were "running around with digital cameras and taking these unbelievable photographs and then passing them off, against the law, to the media, to our surprise."[41] With U.S. troops thus acting like an extremely malevolent form of Trieste's Sunday promenaders, Calvino's story gives an imaginative account of photographic excesses whilst Rumsfeld's complaint provides a more practical illustration of its dynamics. Sontag's, Calvino's, and Holmes' descriptions are all seen combined in the aggressive, acquisitive, trophy-seeking behavior of the Abu Ghraib photographers, which so dramatically undermined the coalition's attempts to brand itself as *Occupation Lite*.

THE GEO-POLITICAL CONSEQUENCES: THE POST 9/11 WAR OF IMAGES

"Of all nations in the world, the United States was built in nobody's image. It was the land of the unexpected, of unbounded hope, of ideals, of quest for an unknown perfection. It is all the more unfitting that we should offer ourselves in images. *And all the more fitting that the images which we make wittingly or unwittingly to sell America to the world should come back to haunt and curse us.*"[42] I have focused here on the Abu Ghraib pictures, but their significance can be more broadly linked to the events of 9/11. Daniel Boorstin feared that America's over-reliance upon images would come back to haunt it. With the events of September 11 2001, Osama bin Laden confirmed Boorstin's foresight in a terrible fashion with an attack deliberately designed to be consumed as a media event. Writing a full forty years before 9/11, Boorstin feared the displacement of ideals by images. His fears have been realized to the extent that the emotional charge of the 9/11 images has been skillfully manipulated for the non sequitur of *the "war on terror."* Writing at the height of the cold war, Boorstin focused upon communism, but his words are now painfully relevant to the gulf that exists not only as a geographical area to which troops are periodically dispatched but also and more significantly as an ever-widening gap between Western and Islamic sensitivities:

> Accustomed to live in a world of pseudo-events, celebrities, dissolving forms, and shadowy but overshadowing images, we mistake our shadows for ourselves. To us they seem more real than the reality. . . . Our technique seems direct only because in our daily lives the pseudo-event always seems destined to dominate the natural facts. We no longer even recognize that our technique is indirect, that we have

committed ourselves to managing shadows. We can live in our world of illusions. Although we find it hard to imagine, other peoples still live in the world of dreams. We live in a world of our making. Can we conjure others to live there too? We love the image, and believe it. But will they?[43]

The images of prisoner abuse reflect the West's narcissistic obsession with the screen, and it is this unhealthy obsession that increasingly fuels Said's concept of neo-Orientalism.[44] A keen awareness of this process arguably marks the malevolent acuity of bin Laden. He is the latest in a string of key Islamic hate-figures that previously included the Ayatollah Khomeni and who all have in common being bracketed within a discourse of evil.[45] Osama bin Laden fulfills the role portrayed in Baudrillard's work of the Manichean demiurge, who creates the evil illusions against which God and goodness avail themselves. The biggest danger for the West, however, is that bin Laden and others play this role self-consciously. They know which buttons to press in order to produce effects that go right to the core of the West's own deeply embedded social pornography of which Abu Ghraib was a particularly shocking example. An implicit notion of this chapter is, therefore, that the media's role in the facilitation of America's increasingly myopic separation from the Islamic Other has been incorporated into the terrorist game plan.[46]

In his *Contributions to Analytical Psychology*, Jung argued that an individual's psychology could be profoundly, albeit unwittingly, influenced by an underpinning dependency of the wider society.[47] He used the example of the average Roman citizen who was inevitably infected by a general social atmosphere permeated by slavery and claimed that the individual is powerless to resist such an influence. McLuhan and Innis[48] used a similar argument to describe the cultural impact of media technologies through history. This chapter suggests that social pornography now permeates media discourse in the West and the *Jerry Springer* nature of the Iraqi pictures implies the validity of Jung's analysis. The social pornography of the image is a fertile resource from which bin Laden and others base their media-savvy strategies. Social pornography facilitates the post-9/11 knee-jerk and unfocused political responses and provides bin Laden with opportunities to further exacerbate the situation with such politically pornographic events as the tragically iconic 9/11 attack.

The true malevolent ingenuity of bin Laden's outrage thus resides in his knowing incorporation of the West's inability to look beyond its own biased and distorted social porn. His malevolent success has been heightened by the repetitive nature and simply overwhelming presence of 9/11 images and their displacement of more considered debate. For example, Osama bin Laden's image is now readily familiar to all but a tiny proportion of Western populations, but a similarly small number are likely to be aware of the more substantive issues lying behind the image. There is, for example, no significant public discussion of the historical parallels and links that can be made between his acts and the Royal House of Saud's uneasy yet perennially intertwined relationship with the Ikhwan bedouin fighters and the Wahabi fundamentalist strand of Islam. The United States was traumatized, yet fundamentally unenlightened, by the shocking, constantly repeated images of the Twin Towers being hit. Unaccompanied by significant efforts to understand, mere repetition of the images reflected the fundamentally distorted perspective of a society increasingly incapable of thinking outside the self-referential media realm alluded to throughout this chapter.

Despite the very real effects experienced by those New Yorkers in the immediate vicinity and aftermath, the rest of the United States experienced the WTC attack Hollywood-style. The pictures of destruction were already disturbingly familiar to a public regularly exposed to the Hollywood imagination of disaster films. Soon after the tragedy, U.S. intelligence services consulted Hollywood figures to brainstorm scenarios for possible future terrorist attacks whilst the release of several movies was postponed because of their perceived similarity to actual events. The media's post-9/11 coverage consisted of an excessive, pornographic dose of the act of destruction and then a matching pornographic exploration of the personal suffering by the victims' families. The emergency workers of Ground Zero quickly became emotive icons and fodder for daytime TV. Hollywood's image-driven influence was much in evidence in the post-September 11 political response as Ronald Reagan's *Star Wars*-sounding cold war "Empire of Evil" was quickly revised to the "Axis of Evil" and discussed in colloquial terms borrowed liberally from the Western film genre. In terms of Calvino's previously cited characterization of the photographic impulse, the madness of bin Laden's designed-for-TV terrorist act was quickly matched by the stupidity of the media's response.

CONCLUSION:
GULF WAR II AS THE REVENGE OF THE IMAGE

> The same law holds for evil as pornography. The shock of pho-
> tographed atrocities wears off with repeated viewings, just as the sur-
> prise and bemusement felt the first time one sees a pornographic
> movie wear off after one sees a few more.[49]

> Have you seen the cicadas? These insects wake up every 17 years.
> These cicadas are brazen. Just today they made some cockroaches line
> up in a pyramid.[50]

A key element of Pornography is the short-lived nature of the
viewer's attention span. Its nature is such that once consumed there
is an almost immediate demand for fresh images. The same tendency
is evident in social pornography in which political discourse requires
fresh images and the impact of the old ones fades rapidly. This perhaps, at least partially, explains the insensitivity of David Letterman,
the most successful late-night talk show host on U.S. television, and
his "joke." It was made less than a month after the Abu Ghraib pictures first appeared in the U.S. press and, when delivered, produced
a large amount of laughter in the New York theatre audience to
whom Letterman presents his show each weeknight. Žižek delin-
eates two major post-September 11 options open to America: "it can
either further fortify its sphere from which it watches world tragedies
via a TV screen or it can 'finally risk stepping through the fantasmatic
screen that separates it from the Outside World, accepting its arrival
in the Real World.'"[51]

The Letterman incident suggests that Žižck's second option is
unlikely to be taken up by America in the near future and the complex reasons for this is a major theme of Baudrillard's work, and
something we have only been able to touch upon here. What I have
tried to show, however, is the deep-rooted nature of the West's
unhealthy relationship to the image and the way in which this has
repeatedly prevented the West from stepping through that fantastic
screen and engaging meaningfully with the Muslim Other. This is a
failure that has typified the post September 11 political response,
from its immediate aftermath right up to recent events in Iraq.

The apparently benign concept of *branding* the United States like
any other commodity image is in fact a stark indication of how "the
land of the free" is imprisoned whether it is thought of in terms of

Narcissus's pond surface or Žižek's screen. In keeping with Jung's insight, social pornography reveals the darker, slavish element of the term *brand*. In order to provide the video's publicity shot, Rufus Hannah and Donnie Brennan, two of the homeless protagonists from *Bumfights*, were paid two hundred dollars, whilst drunk, to have the show's logo tattooed in ink on the former's knuckles and the latter's forehead.[52] Sometimes a brand connotes more than we would wish.

POSTSCRIPT

Almost immediately prior to publication of this book chapter in *Media and Political Violence*, I encountered a series of photographs presented as a fashion shoot in *Italian Vogue* magazine. It reminded me of an interview in which Baudrillard mentions how he is no longer read much in Japan, because the perception is that his work has been overtaken by reality. This seems to be the fate this chapter has already suffered. I naïvely thought that the jokes David Letterman made about the Abu Ghraib abuse could represent the nadir of Western insensitivity to the Muslim Other, but I seriously underestimated the recuperative ability of a media system in which moral condemnation and visual titillation are inextricably intertwined in an unprecedentedly malignant form of caducean commercialism.

At the recent *Engaging Baudrillard* conference held at the University of Swansea, Mark Poster interpreted the U.S. TV series *The Swan* via Foucault's notion of *care of the self* in a positive light rather than as a panegyric for culturally endorsed, narcissistic, self-mutilation. Contra Poster, I would suggest that *The Swan* is of a part with the images from *Italian Vogue*. They portray much more eloquently than mere words the seamless web between the darkest parts of our abusive, pornographic social psyche and institutions as nominally distinct as the U.S. army and the Italian fashion industry. Notwithstanding cultural populism's ongoing attempts to create a more palatable brand of Baudrillard-lite, we should not forget that the real import of Baudrillard's work resides in his unabashed critique of our society's seemingly inexhaustible (and highly profitable) appetite for such recuperations. It is difficult to envisage a better example than these *Italian Vogue* images of the "cold collage" and "cool promiscuity"[53] that constitute the current evil demon of images.

NOTES

1. This paper is an edited version of a similarly entitled book chapter from: Hillel Nossek, Annabelle Sreberny, and Prasun Sonwalkar, eds., *Media and Political Violence* (Creskill, NJ: Hampton Press, 2005), 349–66; and also an edited version of a similar article in *International Journal of Baudrillard Studies* 4, no. 1 (January 2007), http://www.ubishops .ca/BaudrillardStudies/vol4_1/taylor.htm..

2. Jean Baudrillard, *The Transparency of Evil* (New York: Semiotext(e), 1993), 76; emphasis original.

3. Marshall McLuhan, *Understanding Media* (London: Routledge, 1995).

4. Michael Bracewell, *The Nineties: When Surface Was Depth* (London: Flamingo, 2002), 72.

5. Jonathan Raban, "Emasculating Arabia," *The Guardian*, May 13, 2004.

6. "Rumsfeld Testifies before Senate Armed Services Committee," *Washington Post*, May 7, 2004, http://www.washingtonpost.com/wp-dyn/ articles/A8575-2004May7.html (accessed May 25, 2004).

7. Susan Sontag, "What Have We Done?" *The Guardian*, May 23, 2004.

8. Bracewell, *The Nineties*, 66; emphasis added.

9. Baudrillard, *Simulations* (New York: Semiotext(e), 1983); Umberto Eco, *Travels in Hyperreality* (London: Picador, 1987).

10. Barbara Bush speaking on the American television show *Good Morning America*, March 18, 2003.

11. "Violence," *Collins Softback English Dictionary*, 3rd ed. (Glasgow, UK: HarperCollins, 1991).

12. Sontag, "What Have We Done?" http://www.commondreams.org/ views04/0524-09.htm.

13. Martin Amis, "A Rough Trade," *The Guardian Online*, March 17, 2001, http://books.guardian.co.uk/departments/politicsphilosophyandsociety/ story/0,6000,458058,00.html.

14. Ibid.

15. A 1970s U.S. and British TV show that caught unsuspecting members of the public on camera in foolish situations.

16. *Cribs* is an MTV series that takes the viewer into the homes of various celebrities for an unabashed celebration of their conspicuous consumption. *Celebrity Detox* was a May 2003 program in which British B-list celebrities were filmed at a heath spa in Thailand undergoing a rigorous program of enemas. *Jackass* involves a group of U.S. friends performing dangerous physical stunts involving either violence, nudity, bodily excretions, or, at times, all three.

17. *Ghetto Brawls* is a similar product.

18. Sontag, "What Have We Done?"

19. Andre Dubus, *House of Sand and Fog* (London: Vintage, 2001).

20. Irvine Welsh, *Porno* (London: Jonathan Cape, 2002), 450.

21. Bracewell, *Perfect Tense* (London: Vintage, 2002), 8–9.

22. Paul A. Taylor, "Hackers: Cyberpunks or Microserfs?" *Information, Communication & Society* 1, no. 4 (1998): 401–19; Paul A. Taylor, "Informational Intimacy and Futuristic Flu: Love and Confusion in the Matrix," *Information, Communication & Society* 4, no. 1 (2001): 74–94.

23. Sontag, "What Have We Done?" http://www.commondreams.org/views04/0524-09.htm.

24. Phil Taylor, "Image and Reality," *Al-Ahram Weekly*, no. 691, May 20–26, 2004, http://weekly.ahram.org.eg/2004/691/re9.htm (accessed May 25, 2004); emphasis original.

25. William Mitchell, *Iconology: Image, Text, Ideology* (Chicago: University of Chicago Press, 1986), 164.

26. Ibid., 167.

27. Ibid.

28. Baudrillard, *Seduction* (Montreal: New World Perspectives, 1990), 35.

29. Baudrillard, *The Ecstasy of Communication* (New York: Semiotext(e), 1988), 36.

30. Baudrillard, *Fatal Strategies* (New York: Semiotext(e),1990), 60.

31. Baudrillard, *The Ecstasy of Communication*, 44.

32. Baudrillard, *Fatal Strategies*, 58.

33. Sontag, "What Have We Done?"

34. Baudrillard, *Seduction*, 63.

35. Sontag, *On Photography* (London: Penguin, 1979), 9.

36. Ibid., 7.

37. Sontag, "What Have We Done?"

38. Italo Calvino, "The Adventure of a Photographer," in *Difficult Loves* (London: Picador, 1983), 43.

39. Ibid., 40.

40. Joshua Gamson, *Claims to Fame: Celebrity in Contemporary America* (Berkeley: University of California Press, 1994), 20; emphasis original.

41. Sontag, "What Have We Done?"

42. Daniel Boorstin, *The Image: A Guide to Pseudo-Events in America* (New York: Vintage, 1992), 245–46; emphasis added.

43. Ibid., 249.

44. Edward Said, *Orientalism* (London: Penguin, 2003).

45. See Baudrillard, "Whatever Happened to Evil?" in *The Transparency of Evil*, for a full discussion of this theme.

46. Baudrillard has also recently noted that those who live by the image might die by it. See Baudrillard, "War Porn," trans. Paul Taylor, in *International Journal of Baudrillard Studies* 2, no. 1 (January 2005), http://www.ubishops.ca/baudrillardstudies/vol2_1/taylor.htm.

47. Jung cited in Marshall McLuhan, *Understanding Media* (London: Routledge, 1995), 21.
48. McLuhan and Harold Innis, *The Bias of Communication* (Toronto: University of Toronto Press, 2003).
49. Sontag, *On Photography*, 20.
50. David Letterman, *The Late Show*, May 26, 2004.
51. Slavoj Žižek, *Welcome to the Desert of the Real* (London: Verso, 2002), 49.
52. J. Doward and S. Deen, "Outrage as TV Plans to Screen Brawling Tramps," *The Observer*, May 16, 2004.
53. Baudrillard, *The Evil Demon of Images* (Sydney: Power Institute, 1987).

WARLORDS OF THE IRAQI BLOGOSPHERE

Priscilla Ringrose

This chapter addresses the warblogging phenomenon and looks at four case studies of warblogs authored in Iraq in the pre-or immediately post-conflict period. The Iraq War is the first war to be "blogged" on a significant scale and provides prototypical cases of warblogs, including Salam Pax's blog, *Where is Raed?*, widely cited as a significant factor in the popularizing of blogs worldwide, and *My War*, one of the first examples of milblogs (military blogs) to be censored by the U.S. Defense Department, as well as early examples of blogs authored by non-embedded war journalists.

A SHADOW MEDIA EMPIRE?

According to David Kline and Dan Burnstein, the veteran British war correspondent Robert Fisk has become the poster-man for "sloppy" and "anti-American reporting" amongst warbloggers in the *pro*-Iraqi "occupation" camp (2005, 379). Within this section of the blogosphere, "fisk" has come to be used as a verb meaning "to disprove loudly, point by point" (Kline and Burnstein 2005, 379). On March 30, 2003, Fisk reported that a bomb hitting a crowded Baghdad market and killing dozens must have been fired by U.S.

troops, using as evidence the Western numerals he found on a piece of twisted metal lying nearby (Kline and Burnstein 2005, 379). Australian blogger Tim Blair reprinted the partial numbers and asked any of his readers with military knowledge for clues: "Within 24 hours, more than a dozen readers with specialized knowledge had identified the weapon, providing other minute details never picked up by the press (U.S. high-speed anti-radiation missile, man-ufactured by Raytheon, launch point F-16)" (Kline and Burnstein 2005, 379). Although for Kline and Bernstein the "unfortunate moral" of this tale was that Fisk could not be "fisked" on this issue, the story also points to the function of blogs, in Lev Grossman's (2004) words, as "a genuine alternative to main-stream news outlets."

Grossman's (2004) *Time* article subsequently goes further, describing the blogosphere as "a *shadow* media *empire* that is rivaling networks and newspapers in power and influence."

Blogging's media-shadowing role is hardly controversial. Bloggers' habit of providing nearly instant commentary on televised events has created a secondary meaning of the word "blogging"—simultane-ously transcribing and criticizing speeches and events shown on tel-evision online. Political scientists such as Daniel Drezner and Henry Farrell are, however, more circumspect about blogging's "imperial" powers. Drezner and Farrell wonder how "given the disparity in resources and organization vis-à-vis other actors . . . a collection of decentralized, non-profit, contrarian, and discordant Web sites [can] exercise any influence over politics and political outputs?" (2004, 2). They refer to the widely quoted incident leading to the resignation of Senate Majority Leader Trent Lott as the first example of the power of bloggers to influence political outcomes. On December 5, 2002, Lott made some inflammatory remarks at former Senator Strom Thurmond's one hundredth birthday party that were largely ignored by the mainstream media. The blogging community, how-ever, refused to let the story go and five days later the story was picked up by all the major news networks, forcing Lott's hand. Drezner and Farrell do not accept that weblogs were a "causal vari-able" in Lott's downfall but concede that they constituted an impor-tant "intervening variable" (2004, 3). They conclude that blogging *is* politically important in large part because "the rapidity of blogger interactions affects political communication in the mainstream media through agenda setting and framing effects" (Drezner and Farrell 2004, 17).

Drezner and Farrell argue that the blogosphere has capacities similar to that of the media to "elevate issues and devise interpretive frames for them that shape the boundaries and content of political discourse and public opinion" (2004, 17). When, as in the Trent Lott case, a flurry of blogs "frame" a single issue, generating a consensus view, the media pays attention and political opinion can be affected. Although blogs authored by Iraqis in the conflict and post-conflict period were not numerous enough to create the kind of "framing blogathon" Drezner and Farrell refer to, the subset of these blogs, which were popularized in the blogospheres and mediaspheres constituted significant voices in the political debate around the legality of the war in Iraq. Antiwar commentators such as Kelly Dougherty, cofounder of *Iraq Veterans Against the War*, credit Iraqi blogs such as *Baghdad Burning* with contributing to the mobilizing of public opinion against the war.[1]

Blogs and War

Although the first blogs were launched between 1994 and 1998, the first blog explosion did not occur until July 1999 when "several no-cost, easy-to-use weblog content management tools were created" making blogging a straightforward task that required no more technological knowledge than sending an e-mail (Gurak, Antonijevik, Johnson, Ratcliff and Reyman, 2004, Definition of weblogs section, para. 2, 3). While the expansion of blogging is generally attributed to the introduction of these blogging services, U.S.-led wars are also considered an equally significant factor in its exponential growth. The rise of blogging is traced to the period immediately following the events of September 1, 2001, when "the country went on a war footing" and "warblogs" started to proliferate (Reynold as cited in Carl 2005, 21). The month of October 2001, which marked the invasion of Afghanistan and the beginning of the U.S. "war on terrorism" campaign, signaled a second surge in warblog production and led to the emergence of scholarly conventions on warblogging that was mainly focused on blogging's effect on journalism (Boese 2004). Blogs "fully landed on the scholarly radar in 2003," and although this is partly attributed to the Howard Dean blogs (Dean's presidential campaign was remarkable at the time for its extensive use of blogs to solicit contributions online, shattering previous fundraising records for the Democratic presidential primary), it was primarily due to the ongoing Iraq War–blogging phenomenon (Boese 2004).

The pseudonymous Iraqi blogger Salam Pax, the Iraqi architect who began his now famous blog, *Where is Raed?*, in which he openly criticized Saddam's regime, is widely recognized as a significant contributor to the popularity of blogging (Gurak 2004, Definition of weblogs section, para. 3). Salam Pax's blog attracted worldwide readership and global media attention and also served to raise public understanding of the power of blogging as did another popular blog, *warblogging.com*, set up by another pseudonymous blogger, George Paine (an allusion to the eighteenth-century American patriot and pamphleteer Thomas Paine). Paine's blog aimed to provide "a bird's eye view of the perpetual, 1984-style war we've found ourselves in."[2] When hostilities began in March 2003, the number of visitors to the site rose from an average of three thousand to six thousand visitors a day to tens of thousands of visitors from all over the world, including the U.S. House of Representatives, the Department of Defense, the British House of Commons, and the Government of Syria.[3]

On March 21, 2005, Francisco Martinez, a U.S. soldier serving in Iraq, was the first milblogger to be killed in combat.[4] His death was announced by his father on his blog.[5] Although the majority of warbloggers are civilians, military personnel, in particular the U.S. military, form a significant subset of warbloggers. In April 2005, the U.S. military clamped down on U.S. milbloggers, insisting that their postings had to be cleared by unit commanders in the interests of operational security.[6] Although these sanctions led to a minority of milblogs being abandoned, milblogs, particularly U.S. milblogs, are proliferating. In January 2006, a U.S. milblogging community joined a U.S. military site, (http://www.military.com), described as "the largest online military destination" serving "the 30 million Americans with military affinity."[7] As a result of this affiliation (at the time of writing), this site is now offering members access to 1,100 military blogs from 23 countries segmented by country, branch of service, gender, and popularity. [8]

DEFINITIONS AND MUTATIONS

A blog, a contraction of the term "weblog," is a Web site in which items are posted on a regular basis and displayed in reverse chronological order. A blog comprises hypertext and may include images and links (to other Web pages and to video, audio, and other files). Blogging is often characterized as socially interactive since blogging software allows blog authors to link to one another and allows blog readers to post comments to individual entries, giving rise to conversational exchanges. Many blogs contain blogrolls, a collection of links to other weblogs often found on the front page sidebar.

Rebecca Blood distinguishes three types of weblogs: filters, journals, and notebooks (2002, 6–9). Filters are focused around links to other sites on the Web, which include other blogs. Their content is generally external to the blogger (world events, online happenings). The content of journals is personal and focuses on the weblogger's inner world or their reactions to events around them, while notebooks are distinguished from journals by longer, more focused essays (Blood 2002, 6–7). Since Blood identified these distinctions in 2002, the genre has evolved in multiple directions. In 2004, blogs started to become mainstream as political consultants and news services began using them as tools for outreach and opinion forming. Blogs are now found on the online pages of news channels; they have been adopted by commercial businesses for promotional campaigns and are used in political campaigning (Drezner and Farrell 2004, 6). Blogs are becoming an industry in themselves with entrepreneurs such as *Financial Times* reporter Nick Denton, "founder of the first fledgling blog empire," hiring popular blog writers to write on umbrella sites that feed on advertising revenue (Kline and Burnstein 2005, 151). Despite these mutations, Blood's assertion that the vast majority of blogs are personal journals undertaken by single authors still holds true (70 percent) and despite commercial, journalistic, and pedagogic spin-offs, the prototypical blogger is described as a young adult male residing in the United States (Herring, Scheidt, Bonus, and Wright 2005, 5).

In July 1999, the total number of blogs was estimated at around fifty. By March 2005, Technorati was tracking over 7.8 million weblogs and 937 million links, which is almost double the number of weblogs tracked in October 2004, confirming David Sifry's calculations that the blogosphere is doubling in size about once every five months.[9] Drezner and Farrell point out, however, that the skewed distribution of links among blogs means that "[o]nly a few blogs are likely to become focal points, those with very high numbers of links, or with some other characteristic that makes them salient" (2004, 12, 13).

ENTER THE IRAQI BLOGOSPHERE

This chapter proposes to look at four "salient" blogs representing some of the first examples of blogs authored in Iraq but will focus mainly on the two authored by Iraqi citizens. All four are English-language blogs, which attracted the attention of mainstream media and were authored in the pre- or post-conflict period.[10] Three of the bloggers concerned have since secured book deals, illustrating the phenomenon of bloggers crossing back into traditional print media. While two of these works (*Baghdad Blog* and *Baghdad Burning*) reproduce the blog format (including selected materials form the blog's hyperlinks), another (*My War*) rewrites the experiences related in the original blog in a conventional narrative format. One of the books, *Baghdad Blog*, is to be adapted to a film script by media group *Intermedia*,[11] while another, *Baghdad Burning*, has already crossed over further into performance arts, having been adapted to a dramatic production performed at the West End Theatre in New York in March 2005.[12]

These blogs also illustrate the increasing crossovers between the media and blogospheres. One of them was authored by independent journalist, Josh Kucera, who opted to blog the war in addition to writing for *Time magazine*. Another independent journalist, former *New York Daily News* reporter Christoper Allbritton, used the blogging form exclusively to post his reports on the humanitarian conditions in the Kurdish-controlled northern territory. Allbritton raised money for his journey to Iraq by soliciting donations on his blog in exchange for contributors receiving daily dispatches and photos before they were posted on his blog. His story not only demonstrates that single-author blogs can double as a fundraising mechanisms but also that there is a market for "personalized" independent reports from a conflict zone.

For Iraqi civilians in the lead up to the war in Iraq, in the words of Salam Pax: "Internet [blogging] was really very new. It was new for us and new for the government and new for the people who where trying to control the firewall." The first state-operated Internet center in Iraq was opened in 2000, complete with in-house "minders" but home-access was not permitted until 2001.[13] Since then the number of Iraqi bloggers has grown rapidly with the current estimates ranging around two hundred.[14]

The *Kairos* of Blogs

The four weblogs will be examined within the framework of Carolyn R. Miller and Dawn Shepherd's (2004) "Darwinian" style analysis of blogging as a rhetorical gesture which *evolved* to "fit" within a specific cultural context. Miller and Shepherd situate the emergence of blogging in the context of the *kairos* that makes the genre possible, and they focus on the cultural trends of the late 1990s related to the increasingly weakening border between the private and public spheres. In particular, they point to the rise of *exhibitionism* and its correlate, *mediated voyeurism.* In this chapter, I will examine the functions that the four blogs below performed both *for their authors and for their readership communities* and assess to what extent Miller and Shepherd's framework can be considered an appropriate mechanism to account for them.[15]

1. *Where is Raed?* (begun September 7, 2002, http://dear_raed.blogspot .com/)16 by pseudonymous author Salam Pax. In May 2003, the *Guardian* newspaper tracked down Salam and printed a story indicating that he was a twenty-nine-year-old Iraqi architect living in Iraq.[17] Like Riverbend (see below), Salam was partly educated in the West and writes in idiomatic English.
2. *Baghdad Burning* (begun September 2002, http://riverbendblog .blogspot.com/). Author Riverbend's identity is carefully hidden, the weblog entries indicate that she is a young, unmarried Iraqi woman from a Sunni family living with her parents and brother in a middle class neighborhood in the north of Baghdad. Before the war, she was a computer programmer.
3. *My War* (begun June 2004, http://cbftw.blogspot.com/), author Colby Buzzell is a former U.S. Army Specialist and an ex-Styrker Brigade gunner who started to blog when based in Mosul, Iraq.
4. *The Other Side* (begun March 9, 2003, http://www.serendipit-e .com/otherside/) by independent journalist Josh Kucera. Kucera

worked as a foreign correspondent in Bosnia before going to Erbil, Kurdistan just before the start of the war (Boese 2004, Iraq Warblogs section, para. 1).

For Miller and Shepherd, the blogging phenomenon evolves from two cultural trends increasing destabilization of the separation between the private and public realms—the *democratization of celebrity* as advanced by Myra Stark and *mediated voyeurism* as theorized by Clay Calvert. According to Stark (2003), the age of "democratic celebrity" was ushered in the attacks of September 11, 2001, which heralded the end of the celebrity culture of sports heroes and entertainers of the 1980s and 1990s and brought into being a new heroic prototype, *the ordinary celebrity*, typified by fire fighters and policemen who emerged from the Twin Towers (para. 7). Stark points to the blurring of the distinction between celebrities and ordinary people in many areas of life: the entertainment industry (reality TV shows, talk shows), politics (awards to ordinary activists), and on the Internet (where blogs "mak[e] it possible for people to reach out of obscurity . . . and become known to millions") (2003, para. 11). This was the case for Salam Pax whose blog became an international sensation within weeks of being linked to Glenn Reynold's *Instapundit* blog, one of the consistently highest ranking blogs in the world. Salam has gone on to become a media celebrity, treading the international book promotion circuit as well as a media player with a *Guardian* column and appearing as a guest television shows.

The democratization of celebrity is, according to Calvert, fed by the willingness of many "to overshare as it were, so much about their lives with so many people" (2000, 83). Mediated voyeurism, which feeds on the increasing normalization of exhibitionism, is defined by Calvert as "*the consumption of revealing images of and information about others' apparently real and unguarded lives, often yet not always for the purposes of entertainment but frequently at the expense of privacy and discourse, through the means of the mass media and Internet*" (2002, 2–3). Both exhibitionism and voyeurism relate to the shifting expectations associated with the increasingly fluid boundary between public and private: "As our expectations of privacy increase, our expectations for receiving more information—our expectations about what is public—increase" (Calvert 2000, 78). The materiality of the Internet has enabled these expectations to be taken to new limits: "On personal home pages and message boards, in chat rooms and on listservs, and most especially on blogs, people are sharing unprecedented amounts of personal information with total strangers, potentially millions of them. The technology of the Internet makes it easier than ever for anyone to be either a voyeur or an exhibitionist—or both" (Miller and Shepherd 2004).

Most bloggers chose to expose their "private" lives to a "public" composed of a potential mass audience. Although, in Mortensen and Walker's words, blogs "exist right on this border between what's private and what's public," they nevertheless redefine the nature of control associated with definitions of privacy (2002, 256). Sissela Bok defines privacy "as the condition of being protected from unwanted access by others—either physical access, personal information or attention. Claims to privacy are claims to control access to what one takes—however grandiosely—to be one's personal domain" (Calvert 2000, 79). The majority of bloggers actively woo their readership communities and allow unrestricted access to their site, subverting the notion of border demarcation traditionally associated with privacy.

BLOGGING—MORE THAN EXHIBITIONISM?

Does the "abandon" inherent in the blogging act—the relinquishment of "border-control," whether in the sense of unrestricted audience access or in terms of the surrender of personal information—make blogging an exhibitionist occupation by default? Are warbloggers exhibitionists who profit from the sensationalism of their personal circumstances? Although the increasing blurring between public and private is a useful prism through which to understand the *kairos* of the blogs, I will examine other related cultural trends, *in addition to* the rise of exhibitionism/mediated voyeurism, which must be taken into account. In particular, I will refer to Yochai Benkler's (2004) concept of *the Sharing Economy* and David Bollier's (2002) notion of the *information commons.*

Although not all bloggers fit into Calvert's definition of "oversharing" in the sense of inappropriately sharing intimate information, all bloggers "overshare" in the sense that they share with an "unnecessarily" large audience. Because bloggers chose to "exhibit" themselves on a potentially global level and derive gratification from their online visibility, they circulate within a scopophilic economy.

Riverbend's opening post demonstrates that the existence of an audience is intrinsic to her conception of the viability of her blog: "So this is the beginning for me I guess. I never thought I'd start my own weblog. All I could think, every time I wanted to start one was 'but who will read it?'" (2005, 5). Warbloggers may even derive some gratification from the risks involved in politically subversive acts of self-disclosure. Salam Pax (2004) describes his compulsive need to continue blogging in the highly charged pre-invasion period despite the risks of being apprehended by the Iraqi security services: "When [the blog] took a more political turn, my friend Raj in Jordan e-mailed me and said 'look you are turning into warblogger, be careful.' But by that time, I was too hooked, too excited about it and having so much fun that I couldn't stop" (Pax, 2004, television broadcast). For Salam Pax, however, the personal risks of anti-regime blogging from within Iraq before "regime change" were so high that his action had the unexpected benefit of defying belief: "People [in Iraq] are taught to act like sheep. They are totally depoliticized so you don't discuss political affairs with your peers. You don't discuss it. Definitely not with foreigners online because then you could be labeled as a spy or a collaborator with the West. They thought it could never be an Iraqi from within Iraq because it's just so foolish, so stupid to write something bad about Iraq or Saddam from within Iraq because obviously you end up in a very uncomfortable place"(Pax 2004, television broadcast).

Salam Pax's chosen anonymity, a necessary precaution given his "almost giddy irreverence about Saddam's regime," points to another function of self-disclosure common to webloggers writing in war zones (Katz 2003, ix). In contexts where the public sphere is closely monitored and regulated by state forces, blogs act as *spaces of political resistance*. To the extent that this resistance is externally directed and that the blog functions as a conduit for commentary on external events, warblogs "resist" the narcissism associated with exhibitionism; to the extent that warblog readers are "stimulated" by the desire to access uncensored, unedited "independent" accounts of war, they resist the thirst for sensationalism associated with voyeurism. For journalists and civilians living in war zones, the blogging form presents the obvious and perhaps sole mechanism of expressing opinions without censure. Reporters Without Borders' *Handbook for Bloggers and Cyber-dissidents* puts it this way: "Bloggers are often the only real journalists in countries where the mainstream media is censured or under pressure" (2005, 5). The handbook aims to help bloggers living under repressive regimes to acquire the technical expertise to blog anonymously, to enable them to circumvent state-directed Internet filtering and monitoring (to access blocked sites), and at the same time to ensure that their blog is picked up by major search engines in order to maximize the diffusion of their uncensored contents (Reporters 2005, 64).

Iranian urban sociologist Masserat Amir-Ebrahimi (2004) points to the meaning public spaces acquire in nondemocratic societies to explain the different ways blogs functions within such contexts: "In democratic societies, cyberspace is often viewed as an 'alter' space of information, research and leisure that functions in a parallel or complementary fashion to existing public spaces and institutions. In countries where public spaces are controlled by traditional or restrictive cultural forces, however, the internet can take on varied signification. In Iran, where the public sphere is closely monitored and regulated by traditional and state forces, the internet has become a means to resist the restrictions imposed on these spaces."

In the pre-conflict period, blogging provided Salam Pax with a "safe" mechanism for discussing the impending "de-Saddamization" of Iraq and for exposing examples of "Daddy Saddam's" corruption: "But the best gifts is [sic] the car gifts everybody (except *me*) is getting. The latest addition to the list of recipients of $30,000 car gift are judges" (Pax, 2003, 41, 62).

Apart from state monitoring, other forms of outside intervention may threaten the life-cycle of warblogs. Sanctions against blogs often result from a complex circularity of interactions between private and public spheres in which the mediasphere plays an intermediary role, as in the case of Josh Kucera. The day after Kucera's blog was picked up by *the Boston Globe* (who pronounced it "more compelling" than his offline reporting published in *Time*), *Time* requested him to stop publishing the blog (Boese 2004). Mainstream media intervention also played a part in the demise of Colby Buzzell's blog. The (then) *News Tribune* of Tacoma, Washington quoted one particular post entitled *Men in Black* in which Buzzell gave a dramatic account of an insurgent ambush on his patrol. While the post propelled him to instant celebrity status in the blogosphere, the article was picked up by the Pentagon's in-house clipping service, and as a result, Buzzell was asked to clear his postings with his platoon sergeant (Kline and Burnstein 2005, 265). Buzzell ended up being confined to camp for posting a mocking dig at his "editors" before coming to the decision to abandon blog camp (Kline and Burnstein 2005, 265). Neither Buzzell nor Kucera perceived their employers' responses to their non-professional activities as political censorship. Kucera cited commercial interests rather than political censorship as the motive behind *Time*'s move. Buzzell's blog did not contain any ideologically sensitive material (he was commended for "performing gallantly" as a soldier), but he was nevertheless sanctioned on the grounds that the information it contained posed a potential risk to operational security (Kline and Burnstein 2005, 265).

For warbloggers *the political is personal.* Blogging, and warblogging in particular, functions as an important mechanism not only to carry firsthand information and comments on political and military actions to the outside world but also to *mentally process the personal traumas* that these actions generate in the bloggers' everyday lives. Bloggers have irreverently been dubbed the "pajamahadeen" or the "the insurrectionary pajama people" (Kline and Burnstein 2005, 369). This image conveys both the individual blogger's potential to activate political resistance *and* the solitary figure of one man and his computer, recalling the lone musings associated with the one of the warblog's many generic ancestors—the war-diary. In times of conflict, the "pajama" or "private" side of blogging functions as a cutting-off from, a "safe-haven" from the outside world. The image of blogging as a space of private sanctuary resurfaces in Tom Matrullo's comparison of blogs with *loci amoeni,* "safe, idyllic, enclosed gardens where heroes of romance literature would recover from the battles of the outside world" (as cited Walker and Mortensen 2002, 259):

> The blog takes on some of the characteristics of the enclosed Renaissance garden, the interior plenitude of the autonomous voice reflecting upon and responding to other voices. . . . If one goes back and looks into the worlds of folks like Ariosto, Tasso, Cervantes, etc., one begins to see that the gardens in their works are places of rebirth where the battered warriors briefly stop outside the battle to recollect themselves. (Matrullo, as cited in Walker and Mortenson 2002, 260)

This image, as Walker and Mortensen point out, "encompasses the seemingly paradoxical mixture of private and public that is evident in weblogs. Blogs are visible, open spaces that encourage linking and conversation but they are also enclosed and private spaces that allow the writer to process the experiences of daily life" (2002, 260). In extreme conditions such as war, where everyday life is both stressful and unpredictable, blogging provides individuals with a routine and creative activity that allows them to "step outside the battle" in order to "digest" the traumatic situation they find themselves in. According to Rebecca Blood (2000), one of the world's first bloggers, the act of blogging may have the effect of making the individual more aware not only of his own situation but also of his own opinions:

> Shortly after I began producing Rebecca's Pocket I noticed two side effects I had not expected. First, I discovered my own interests. More importantly, I began to value more highly my own point of view. . . . In composing my link text everyday I carefully considered my own opinions and ideas, and I began to feel that my perspective was unique and important.
>
> This profound experience may be most purely realized in the blog-style weblog. . . . [T]he blogger, by virtue of simply writing down whatever is on his mind, will be confronted with his own thoughts and opinions. Blogging every day, he will become a more confident writer. A community of 100 or 20 or 3 people may spring up around the public record of his thoughts. As he enunciates his opinions daily, this new awareness of his inner life may develop into a trust in his own perspective.

Blood's comments on the effects of a growing readership community on the blogger help to explain why such responses can play a role in opening up journal-style blogs into political-opinion pieces, a transformation that is common in warblogs. In Salam Pax's case, the role of the readership community in this process was explicit—they actively solicited his opinions: "[The blog] was going to be very personal, nothing to do with politics, just about what we're doing in Baghdad. Later on when more and more people started to come and read it and ask all these questions about Baghdad . . . [is] when it took a more political turn" (Pax 2004, television broadcast) Various other factors motivate warblogs' propensity toward its political subgenre. Warbloggers have "privileged" access to local knowledge of, and responses to, political and military actions as well immediate access to global media. Because of their rootedness between local experiences of war and global access to news-network reporting, blogs (and even individual posts) authored in conflict zones tend to oscillate between the journal and opinion-piece genres:

Tuesday August 19, 2003

Tired

How is it possible to wake up tired? It feels like I've been struggling
in my sleep . . . struggling with nightmares, struggling with fears . . .
struggling to listen for gunshots or tanks. I'm just so tired today. It's
not the sort of 'tired' where I want to sleep- it's the sort of tired
where I just want to completely shut down . . . put myself on
standby, if you will.

I think everyone feels that way lately.

Today a child was killed in Anbar, a governorate north-west of
Baghdad. His name was Omar Jassim and he was no more than 10
years old, maybe 11. Does anyone hear of that? Does it matter any-
more? Do they show that on Fox News or CNN? He was killed during an American raid—no one knows why. His family are [sic]
devastated—nothing was taken from the house because nothing was
found in the house. It was just one of those raids. People are terrified
of the raids. You never know what will happen—who might be shot,
who might react wrong—what exactly the wrong reaction might
be. . . . Things are getting stolen too—gold, watches, money (dollars). . . . That's not to say ALL the troops steal—that's unfair. It's like
saying all of Iraq was out there looting. But it really is difficult having
to worry about looters, murderers, gangs, militias and now American
troops. I know, I know—someone is saying, "You ungrateful Iraqis!
They are doing this for YOU . . . the raids are for YOU!" But the
truth is, the raids only accomplish one thing: they act as a constant
reminder that we are under occupation, we are not independent, we
are not free, we are not liberated. . . . We're living, this moment, the
future we were afraid to contemplate 6 months ago. It's like trying to
find your way out of a nightmare. I just wish they would take the oil
and go. (Riverbend 2005, 7–8)

REALITY: THE BEST SHOW

Calvert identifies one of the social forces motivating mediated
voyeurism as the desire for truth in a media-saturated world, point-
ing to dissatisfaction with mainstream media as one of the reasons
for the shift toward reality-based mediated voyeurism (Calvert 2000,
61). Warblogging actively plays to this desire for alternative sources

of "truth" and warbloggers often situate their writing explicitly in a complementary or compensatory relation to the mediasphere. The title of Josh Kucera's blog *The Other Side* implies, as his opening post states explicitly, that his blog should be viewed "not [as] a substitute to ordinary media but a[s] complement to it," offering more of everyday life and topics not conventionally covered by political reporting: "You can get good information from the *New York Times*, BBC and Associate press. But you won't hear unvarnished opinion from a guy on the ground, or what ordinary days are like for the people on the ground: about pornographic movie theatres, tragic love stories or the sunset over Erbil" (2003).

Colby Buzzell viewed his blog as redressing the geographical limits of media coverage: "A big thing for me was that a lot of stories never got any coverage whatsoever. We were in the northern theater in Iraq and my whole time there I never saw an embedded reporter. I have gotten e-mails from other soldiers in different theaters of Iraq that were also e-mailing me saying the same thing. 'We get no media here and a lot of stuff that happens here never even gets mentioned back home'" (as cited in Burnstein and Kline, 266). But while Buzzell laments the scarcity of embedded reporters, Salam opposes the skewed vantage point of such journalists with the ordinary civilian-warblogger's unprotected view from the ground: "What [they] see is people shooting, not the people getting shot at." Salam's comment on the importance of warblogs in "giving news more context" and "making news more real" points to what Kitzmann (2003) refers to as the "fetishization" of notions of "reality" and "liveness" within Web-based forms of self-documentation (60).

Mediated voyeurism is also driven by "the chance to observe real people as they face their moments of reckoning" or "moment of truth attraction" (Calvert 2000, 64). For Calvert, such attraction is related to a displaced sense of identification: "As we watch these people confront these "pulse-pounding" moments, we are allowed not only to view these responses but to speculate about our own. A sense of 'it could happen to me' amongst audience members leads, in turn, to speculation about 'what if it really did happen to me'" (ibid.). The inherent unpredictability and danger of war situations augments the sense of suspense generated by narratives of the real: "If the basis of storytelling is the surprise of what is going to happen next, reality can be better than fiction because no one, not even the protagonists themselves, can predict the outcome. Without a script but with a barrel full of plot elements, the story just keeps unfolding" (Gabler 2000). Like video vérité and tell-all talk show voyeurisms, warblogs play to the phenomenon of "moment of truth" attraction and regularly provide readers with accounts of "fateful" situations. Buzzell's infamous *Men in Black* post, offering a "riveting account of a bloody firefight between his unit and scores of black-clad insurgents" describes such a moment (Kline and Burnstein 2005, 265): "People were hooting and hollering, yelling their war cries and doing the Indian yell thing as they drove off and locked and loaded their weapons. Bullets were pinging off our armor and you could hear multiple RPGs [rocket-propelled grenades] being fired and flying through the air and impacting all around us. I never felt fear like this. I was like, this is it, I'm going to die."

Mediated voyeurism may also create the illusion that "viewers" are actively involved in the world around them: "Updating ourselves on other's real-life extreme situations may give us the sense that, in some manner, we are helping them" (Calvert, 2000, 72). Calvert claims, however, that this feeling often has the converse effect of breeding the learned passivity associated with the "narcotizing dysfunction" of massive media consumption where viewers gain the impression of being actively involved but watching is substituted for action. For the active members of the readership community, the "feeling of being involved" in the limited sense of "helping" the blog author, might not be illusory. Many blog authors and readers claim to receive emotional support through blogs. Novelist and ex-blogger Ayelet Waldman describes how she and other women are vicariously attracted by the "emotional pull" of blogs whose authors face radical life situations (such as infertility and miscarriage weblogs), even when they (as in the case of Waldman, a mother of four) have no personal stake in the issue: "It's a remarkable phenomenon to meet thousands of strangers who lend each other emotional support. It's also a phenomenon to see people open up this intimate and heart-breaking aspect of their lives for perusal by strangers" (Kline and Bunstein 2005, 313).

Digital Intimacy?

Blogs written by ordinary people in extreme situations produce a powerful identification in their readers. When these daily experiences involve risk-taking or are life-threatening, the emotional investment of readers increases. The personal investment of the *author* is also key, as the engaged reader-responses to Kucera's blog writing (in contrast to his professional output) reveal: "Still, [Kucera] said, in the four years working as a freelancer overseas, he had not ever gotten as much feedback and interest in his work as he had in the weeks of the Iraq war though his blog. His writing was being published by one of the largest circulation news magazines [*Time*] in the West yet his blog audience cared about him, worried about him, gave his work constant dialogue and feedback" (Boese 2004).

Salam Pax and Riverbend's blogs are similarly interspersed with messages of gratitude to their readers, addressed both individually and as a group: "Thank you for making the last couple of months just great. For taking the time to read this weblog, to link, write an e-mail or comment. *Most of you know more about what I think and feel than my family does. For starters, none of them know that I blog. You do. And Diane knows way too much for my own good*" (Pax 2003, 88) [My emphasis].

For bloggers, the context of war may exacerbate the blurring between lived experience rooted in spatial proximity and mediated experience. On the one hand, they experience events through the media that are not longer spatially distant from the practical contexts of day to life. On the other hand, mediated experience may take on more significance as a source of interpersonal connections as regular social and workplace networks are disrupted. But do blogs such as Salam Pax's represent "the voice of an Internet generation alienated from nations and tribes but connected to one another in the most intimate of digital ways?"[18] How strong are the ties that bind blog authors and readerships? Do such ties equate to a sense of community? Are such ties stronger in a conflict situation?

Anita Blanchard's (2004) survey of research on SOC (sense of community) in virtual communities identifies four features, which computer media communication must fulfill to qualify as a community: membership (boundaries, belongings, and group symbols); influence (in terms of enforcing and challenging norms); exchange of support among members; and shared emotional connections among members. Research on whether popular blogs constitute virtual communities has yielded equivocal results. Given that blogs are heavily reliant on the centrality of their author and that blogs do not privilege public spaces for public interaction, Blanchard (2004) concludes that blogs have "some particular challenges in creating *a critical mass* of participants with a sense of community."[19]

Analyses of the way individuals (rather than communities) form ties may be more relevant to the way single author blogs functions. Evolutionary anthropologist Robin Dunbar's "social brain hypothesis"[20] has been used to advance the *cognitive* limit to the number of individuals with whom any one individual can maintain stable relationships—estimated at 150 (Zhou, Sornette, Hill, and Dunbar 2005, 2). Further related empirical research on average sizes of smaller core social groupings sets the average size of an individual's "support clique" (identified as the set of individuals from whom individuals would seek advice or help from in severe emotional and financial distress) as between three to five individuals, and the size of the average "sympathy groups" (the number of individuals with whom one has special ties) as twelve to twenty (ibid., 3).

In *Weblogs and Emergent Democracy*[21] Internet entrepreneur Joishi Ito (2003), in consultation with Socialtext CEO Ross Mayfield, discusses typical and maximum group sizes operating within the blogosphere and identifies three types of networks developing amongst weblogs. Mayfield suggests a first level "flat" network of twelve as the maximum number of "associates" one can develop dense interlinking with (Mayfield's comments are more relevant to "production-oriented blogs" where an individual uses the blog to exchange ideas or to develop an intellectual or other product with colleagues); the second level network, consisting of weaker social ties, is "bell-shaped" (normal distribution) and adopts Dunbar's law of 150 to quantify the maximum number of individuals with whom popular bloggers could typically sustain contact (Ito 2003). Finally, blogs can sustain a third, political, level of networking. Such networks are described in terms of a "power-law curve," with each "hit" functioning as a vote, and where the weblogs with the "most votes" or in the top of this power curve are the most influential (Ito 2003).

The interest of this type of extrapolation with reference to weblogs in general and warblogs in particular resides in Ito's observation that the power of weblogs resides in their capacity to operate in all three "clusters" mentioned above: "A single weblog and even a single entry in a weblog can have an operational purpose, a social purpose and a political purpose." *Where is Raed?*, for example, was initiated in order to sustain a single one-to-one contact (Salam Pax wanted to keep in touch his friend Raed, who had moved to Jordan and did not respond to e-mail). From the repeated references to a small cluster of named close friends, there is evidence from the blog that Pax's *support clique* consists of old friends that pre-date the blog (Raed, G.) but expands, as a result of the blog, to include one new Web-friend (Diane). References to regular e-mail exchanges with both named and unnamed individuals attest to connections to a wider social network of regular readers. But the blog also functioned on a political level, since it was read by a vast number of readers who were interested (and potentially influenced by) Salam's opinions.

Cyberapartheid?

Popular opinion blogs wind up to the political network level. But do political blogs and warblogs in particular self-segregate in terms of political alignment? Did blog readers in the pre-conflict period fall into either pro-war or antiwar camps? Cass Sunstein's observation that "new technologies, emphatically including the Internet, are dramatically increasing people's ability to hear echoes of their own voices and to wall themselves off from others" has fuelled fears about the perceived emergence of "cyberapartheid" and "cyberbalkanization" (as cited in Drezner and Farrell 2004, 21). On the other hand, cybercommentators such as law professor Jack Balkin (2004) dismisses this threat and argues that the intense inter-commenting and cross-linking intrinsic to blogging works against this kind of sequestration:

> [M]ost bloggers who write about political subjects cannot avoid addressing (and, more importantly, linking to) arguments made by people with different views. The reason is that much of the blogosphere is devoted to criticizing what other people have to say. It's hard to argue with what the folks at National Review Online or Salon are saying unless you go read their articles, and, in writing a post about them, you will almost always either quote or link to the article, or both. Ditto for people who criticize Glenn Reynolds, Andrew Sullivan, or Kos, or Atrios. If you don't like what Glenn said about

Iraq, you quote a bit of his posting, link to it, and then make fun of him. These links are the most important way that people travel on the Web from one view to its opposite. (And linking also produces a good check on criticism because you can actually go and read what the person being criticized has said.)

In addition, most bloggers have blogrolls which include a wide variety of different sources with very different ideological views.

The Iraq War demonstrated that weblogging can in fact create connections between individuals with radically different political views. In February 2003, bloggers from the pro-war and antiwar camps came together for a "structured debate to exchange ideas and argue our respective positions." Bloggers associated with the pro-war blog, *The Truth Laid Bear*, and the antiwar blog *Stand Down: The Left-Right Blog Opposing an Invasion of Iraq* hosted a "Cross-blog Iraq Debate—a structured debate to exchange ideas and argue our respective positions." The debate took the form of a call for questions (to be answered by the "opposing camp") followed by the publication of selected questions and the compilation of corresponding replies.[22]

Salam Pax's blog also points to the existence of readers from a wide range of the political spectrum, as the conflicting conspiracy theories surrounding his political allegiance confirm: "Wonderfully, the conviction of those that he [Salam Pax] was a Baathist agent was matched only by the suspicion of others that he was a Mossad or CIA operative" (Katz 2003, x). These antagonistic reader-responses not only create problems for the thesis of political self-segregation, they also attest to what Katz (2003) identifies as "the most compelling attributes of Salam's diaries: he directs vitriol in all directions" (xiii). The Manichaeism of Putnam and Sunstein's arguments is thus not only undermined by the plurality of political views represented in Salam Pax's readership community but also by Salam's own refusal to be "cocooned" into any particular political camp. On November 15, 2002, he voices his ambivalence about the impending hostilities:

> I know the war is inevitable . . . and I know Saddam is a nutcase with a finger on the trigger. But this is my country and I love its people. There is not way you can convince me that war is OK. . . . On an emotional level I cannot and will not accept a war in Iraq. But on the other hand . . .

Look, there is no way I am going to say it, mainly because I don't
trust the intentions of the American government. (Pax 2003, 38)

PUTTING THE BRIDGE THERE

Salam Pax and Riverbend's refusal to be pinned down to a simplistic
or closed narrative of war might have made them some cyberene-
mies, but it is also represents an important factor in their global
appeal. Their capacities to engage creatively with multiple perspectives and to create dialogues with individuals outside their own culture qualify them as "bridge blogs," which is a term coined by
Iranian-Canadian journalist and weblogger Hossein Derakhshan. In
Global Voices' Bridge Blog Index, Derakhshan (2004) proposes three
models for the ways people can use weblogs to communicate
between cultures: windows, bridges and cafés:

> Windows allow us to look into another culture, but not interact. . . .
> Cafés are complex spaces where groups of people can meet to discuss
> in ways that they can't meet in the real world, due to geography, pol-
> itics or language. . . . Bridges are more interactive than windows, but
> less complex than cafés. They are usually the project of a single blog-
> ger or a small group of authors. Bridge bloggers write for an audience
> outside their everyday reality—for instance, when Ory Okolloh writes
> about corruption in Kenya, reaching family at home and readers at
> Harvard, she is bridge blogging.

The concept of bridge bloggers has been adopted by Erhan
Zuckerman and Rebecca MacKinnon of Harvard Law School's
Berkman Center for Internet and Society as the basis of for the
Global Voices Wiki,[23] which contains a global index of bridge bloggers, categorized non-hierarchically—by continent and country. The
rationale behind the compilation of bridge blogs worldwide, according to MacKinnon, was to create a counter to the political and geographical biases of the mediasphere: "It [mainstream media] ignores
many international stories . . . and when it does tackle then it tends
to reinforce stereotypes about foreign countries rather than shed
new light on them" (Boyd 2005).

Surprisingly, the drive to remedy stereotypes, which is a central
feature of bridge blogs, brings us back to Calvert's discussion of
exhibitionism. In the context of the exhibitionist self-disclosure,
Calvert quotes the results of Patricia Joyner Priest's study of the

motivations of participants in the sensationalist U.S. TV talk show *Donahue*. In addition to financial motivations, Priest finds that "the driving motivation expressed by most informants, especially for those who represented severely marginalized groups, was a desire to *remedy stereotypes* and *to educate a national audience* about discrimination and alternative lifestyles" [My emphasis] (Calvert 2000, 85). Similarly, two of the driving forces in the writing of bridge bloggers during the Iraq War were the desire to *educate global audiences* and to *combat Western stereotypes* of Iraqi culture: "I am female and Muslim. Before the occupation, I more or less dressed the way I wanted to. I lived in jeans and cotton pants and comfortable shirts. Now, I don't dare leave the house in pants. A long skirt and loose shirt (preferably with loose sleeves) has become necessary. A girl wearing jeans risks being attacked, abducted, or insulted by fundamentalists who have been . . . liberated!" (Riverbend 2005, 17)

As the following excerpt reveals, Riverbend's texts also actively deconstruct the Huntington-style "us"–versus–"them" dogmas, which in Edward Said's (2002) formulation "pretend that the principal consideration is epistemological and natural—[that] our civilization is known and accepted, [and that] theirs is different and strange, whereas in fact the framework separating us from them is belligerent, constructed and situational" (577):

Setting the Record Straight

I'm going to set the record straight, once and for all.

I don't hate Americans, contrary to what many people seem to believe. Not because I love Americans, but simply because I don't hate Americans, like I don't hate the French, Canadians, Brits, Saudis, Jordanians, Micronesians, etc. It's that simple. I was brought up, like millions of Iraqis, to have pride in my own culture and nationality. At the same time, like millions of Iraqis, I was also brought up to respect other cultures, nations and religions. Iraqi people are inquisitive, by nature, and accepting of different values—as long as you do not try to impose those values and beliefs upon them.

Although I hate the American military presence in Iraq in its current form, I don't even hate the American troops . . . or wait, sometimes I do:

—I hated them on April 11—a cool, gray day: the day our family friend lost her husband, her son and toddler daughter when a tank hit the family car as they were trying to evacuate the house in Al-A'adhamiya district—an area that saw heavy fighting.

—I hated them on June 3 when our car was pulled over for some strange reason in the middle of Baghdad and we (3 women, a man and a child) were made to get out and stand in a row, while our hand-bags were rummaged, the men were frisked and the car was thoroughly checked by angry, brisk soldiers. I don't think I'll ever be able to put into words the humiliation of being searched. . . .

On the other hand . . .

—I feel terrible seeing the troops standing in this merciless sun—wearing heavy clothes . . . looking longingly into the air-conditioned interiors of our cars. After all, in the end this is Baghdad, we're Iraqi—we've seen this heat before.

—I feel bad seeing them stand around, drinking what can only be lukewarm water after hours in the sun—too afraid to accept any proffered ice water from "strange Iraqis."

—I feel pity watching their confused, frightened expressions as some outraged, jobless, father of five shouts at them in a language they can't even begin to understand. . . .

So now you know. Mixed feelings in a messed up world (Riverbend 2005, 14–15).

Bridge bloggers serve as cultural interpreters. Riverbend's bridge building often takes the form of "cultural object lessons" which she gives on "everything form the changing status of Iraqi women to Ramadan, the Iraqi educational system, the significance of date palms, and the details of mourning rituals."[24] Salam Pax's bridge building style, on the other hand, relies principally on a particular form of humor which allows him to confront the sensitive ethnic, religious, and political differences "framing" the conflict situation. According to frame theories of humor, the mechanism of "joking" functions as a break from everyday serious life: "The joker makes a shift from the serious frame to the humorous frame and is allowed to present criticism without fear of retribution" (Mulder and Nijholt 2002, 7).

For Salam, the diversionary function of blogging repeats the diversionary mechanism of his humor—blogging as an activity and "joking" as a rhetorical device fulfill the paradoxical functions of enabling him to simultaneously escape from, and yet engage with, the seriousness of war. Salam's references to the "serious issue" of Sunni/Shiite sectarian divide in Iraq include explanations of their different prayer rituals, which are incongruously reframed in relation to Salam's own body. Here, he posits himself as a kind of human bridge between Shiites and Sunnis (Salam has earlier explained that his mum is Shia and his father is Sunni): "There is also the debate about whether to cross your arms or let them dangle by your sides during prayer. Who cares? Just get on with it! And what am I supposed to do if I ever decided to pray? Hang on to my belly with one hand and let the other dangle? But I give one piece of advice. If you were ever cornered and had to choose, go for Shia. Very dramatic. They love ceremonies and during Ashur it is OK for men to cry, wail and generally be drama queens—everyone will consider you very devout. (Pax 2003, 43)

THE ECONOMY OF RECOGNITION VERSUS THE SHARING ECONOMY

Riverbend and Salam's blogs function within two conflicting economies. As blogs they are situated by default within what Miller and Shepherd (2004) refer to as the culture of exhibitionism or within what Andrew Kizmann (2003) terms an "economy of recognition" (58). Blogs are ranked by popularity by weblog search engines (such as Technorati), which track the number of links to each blog, or by RSS readers (such as Rojo and Bloglines), which tally the numbers of the blogs' subscribers. These systems generate lists of the top one hundred blogs that, along with reader polls, are used to assign an increasingly wide range of blog awards.[25] As Kitzmann (2003) notes, the function of such "digital seals of approval" is to create "a kind of economy of recognition, one often closely paralleling the tropes and discourses of mainstream media" (58).

Bloggers have instant access to popularity rankings and often explicitly situate themselves within the economy of recognition.

Salam, for example, farcically equates incoming links as expressions of sexual passion: "I checked my stats today and found out that I had been linked by Pandavox. . . . The goddess of linkylove has blessed me. Burning that modem and doing my sacred linkwhore dance around it worked" (2003, 3).

As popular blogs, Riverbend and Salam Pax's blogs are situated and situate themselves within the economy of recognition. On the other hand, I suggest that as cultural bridge builders, both Salam Pax and Riverbends' blogs move beyond the self-promotional economy of recognition and enter into what David Bollier terms the *information commons.* Bollier uses the term *commons* to refer to a wide range of *shared assets* and forms of community governance. The *commons* consists both of tangible assets—such as natural resources on public lands, public facilities, and the broadcast airwaves—and intangibles assets less readily identified as belonging to the public, including "a large expanse of cultural resources," dubbed the *information commons,* and consisting of "creative works and public knowledge not privatized under copyright law" (Bollier 2002).

Yale Law Professor Yochai Benkler (2004) also refers to the commons in his elaboration of *the Sharing Economy,* a term used to describe an emerging Internet-based model of economic production, based on commons-type behaviors. *The Sharing Economy* encompasses large-scale Internet-based projects that are produced as the result of the participation of large numbers of individuals (examples given are open-source software, such as Linux or the volunteer-written online encyclopedia Wikipedia) (Benkler 2004, 275–81). Benkler (2004) explains the *kairos* that makes this economy possible in terms of technological developments, which facilitate increasing levels of individual control over production: "My claim is not, of course, that we live in a unique moment of humanistic sharing. It is, rather, that our own moment in history suggests a more general observation: that the technological state of a society, particularly the extent to which individual agents can engage in efficacious production activities with material resources under their individual control, affects the opportunities for, and hence the comparative prevalence and salience of social market . . . and state production modalities" (278).

While Benkler argues that new technologies are increasing the *economic value* of social behavior, turning peer-production into something economically valuable, he does not expect this kind of production to pose a major challenge to the market system. He does, however, highlight a range of products that are particularly amenable to this form of production: "It so happens that a lot of the most valuable products of the Information Economy can be produced this way: software, most information, most knowledge, a lot of computation, a lot of storage, a lot of connectivity" (Hof 2005).

Both Riverbend and Salam's blogs are listed within the peer-produced *Global Voices Wiki's* Bridge Blog Index, which functions as a global news and information resource. *Where is Raed?* is cited in the introduction as an exemplary bridge blog, and Riverbend's blog is indexed under Iraqi blogs. As components of *the Global Voices Wiki*, I suggest that both these blogs circulate within this *Sharing Economy* and that the information, connectivity, and knowledge they produce contribute toward what I would call the *cultural commons*.

The two conflicting economies within which the two blogs circulated can be related to Hélène Cixous' Realms of the *Proper* and of the *Gift*. The Realm of the *Proper*, like Kitzmann's "economy of recognition", relates to values systems structured by an "economy of the proper." The desire for a "proper" return signals an emphasis on "self-identity, self-aggrandizement and arrogative dominance" and leads to "the obsession with classification, systematization and hierarchization" (Moi 1985, 110–11). The Realm of the *Gift*, on the other hand, corresponds "fairly closely to a Derridean definition of writing: is open to difference, willing to be 'traversed by the other,' characterized by spontaneous generosity . . . a deconstructive space of . . . interchange with the other" (Moi 1985, 113). War bridge bloggers inhabit these deconstructive spaces of exchange as they break down ethnic and religious differences exacerbated by conflict and geographical distance.

In *The Media and Modernity*, John B. Thompson (1995) contrasts the *institutional sequestration of experience* (death, illness) with the *desequestration of experience* effected through mediated experiences of desperate life conditions, injuries, and fatalities. War bridge blogging amplifies this desequestration of experience in its capacity to creating virtual proximity, enabling large numbers of individuals outside a war zone to make intimate connections (whether reciprocal or non-reciprocal) with the "enemy out there": "People in the West never saw the people of Iraq, never understood the people of Iraq or saw the individual. It was always Saddam. Wars, sanctions, occupations, invasion of Kuwait and the rallies Saddam would hold—'Long live Saddam, we love you, we go to death with you.' But we're not so very different from you. We have to do certain things because we need to live. At some point I realized that this is what the weblog is good for, basically putting the bridge there" (Pax 2004, television broadcast).

"We're Not So Different From You . . . "

Salam and Riverbend's blogs put "the portrayal of Iraqis as poor, anti-Western, frequently hysterical and altogether very different from us" (Katz 2003, ix). According to Edward Said (2002), such acts of deconstruction may incite fear: "For there are closing ties between apparently warring civilizations than most of us would like to believe; both Freud and Nietzsche showed how the traffic across carefully maintained, even policed boundaries moves with often terrifying ease. . . . Hence the altogether more reassuring battle orders (a crusade, good versus evil, freedom against fear, etc.) drawn out of Huntington's alleged opposition between Islam and the West."

Acting as a countercurrent to the kind of facile reassurance provided by Huntington-style ideology, the fast flow of Internet traffic associated with Riverbend and Salam's blogs nevertheless provides, I believe, a different kind of reassurance, a closer comfort—not the "comfort of strangers" but the knowledge that "you are not so different from me."

Notes

1. Citation taken from inside cover of Pax, S. 2003. *The Baghdad Blog.* London: Atlantic.
2. http://www.warblogging.com.
3. http://www.warblogging.com/archives/000001.php.
4. http://www.pointblog.com/past/cat_warblogs.htm.
5. http://www.mfconsulting.com/blog/archives/000076.html.
6. http://www.pointblog.com/past/2005/08/03/warblogs_en_irak_declaration_obligatoire.htm.
7. http://www.military.com.
8. http://www.milblogging.com.
9. http://www.sifry.com/alerts/archives/000298.html.
10. Only one of these warblogs, Riverbend's, is still online at the time of

writing. Salam Pax has started a new blog, *Shut Up You Fat Whiner*, see http://justzipit.blogspot.com.

11. http://news.bbc.co.uk/2/hi/entertainment/3707111.stm.

12. http://www.sixfigures.com/pr01.html.

13. http://www.guardian.co.uk/Iraq/Story/0,2763,1038253,00.html.

14. http://iraqblogcount.blogspot.com/ listed 188 Iraqi blogs as of January 2006. This figure includes non-Iraqis writing in Iraq and ex-patriot Iraqis.

15. When discussing the four case studies, I use the term "warblog" in the sense of a blog that is written during a conflict or immediately post-conflict situation. The term is also commonly used to denote blogs whose content relates to commentary about war.

16. Citations from Riverbend and Salam Pax's blogs will be taken from the book versions of their blogs and the relevant page number will be used as reference.

17. http://www.guardian.co.uk/g2/story/0,3604,966768,00.html.

18. Quotation from Los Angeles Times, taken from the back cover of Pax, S. 2003. *The Baghdad Blog*. London: Atlantic.

19. Although this may still be true of single-author blogs, the emergence of *community weblogs*, where anyone can add posts, and *group weblog*s, where only members of a designed group may enter posts is meeting that challenge.

20. Dunbar found correlations between neocortex size and maximum group sizes in non-human mammals, from which figures for modern human interaction were later extrapolated.

21. A community-written document, mostly written by Joichi Ito.

22. http://www.truthlaidbear.com/archives/2003/02/10/crossblog _iraq_debate_the_questions.php#000937

23. A "wiki" is a website that allows users to easily add and edit content and is especially suited for collaborative writing. See http://cyber.law.har-vard.edu:8080/globalvoices/wiki/index.php/BridgeBlog.

24. *Publisher's Weekly* quote on inside cover of Riverbend. 2005. *Baghdad Burning*. London: Marion Boyars.

25. The awards genre includes multi-category awards (*Blog Awards* and *Bloggies*), specialist awards (*Reporters Without Frontiers Freedom Blog Awards*), sectarian awards (*Catholic Blog Awards*), country-indexed awards (*Philippine Blog Awards*), and regional awards (*Asian Blog Awards*).

REFERENCES

Amir-Ebrahimi, M. 2004. Performance in everyday life and the rediscovery of the "self" in Iranian weblogs. Bad Jens: *Iranian Feminist Newsletter* 7. http://www.badjens.com/rediscovery.html (accessed August 21, 2005).

Balkin, J. 2004. What I learned about blogging in a year. *Balkanization Blog.* January 23. http://balkin.blogspot.com/2004_01_18_balkin_archive .html#107480769112109137 (accessed September 3, 2005).

Benkler, Yochai. 2004. Sharing nicely: On shareable goods and the emergence of sharing as a modality of economic production [electronic version]. *The Yale Law Journal* 114:273–358.

Blanchard, A. 2004. Blogs as virtual communities: Identifying a sense of community in the Julie/Julia project. In *Into the bloggosphere: Rhetoric, community and culture of weblogs.* http://blog.lib.umn.edu/blogosphere/ blogs_as_virtual.html (accessed January 5, 2006).

Blood, R. 2000. Weblogs: A history and perspective. *Rebecca's pocket blog.* September 7. http://www.rebeccablood.net/essays/weblog_history.html *(accessed* December 15, 2005).

———. 2002. *The weblog handbook: Practical advice on creating and maintaining your blog.* Cambridge MA: Perseus.

Boese, C. 2004. The spirit of Paulo Freire in blogland: Struggling for a knowledge-log revolution. In *Into the bloggosphere: Rhetoric, community and culture of weblogs.* http://blog.lib.umn.edu/blogosphere/the _spirit_of_paulo_freire.html (accessed January 5, 2006).

Bollier, D. 2002. Reclaiming the commons. *Boston Review* 27:3–4. http://www.bostonreview.net/BR27.3/bollier.html (accessed January 14, 2006).

Boyd, C. 2005. Global voices speak through blogs. *BBC News/Technology.* April 6. http://news.bbc.co.uk/2/low/technology/4414247.stm (accessed July 3, 2005).

Buzzell, C. 2005. *My war: Killing time in Iraq.* New York: Putnam.

Calvert, C. 2000. *Voyeur nation.* Boulder: Westview Press.

Carl, C. R. 2005. *Bloggers and their blogs: A depiction of the uses and usages of weblogs on the World Wide Web.* MA Thesis, Georgetown University. http://cct.georgetown.edu/thesis/ChristineCarl.pdf (accessed February 3, 2006).

Derakhshan, H. 2004. What are BridgeBlogs? *Global voices online.* http://globalvoicesonline.org/wiki/index.php/Bridge_Blog_Index (accessed September 7, 2005).

Drezner, D. W., and Farrell, H. 2004. *The power and politics of blogs.* August 2004. http://www.danieldrezner.com/research/blogpaperfinal.pdf (accessed August 20, 2005).

Dunbar, R. I. M. 1992. Neocortex size as a constraint on group size in primates [Electronic version]. *Journal of Human Evolution* 22 (6):469–93.

Gabler, N. 2000. Behind the curtain of TV voyeurism. *The Christian Science Monitor.* July 7. http://csmonitor.com/cgibin/durableRedirect.pl?/durable/2000/07/07/p1s4.htm (accessed August 29, 2005).

Gurak, L., S. Antonijevik, L. Johnson, C. Ratliff, and J. Reyman. 2004. Introduction: weblogs, rhetoric, community, and culture. In *Into the bloggosphere: Rhetoric, community and culture of weblogs.* http://blog.lib.umn.edu/blogosphere/introduction.html (accessed January 18, 2006).

Grossman, L. 2004. Meet Joe Blog. *Time.* June 13. http://www.time.com/time/magazine/article/0,9171,1101040621-650732-1,00.html (accessed August 3, 2005).

Herring, S. C., L. A. Scheidt, S. Bonus, and E. Wright. 2004. Bridging the gap: A genre analysis of weblogs. *Proceedings of the 37th annual Hawaii international conference on system sciences.* http://csdl2.computer.org/comp/proceedings/hicss/2004/2056/04/205640101b.pdf (accessed August 5, 2005).

Hof, R. D. 2005. The sharing economy. *Business Week Online.* June 20. http://www.businessweek.com/magazine/content/05_25/b3938902.htm (accessed August 10, 2005).

Ito, J., and Jon Lebrowsky, eds. 2003. *Weblogs and Emergent Democracy.* http://joi.ito.com/static/emergentdemocracy.html (accessed January 10, 2006).

Katz, I. 2003. Introduction to Pax. S. *The Baghdad blogger.* London: Atlantic.

Kitzmann, A. 2003. That different place: Documenting the self within online environments [Electronic version]. *Biography* 26 (1):48–65.

Kline, D., and D. Burnstein. 2005. *Blog! How the newest media revolution is changing politics, business, and culture.* New York: CDS.

Miller, C. R., and D. Shepherd. 2004. Blogging as social action: A genre analysis of the weblog. In *Into the blogosphere: Rhetoric, community and culture of weblogs.* http://blog.lib.umn.edu/blogosphere/blogging_as_social_action_a_genre_analysis_of_the_weblog.html (accessed January 5, 2006).

Moi, T. 1985. *Sexual/textual politics: Feminist literary theory.* London: Routledge.

Morman, T. 2003. Great weblogs for not-so-great times. *Indy.* March 26. http://indyweek.com/durham/2003-03-26/triangles.html (accessed November 24, 2005).

Mulder, M. P., and A. Nijholt. 2002. Humour research: State of the art. *Institutional Repository of the University of Twente.* http://doc.utwente.nl/fid/1183 (accessed January 26, 2006).

Pax, S. 2003. *The Baghdad Blog.* London: Atlantic.

————. 2004. *Baghdad Blogger/Salam Pax: Video Reports from Iraq.* [Online version of Television broadcast interview with Salam Pax]. *CBC Zed Gallery.* November 4. http://zed.cbc.ca/go;jsessionid =aHLiZhWi8ofa?POS=5&CONTENT_ID=186317&c=contentPage (accessed August 28, 2005).

Reporters without Borders. 2005. *Handbook for bloggers and cyber-dissidents.* September. http://www.rsf.org/IMG/pdf/handbook_bloggers _cyberdissidents-GB.pdf (accessed November 8, 2005).

Riverbend. 2005. *Baghdad burning.* London: Marion Boyars.

Said, E. 2001. The clash of ignorance. *The Nation.* October 22. http://www.thenation.com/docprint.mhtml?i=20011022&s=said (accessed November 26, 2005).

————. 2002. The clash of definitions. *Reflections on exile and other essays.* Cambridge: Harvard University Press.

Stark, Myra. 2003. You, me, celebrity. *Saatchi and Saatchi 2003: Ideas from trends.* http://www.showsmart.com/newsarticlesstories/other/ 2003trends.cfm (accessed September 4, 2005).

Thompson, J. B. 1995. *Media and modernity: A social theory of the media.* Cambridge: Polity.

Walker, Jill, and Torill Mortensen. 2002. Blogging thoughts: personal publication as an online research tool. *Researching ICTs in context: SKIKT-researchers' conference 2002.* http://www.intermedia.uio.no/konferanser/ skikt-02/docs/Researching_ICTs_in_context-Ch11-Mortensen-Walker.pdf (accessed August, 3, 2005).

Zhou, W. X., D. Sornette, R. A. Hill, and R. I. M. Dunbar. 2005. Discrete hierarchical organization of social group sizes. *Proceedings of the royal society*, B 272: 439–444. http://www.citebase.org/cgi-bin/citations?id =oai:arXiv.org:cond-mat/0403299 (accessed January 16, 2005).

CHAPTER 8

WARRIORS OR AMAZONS:
HOW OPPOSING THE WAR IN IRAQ
BECAME A GENDER ISSUE IN MEXICO

Maria de la luz Matus-Mendoza

INTRODUCTION

After more than three thousand North American casualties in the Iraq War and a senatorial election showing strong opposition to the war, one might wish to go back in history to analyze the different voices that opposed the armed conflict. Among those countries that opposed the war was Mexico. Mexico acted according to its non-intervention policy. However, sexism in the language was present in the voices expressing opposition. Mexican society has been recognized as a machismo or patriarchal society. Men are the providers in the house: women do not have to work. The sole role of women is to bear and look after their children (Nash 1999; Fought 2003). This ideology in turn permeates language; in Cameron's words (1990, 89) "society holds [these] beliefs about men and women and their relative status; language . . . reflects those beliefs."

One might wonder if this machismo continues to manifest itself in the face of great conflict, especially when directed toward its most important and political partner, the United States. For this reason, editorials and editorial cartoons are analyzed using critical linguistics that indicate the way discourse is ideologically influenced by, and can itself influence, power relations in society. The term discourse has been widely used in social sciences (Foucault 1971; Gutiérrez Vera 2004) and linguistics (Searle 1969; Mills 1995; McConnell-Ginet 1998). Paraphrasing Fairclough (1995), "discourse" here refers to the written language use and visual images[1] (another type of semiotic activity, that is, signs). It is noteworthy to emphasize that the language employed by writers belongs to a system from which it is within the writer's discretion[2] to select how to communicate his message. Meaning involves the process of meaning-production not being accessible at the level of the individual words. "[It] exists in relation to concrete subjects and objects, and is inexplicable except in terms of this set of relationships" (Hodge and Kress 1988, viii). That is why to interpret phrases one should draw on factors other than the literal meaning of words that compose the message (Mills 1995). This analysis will use Brown and Yule's three-step aspect to interpret the writer's meaning when he or she produced the discourse. "First, to try to work out what the intention of the speaker/writer is; second, using general knowledge, at the level both of facts about the world and knowledge which you assume you will be expected to know in the situation; and third, determining the inferences which need to be made" (Brown and Yule 1983, 225).

Sample and Analysis of Written Discourse

A qualitative analysis was carried out by looking repeatedly for patterns (Johnstone 2000) in the headline and bodies of editorials and editorial cartoons on ABYZ News Links[3] from January 1 to March 30, 2003: *El Universal.* Surprisingly, the number of editorials that contain sexist language[4] is rather small compared with the number of editorial cartoons that illustrate a sexist argument against the war in Iraq. The analysis of written discourse starts with the headlines and continues with the patterns found in the body of the editorial. From a total of fifty-eight editorials, seven exhibit sexist language. They can be divided from general to particular in four groups: (1) a letter from a mother to a dangerous man; (2) historic "macho figures" such as Pancho Villa, Ulysses, Hector, Caligula; (3) historic female figures such as Cleopatra and Helen of Troy; and (4) The Trojan War.

The editorial printed in *El Universal* on February 15, 2003, titled "From a Mother-to-be to a Dangerous Man" ("De una futura madre a un hombre peligroso") follows the format of a formal letter addressed to "Mister George W. Bush." It can be divided into two main sections. The first contrasts human capital and economic resources between Iraq and the United States. It seems to be an informative letter that offers information about illiteracy rates in Iraq and health issues that affect Iraqi children, "63% of Iraqis don't know how to read nor write; 71% lack running water." In the second section, motherhood in Mexico, Iraq, and the United States is used as an argument to convince Bush to avoid the war. The first five lines describe mothers-to-be as hopeful and happy individuals who wish the best for their children. On line six, Bush's mother is introduced in an attempt to create empathy toward motherhood and the children to be born in Iraq and the United States. The last three sentences could be related to a macho perspective in relation to marriage and motherhood. First, the phrase, "the husband that was given to her" suggests that she didn't have any control in choosing him. Second, the last two sentences imply that a mother suffers because of her children, and it is her children's responsibility to avoid her suffering.

This editorial portrays women from the traditional perspective that females are depicted in a patriarchal society. "Women [are] more often referred to in terms . . . of their relation to others" (Mills 1995, 163); as a mother-to-be in this case. Furthermore, the fact that the letter is signed using only the first name, Daniela, suggests that this woman can be anybody and everybody.

There are two editorials that refer to historic "macho figures" such as Pancho Villa, Ulysses, Henry VIII, and Hector to oppose the war in Iraq. The editorial titled, "Pancho Villa, Cleopatra and the Iraq War" ("Pancho Villa, Cleopatra y la Guerra de Irak") can also be divided in two main sections. The first part describes how Pancho Villa, Henry VIII, Julius Caesar, and Mark Anthony changed history because of the circumstances they faced and their frivolous reasons: lust and love. The second part compares this rationale to Bush's less romantic, yet also frivolous, reasons. His rationale is based on economic and political reasons: "control of the oil in the region . . . encourage the war industry, . . . the Pentagon pressure to justify its budget, [and] the need to consolidate his leadership in order to be reelected" (*El Universal*, January 26, 2003). The editorial closes reiterating that millions of people's future will change due to reasons that can be found on a psychiatrist's sofa other than reasons that will benefit people. "Cleopatra's nose, Henry's VIII concupiscence and Bush's ignorant stubbornness become the motors of the history" (ibid.).

Without this cattle stealer [Pancho Villa] who became a general because of the circumstances, the Mexican Revolution would have been different. This makes us wonder about the decisive role that individuals who make history have:

> Probably, England would be a Catholic country if Henry VIII would have had the gift of abstinence. But he didn't. . . . He decided to found the Anglican Church for himself and for every Englishman. . . . This changed millions of people's history and the history of Europe.

> The topic might seem frivolous, but it isn't. Some historians have documented the dramatic changes that occurred in Ancient History because of Julius Cesar's and Mark Anthony's decisions when Cleopatra's exotic beauty subdued them. They invaded Egypt. . . . they modified the history of that country. Romans would not have invaded Egypt if the leaders had not been victims of passionate love for the Egyptian queen. (*El Universal*, January 26, 2003)

The editorial titled, "The Trojan War will not occur" ("No ocurrirá la Guerra de Troya") borrows its title from a play by Jean Giraudoux who wrote it in the eve of World War II. It deals with Ulysses' and Hector's unsuccessful efforts to make Helen return to Troy as the only way to avoid the Trojan War. This editorial explores Hussein's multiple violations of UN resolutions and suggests that Hussein's resignation is the only thing that would avoid the Iraq War. However, it compares that with Helen of Troy's unwillingness to leave Paris. Therefore, the war is inevitable. This editorial appeals to the common belief that Paris and Helen's love affair caused the Trojan War. Nevertheless, historians know that the war followed political as well as economic reasons. Once again a sexist perspective can be seen in this editorial. In the war against Iraq, Hussein was unwilling to leave Iraq, but several sources have suggested that economic and political causes motivated the armed conflict.

"An Innocent Girl's Consent" ("El sí a la Guerra") is another editorial that borrows its title from a dramatic Spanish play that deals with the practice of arranged marriages of older men to teenage girls in the 1800s. The editorial suggests that agreeing with the war serves to strengthen political bonds, and it is convenient for economic reasons; it has the same purposes that arranged marriages had among royal families of Europe as the play portrays them. The following quotations from the editorial support this interpretation.

Some national voices have manifested the consent to the war against Iraq in exchange for automatic concessions from the United States:

> The argument in favor to support the war, besides assuming that there would be war between the United States and Iraq, supposes the United States will be governed indefinitely by George Bush. . . . The keen-witted analysts flirting with supporting the war proclaim that they have discovered the reason of the crisis.
>
> The war is to win the presidential reelection.
>
> To support the war would mean the tacit subversion of the international order in favor of an uncertain, violent and arbitrary configuration between the United States and other countries, not only the Islamic world.
>
> To accept the war would mean to encourage the tendencies toward the abandonment of the UN. (First, it would deepen current division, and later through the formation of new blocks, Mexico would be isolated from Europe, Russia and France.) Moreover, Mexico would be at the mercy of the United States. That would mean that our northern neighbor would not treat us better even if we were submissive and obedient. (*El Universal*, March 4, 2003)

The editorial "In the Kingdom of the Absurd" ("En el reino de lo absurdo") compares Bush's irrational decision to start the war against Iraq with Vicente Fox's positive comments on Mexican peasants who do not know how to read; "Both attitudes show the mental derangement that leads the desire to cover [Bush's and Fox's] inefficiencies and errors." The editorial insists that North Americans believe everything that is told to them; it illustrates this by referring to the famous H. G. Wells radio show, "The War of the Worlds," which caused panic in New York sixty-four years ago. The editorial also stresses the fact that finding and killing Saddam Hussein and exhibiting his body would be child's play for the most powerful nation in the world. Therefore, it is irrational to be afraid of a country that hardly has slingshots in comparison to the technically advanced military armament of the United States. Actually, this editorial states that the war against Iraq distracts North Americans from noticing Bush's problems in the administration as well as white collar scandals, such as Enron. On this note, the editorial brings about Fox's illogical praise of illiterate women when he stated, "One lives better without reading the newspapers" (*El Universal*, March 4, 2003). This is interpreted as Fox's wish to have a nation that does not have any possibility of information. The result should be a nation that can be manipulated by the government using television anchors and personal publicity spots as the messengers. What seems to lie beneath this editorial is the idea of controlling women through the lack of instruction, since men are never mentioned in the editorial. In this case both Bush and Fox want to manipulate the public for their own personal and political gains.

The editorial "Caligulas's Epoch" ("época de Calígulas") compares "the Roman political system that allowed Caligula to name his horse a consul with the North American political system that allowed George Bush to become president" (*El Universal*, March 15, 2003). It blames Caligula's mental disorder for his decision. However, it considers Bush's decisions inexcusable and points out the changes that he introduced in his native Texas, such as the death penalty, the ecological destruction, the plutocracy's interests, and the abolition of rights for women and the poor. The editorial also compares Bush's belief that he is God's instrument to impart justice in the world to Caligula's proclamation that he was a god and therefore gave orders to build temples and to hold sacrifices in his honor. Even though there are several references to previous North American presidents who considered themselves instruments of God throughout history, what seems more relevant for the purpose of this chapter is that Condoleezza Rice receives the same label as her male colleagues (Donald Rumsfeld, Dick Cheney, and Colin Powell) in the administration: they are his four [Horsemen] of the Apocalypse.

ANALYSIS OF VISUAL DISCOURSE

There are forty editorial cartoons that have a patriarchal take on the war. These can be divided in three distinct groups: (1) the war represented exclusively as a male issue; (2) women representing Iraqi's

Figure 8.1 "Educastrador" 'Educator-Castrator'
Boligan (*El Universal*, March 7, 2003)

grateful people or revenge against North Americans; (3) Saddam Hussein as a man who obeys his women's desires and performs house chores.

The thirty representations of only males as participants in the war seem to agree with research on women's and men's graphic representations in newspapers (Mills 1995, 161) and English as Foreign Language textbooks (Graci, 1989). Males are presented as physically strong and having stereotypical roles. Two cartoons are especially poignant "Educator-Castrator" ("Educastrador") and "The Resolution" ("La Resolución"). The male soldiers' physical and military powers are stressed. In the first cartoon, the soldier seems to crush Baghdad as an insect under his powerful feet. However, this strong soldier armed with powerful weapons is about to step into the city that resembles a bear trap. After so many casualties and complete chaos in the Iraq War, this cartoon seems to be prophetic. In the second one, the soldier uses the United Nations building to pull the trigger against Iraq. It is noteworthy to notice that both soldiers have an enormous body but a very small head. It may be that the cartoonist is making an additional comment.

The cartoon, "The Resolution" is playing with two ideas. On one hand is the idea that the United States decided to begin a war against

Figure 8.2 "La Resolución" 'The Resolution'
Boligan (*El Universal*, February 22, 2003)

Iraq in spite of the fact that the United Nations did not issue a diplomatic resolution to back up the war. On the other hand, using the building to pull the trigger might suggest that the United Nations' inability to control the most powerful nation in the world contributed to the war; its lack of political and diplomatic power made the United Nations the instrument of the United States and England.

Of the seven cartoons with Bush, there are four that suggest that the war is a game: two show Bush driving a tank and a plane. In another Bush is target shooting. One of the two most striking is seen in Figure 8.3: George Bush wearing a strait-jacket. Actually the title of the cartoon is "Crazy like a Fox" ("Loco Furioso"). The ball that he is about to hit might be the world; Bush's threat to world peace and the United Nations is another criticism stated in different editorials. The nail across the mace might suggest not only an unfair game—that is, there were no truthful reasons to start the war—but also that Bush might deflate the world, that is, it could be interpreted as creating an unstable situation in the Middle East. The capsule in the cartoon reads: "Hussein, You are running out of time!"

Figure 8.3 "Loco Furioso" 'Crazy Like a Fox'
(*El Universal*, January 26, 2003)

Cartoon 4 does not have a title. However, it suggests several ideas that have been written about the war and George Bush. Bush is portrayed as a cowboy from Texas who wants to start a war against Iraq for the wrong reasons. Moreover, the cowboy appeals to the common idea that Texans are virile and courageous individuals who face dangers in their everyday life. Here the cowboy is riding a missile as it were a horse in a rodeo; it seems only another game. This cartoon also might refer to the last scene of *Dr. Strangelove*.[5] Major T. J. manually fixes the mechanism to deploy a nuclear missile against Russia. When the Major manages to deploy the missile, he is riding it and seems extremely happy. The cowboy in the dark might be Vicente Fox who was constantly criticized for not having a definite position against the war. He seems to be the passive observer that editorials portray.

The cartoon called "Team Work" ("Trabajo en Equipo") simply seems to mock the Iraqi society where women do not have any rights and have to always obey males. The two bubbles with Hussein's comments reinforce this idea. He says, "I don't leave Iraq until I check with my 40 wives . . . We are such a happy presidential harem that we take all the decisions together." This cartoon transgresses

Figure 8.4
Boligan (*El Universal*, March 16, 2003)

the traditional role representation in male and female portrayal.
Saddam Hussein is represented performing a stereotypical woman's
job, which is cleaning.

The last two cartoons selected here are the only ones that portray
women. The first one appeals to the traditional representation of a
female as mother, caregiver, and hostess (Mills 1995); she welcomes
the invaders with a bouquet of flowers. It is interesting to notice that
this woman is carrying a baby. Thus, this suggests her vulnerability
and her sincere wish to welcome the North American soldiers. The
unequal representations of the soldiers and the woman also suggest
her weakness and vulnerability. The title though is quite interesting,
"From the Citizens as Stubbornness" ("De la Ciudadania como
Terquedad").

The second cartoon depicting a woman included here seems to
contradict the previous image of women as mothers and victims.
Here this woman represents the terrorist revenge. This woman has
this label on her gown. Hussein and Bush are smaller than her; this
might suggest the power and impact of the terrorist movement
against the United States. She is staring at Bush's club on which is
written: "United States and its allies." Hussein, compared to the terrorism lady, seems to be an innocent child. These cartoons portraying two different images of women are reminiscent of the posters

Figure 8.5 "Trabajo en Equipo" 'Team Work'
Omar (*El Universal*, March 22, 2003)

painted during the Spanish Civil War where women were represented in these two different lights: as a mother and victim of the war
and a courageous fighter against the war. Of course that was a different war, but the point here is that two macho societies decided to
play with these two ideas. Moreover, the woman representing the
terrorist might have a sexism undertone in that women can be really
harmful when they are hurt.

CONCLUSION

Both written and visual discourses discussed in this chapter support
the idea that there was an opposition against the war in Iraq using
sexist language and images. Interestingly, the number of editorials
with this undertone seems relatively low. It might be that the main
reasons for opposing the war were anchored in Mexico's painful

Figure 8.6 "De la Ciudadanía como Terquedad" 'From the Citizens as Stubbornness'
Boligan (*El Universal*, March 2, 2003)

Figure 8.7 'Buscha Pleitos' "Trouble Maker"
Carreño (*El Universal*, March 16, 2003)

history in regards to North American imperialism. Nonetheless, sexism in the language can be found here.

NOTES

1. This is a semiotic analysis approach. In this approach linguistic, psychological, philosophical, and sociological characteristics of communicative signs are studied together. Danesi (1999, 5) defines signs as "gestures, movements, words, word glances, and [images] that human beings routinely enlist to make and send out messages."
2. Of course, the writer is limited by the grammatical parameters of each language.
3. It wasn't possible to use Lexis-Nexis. The available issues published in Spanish-speaking countries are very limited; most of the files end in 1999.
4. Sexist language refers to the unequal representation of men and women. It "also represents stereotypes of women and men, sometimes to the disadvantage of men, but most often to the disadvantage of women" (Wareing 2004, 76).
5. This author would like to thank Dr. Hakanen who suggested this reference to *Dr. Strangelove*, a classic 1964 movie produced and directed by Stanley Kubrick. It is a black comedy loosely based on the novel *Red Alert* by Peter George.

REFERENCES

Boligan. http://www.eluniversal.com.mx/wcarton1883.html (accessed December 5, 2005).

———. 2003. Educastrador. *El Universal*. March 7. http://www.eluniversal.com.mx/wcarton1846.html (accessed December 10, 2005).

———. 2003. La Resolución. *El Universal*. February 22. http://www.eluniversal.com.mx/wcarton1795.html (accessed February 22, 2003).

Brown, Gillian, and George Yule. 1983. *Discourse analysis*. Cambridge, New York: Cambridge University Press.

Cameron, Deborah. 1990. Demythologizing sociolinguistics: Why language does not reflect society. In *Ideologies of language*. New York: Routledge, 79–93.

Carballo, Emmanuel. 2003. La sombra de Poncio Pilatos. *El Universal*. March 4. http://www2.eluniversal.com.mx/pls/impreso/w_editoriales.detalle?var=17559 (accessed December 5, 2005).

Carreño. 2003. Bushca pleitos. *El Universal.* March 4. http://www.eluniversal
.com.mx/wcarton1884.html (accessed December 12, 2005).

Cremoux, Raúl. 2003. De una futura madre a un hombre peligroso. *El
Universal.* February 15. http://www2.eluniversal.com.mx/pls/impreso/
w_editoriales.detalle?var=17421 (accessed December 12, 2005).

Danesi, Marcel. 1999. *Of cigarettes, high heels and other interesting things.
An introduction to semiotics.* New York; St. Martin Press.

Foucault, Michael. 1971. El orden del discurso. Colección cuadernos pop-
ulares, serie archivos de filosofía. México: Universidad Nacional Autónoma
de México.

Graci, Joseph P. 1989. Are foreign language textbooks sexist? An exploration of modes of evaluation. *Foreign Language Annals* 22.5: 477–90.

Hodge, Robert, and Gunther Kress. 1988. *Social semiotics.* Ithaca, New
York: Cornell University Press.

Johnstone, Barbara. 2000. Standards of evidence: How do we know when
you're right? *Qualitative methods in sociolinguistics.* New York: Oxford
University Press.

McConnell-Ginet, Sally. 1998. The sexual (re)production of meaning: A
discourse-based theory. *The feminist critique of language: A reader.*
Deborah Cameron, ed. New York: Routledge, 198–210.

Meyer, Jean. No ocurrirá la guerra de Troya. *El Universal.* http://www2
.eluniversal.com.mx/pls/impreso/w_editoriales.detalle?var=17481
(accessed December 10, 2005).

Meza, Ramón Cota. 2003. El sí a la guerra. *El Universal.* March 4. http://
www2.eluniversal.com.mx/pls/impreso/w_editoriales.detalle?var=1756
0 (accessed December 15, 2005).

Naranjo. 2003. Loco furioso. *El Universal.* January 26. http://www.eluniversal
.com.mx/wcarton1675.html (accessed January 26, 2006).

Nash, June C. 1999. *The transformation of gender roles in migration.* Santa
Cruz, CA: Chicano/Latino Research Center, Merrill College, University
of California.

Omar. 2003. Trabajo en equipo. *El Universal.* March 22. http://www
.eluniversal.com.mx/wcarton1909.html (accessed December 18, 2005).

Patterson, Jorge Zepeda. Pancho Villa, Cleopatra y la guerra de Irak.
El Universal. http://www2.eluniversal.com.mx/pls/impreso/w_
editoriales.detalle?var=17210 (accessed January 26, 2006).

Quiñónez, Guillermo Fabela. 2003. En el reino de lo absurdo. *El
Universal.* February 16. http://www2.eluniversal.com.mx/pls/
impreso/w_editoriales.detalle?var=17441 (accessed February 16, 2006).

Searle, John. 1969. *Speech acts: An essay in the philosophy of language.*
London: Cambridge University Press.

Steffan, Heinz Dieterich. época de Calígulas. El Universal. http://www2
.eluniversal.com.mx/pls/impreso/w_editoriales.detalle?var=17681
(accessed January 10, 2006).

Trimble, Robert G. 2006. *A translation of Leandro Fernández de Moratín's El sí de las niñas / An innocent girl's consent.* Lewiston, NY: The Edwin Mellen Press.

Vera, Daniel Gutiérrez. 2004. La textura de lo social. *Revista Mexicana de sociología* 66 (2): 311–43.

Wareing, Shân. 2004. Language and gender. In *Language, society and power*, by Shân Wareing, 75–79. New York: Routledge.

PART II

WARS THEN AND NOW

CHAPTER 9

NOT SO "FAR FROM VIETNAM": A STUDY OF WAR, FILM, AND THE MEDIA

Jonathan Ervine

This chapter will illustrate film as a medium that, when used effectively, can analyze and criticize war in a manner that reacts against dominant discourses that are the product of mass media coverage or the overly simplistic representations of traditional war films. The prime focus will be on comparing and analyzing the Vietnam War and the ongoing conflict in Iraq from the point of view of filmic representations of war and how these relate to and engage with media representations of war. Films that will be addressed adopt approaches that compliment or go beyond those of the mainstream media (especially television) but can, however, struggle to have the same impact. The term "sign of war" will be used here as an event or action that illustrates that a conflict is taking place. Attention will be paid to events as signs of war, and the number of different wars and conflicts that are referred to in the three films: *Loin du Vietnam*, *11'09"01 September 11th*, and *Fahrenheit 9/11*. The films cover the American Vietnam War, the World Trade Center Attacks of 2001, and the recent Iraq War, respectively. All three films address the way in which media's diffusion of images of events such as the World Trade Center attacks plays a key role in elevating them to the status of events that become perceived as signs of war. These films illustrate

Hayward's definition of counter cinema as: "a cinema that, through its own cinematic practices, questions and subverts existing cinematic codes and conventions" (2000, 75) and is "oppositional, exposes hegemonic practices, unfixes . . . stereotypes, makes visible what has been normalized or marginalized" (ibid., 76). The films redress imbalances of media coverage, which they criticize and assess, as well as encourage people to reflect on signs of war in new and different ways. The fact that the films counteract rather contribute to misrepresentations of conflicts sets them apart from conventional war films, which often "glorify or put forward the heroics of a particular nation" and "rarely look at the horrors of war" (Hayward 2000, 449).

FILM AND WAR FROM VIETNAM TO IRAQ: OBJECTIVES AND APPROACHES

Despite being made almost forty years ago, *Loin du Vietnam* demonstrates an approach to war and representations of war that is similar to those adopted in *11'09"01* and *Fahrenheit 9/11*. According to Laurent Véray (2004), when watching *Loin du Vietnam*, parallels become apparent between the arguments that we hear General Westmoreland using to justify American military intervention in Vietnam and those used by the American government to justify military intervention in Iraq since 2003 (26). Therefore, the legacy of the Vietnam War on the American consciousness has conditioned the official American approach to war. Spencer (2005) refers to "Vietnam Syndrome . . . [as] a condition without end, where political fears about the news media representing wars in ways which are likely to jeopardize public support is ever present" (55). Hoskins (2004) highlights the importance of media representations saying that "the media, as today's principal source of visual images, powerfully shape or direct social memory" (4). Inevitably film can also influence views on conflicts. Philo and Gilmour (2004) note that "in our popular culture, U.S. films have portrayed their forces as involved in heroic and bloody action against a deadly enemy [in Vietnam]" and that such films "do not typically discuss the millions of mostly civilians who were killed or injured" (235). The authors link this approach to the fact that many young people in the United

Kingdom and the United States of America have misplaced ideas about the extent of losses on both sides in the Vietnam War (235–6).

There are similarities regarding how the three films to be studied counteract such misplaced ideas, notably in relation to their method of production and their objectives. *Loin du Vietnam* and *11'09"01 September 11th* are both portmanteau films (films composed of different short films) and feature footage from several different countries and footage filmed by directors from several different countries. *Loin du Vietnam* was coordinated by Chris Marker and comprises short films by several directors associated with the French New Wave cinema of the late 1950s and early 1960s, such as Jean-Luc Godard, Alain Resnais, and Claude Lelouch. It also features contributions from the Dutch documentary filmmaker Joris Ivens and the American filmmaker and photographer William Klein. *11'09"01 September 11th* was coordinated by Alain Brigand and consisted of eleven shorts of eleven minutes, nine seconds and one frame, hence the title (*11'09"01*), which is also close to the European way of writing the date September 11, 2001 (11.09.01 rather than 09.11.01). The eleven short films were made by eleven different directors, each from a different country. Thus, both films' conceptions demonstrate a desire to depict conflict from a variety of different viewpoints and consequently expose the spectator to a range of different reactions. This is part of an attempt to challenge the spectators and encourage them to think differently about events that they might already be aware of and have seen representations of. *Loin du Vietnam* features footage filmed in Vietnam during the war, footage of reactions to the war in America (including pro-war and antiwar demonstrations) as well as reactions to the war in Europe. The short films that make up *11'09"01* are set in a variety of different locations, including the United States, the United Kingdom, Israel, Burkina Faso, Bosnia, and Iran. This multiplicity of perspectives is a means of avoiding reshowing representations of major events that audiences will be familiar with. While Michael Moore's *Fahrenheit 9/11* might appear somewhat different from *Loin du Vietnam* and *11'09"01*, as it is the work of a single director, it nevertheless explores the progression from the World Trade Center attacks to the ongoing conflict in Iraq from the perspectives of citizens of different countries who are on opposing sides in a war. It explores how the case for war was made in America and also the consequences this had on Iraqi civilians and American soldiers serving in Iraq.

What truly brings all three films together is that they were made as a reaction against war and representations of war from the perspective of rich Western countries. On-screen captions are used at the start of both *Loin du Vietnam* and *11'09"01* to inform the spectator of the objectives of those involved in the film. A caption that appears near the start of *Loin du Vietnam* tells us that those who participated in the film did so in order "to express, by the exercise of their profession, their solidarity with the Vietnamese people fighting against aggression." The caption that appears on screen at the start of *11'09"01* tell the viewer that the film features "11 directors from different countries and cultures, 11 visions of the tragic events that occurred in New York City on September 11, 2001, 11 points of view committing their subjective consciousness" and that there was "complete freedom of expression." In a more precise explanation of the film's objectives that features as a bonus on the DVD of the film, Alain Brigand links this diverse approach to "the duty of reflection" linked to evoking the World Trade Center attacks using images other than those beamed around the world in the immediate aftermath of the events and the need to form "a reflection responding to images with other images." Michael Moore's *Fahrenheit 9/11* traces how the aftermath of the Twin Towers collapsing—of which television images were replayed countless times—was used as the start of a process that would be used to attempt to justify the "war on terror," and consequently the Iraq War. However, whether or not depicting this chain of events is Moore's prime objective is open to question. It could be argued that *Fahrenheit 9/11* is a critique of George W. Bush more than it is a critique of war, and that Moore's critique of war is merely part of his critique of George W. Bush. Moore begins *Fahrenheit 9/11* by referring back to Bush's 2000 election victory and ends with Bush losing his track mid-sentence during a speech. His film appears to have been made in an attempt to discredit the American president during the election campaign of 2004 that ultimately led to his reelection. Moore decided to prevent *Fahrenheit 9/11* being put forward for a potential Oscar nomination for best documentary so as to try to get it broadcast on television prior to the November presidential elections. In addition, the DVD of *Fahrenheit 9/11* was released a month before the elections, and the extras section featured additional footage of the suffering in Iraq.

The Use, Misuse, and Reuse of Images

It has been argued (Frodon 2004; Burdeau 2004) that the way in which *Fahrenheit 9/11* was made with a clear political objective in mind—that is, discrediting George W. Bush during his 2004 presidential election campaign—meant that aesthetic issues were neglected. Indeed, during the 2004 Cannes Film Festival, Jean-Luc Godard (one of the directors who contributed to *Loin du Vietnam*) was highly critical of Moore's use of images in *Fahrenheit 9/11*. Godard thought that Moore was mechanically using images as part of his discourse and ignoring their value as images (Frodon 2004, 15). He also accused Moore of being a speechmaker rather than a filmmaker, thus discrediting the cinematic as opposed to thematic aspects of his work (Burdeau 2004, 45). Such comments reflect the tradition of film criticism within France and the value placed on cinema as an art form. Jean-Michel Frodon (2004) has gone as far as saying that *Fahrenheit 9/11* was not so much a film as "a televisual tract aimed at having an influence on the next American [presidential] elections" (14), thus suggesting that cinematic issues had been neglected in favor of a political objective.[1] Aside from the fact that Moore's film draws heavily on televised images, his use of these images has been seen by some as inconsistent. Burdeau (2004) has observed that Moore is sometimes very critical of certain television news images but uses others to try to give weight to his argument (45). On one hand, Moore prefers to have a black screen as the backdrop to the sound of the World Trade Center attacks, and his refusal to replay the iconic images of the planes crashing into the World Trade Center appears linked to his criticism of the American media for cultivating a climate of fear in the aftermath of the attacks. On the other hand, he does use very graphic images of the suffering inflicting by and upon American troops in Iraq. We see charred body parts of Iraqis strewn across a street and also the charred and dismembered bodies of American soldiers being dragged through Baghdad following an ambush. Thus, Moore appears to have an ambiguous attitude toward using what could be considered sensationalist images of war, and he lacks subtlety.

While *Loin du Vietnam* and *11'09"01* do not feature graphic images of the sufferings war can lead to, it does share with *Fahrenheit 9/11* the fact that it uses and reuses images to create political messages. All three films make use of television news clips, which they place within a context that discredits the arguments put forward in the clips. For example, after showing television reports about the post-September 11 climate of fear in the United States, we see Moore following a policeman in Oregon who works part-time at the only police station on a stretch of coastline more than one hundred miles long and whose work has not changed since the World Trade Center attacks. In *Loin du Vietnam*, the clearest example of reappropriation of televised images relating to war occurs when we see General Westmoreland giving a press briefing about the progress of American forces in Vietnam. He admits that civilian deaths are occurring in Vietnam but suggests that this is due to human or mechanical error and not overuse of firepower. He contrasts this with what he describes as "calculated attacks" by the Vietcong on "innocent civilians." While we see and hear this newsreel footage, the image becomes blurred and crackly at points and zooms in and out, reinforcing the fact that we are watching a television broadcast and indeed an event created for, and arguably by, television. The introduction of the cracklings in the footage and the zooming in and out serves to discredit the speaker (Westmoreland) by making the presentation appear considerably less slick than it would have appeared in the original broadcast. The British film theorist and documentary editor Dai Vaughan (1988) has highlighted the way in which such devices can be used to discredit speakers, recalling that while working on one documentary film he was told "you'll have to put this man in, to ensure a fair balance of opinion. If you don't like what he says, you can always cut to a wall being knocked down" (37).

Ken Loach's section of *11'09"01* again demonstrates how archive footage of a press conference can be used to undermine the person giving the press conference. We see a shot of George W. Bush describing the World Trade Center attacks as the actions of "enemies of freedom committing an act of war on our country." Pablo, the central character in Ken Loach's short film, immediately turns this phrase against America by saying that the Santiago massacre of September 11, 1973, was an event that involved enemies of freedom committing an act of war on his country. He highlights this by mentioning that America offered up to ten million dollars to fund the coup led by Augusto Pinochet, which led to the overthrow of a democratically elected communist government. We see newsreel footage of the coup as Pablo talks, and the emotion in his voice is obvious.

Pablo also mentions that the coup resulted in thirty thousand people being killed, a figure which he repeats as if to try to subtly put into perspective the fact that just under three thousand people lost their lives in the World Trade Center attacks on September 11, 2001.

This reference to the attacks on the World Trade Center is one of many that we *hear* in *11'09"01*, but we do not actually *see* many images of the Twin Towers crumbling. Alain Brigand has related this to the need to "evoke the planetary echo of this event other than by these terrible images." This may be a suggestion that he felt that filmmakers have a duty to do more than reuse well-known images or at least make sure that they do something original when they do so. The fact that the first segment of *11'09"01* is shot in Iran rather than New York (the scene of the World Trade Center attacks) helps to provide a series of images far removed from those of the planes crashing into the Twin Towers in Manhattan. The setting is a refugee camp inhabited by Afghans, which provides a backdrop far removed from that of a modern American city. We see a teacher attempting to explain the magnitude of the World Trade Center attacks to a group of children for whom airplanes and skyscrapers are alien images and who are cut off from the world of mass media such as twenty-four-hour television news. The teacher takes the children to a chimney to try to illustrate what happened in New York, and the smoke that billows out of the top of the chimney is reminiscent of the image of smoke billowing out of the Twin Towers before they collapsed. When we do see images of the Twin Towers, including ones of the planes crashing into them in *11'09"01*, they are often on a television screen in the corner of a shot. This reinforces the fact that they are images that owe their iconic status to television news. Hoskins (2004) has stated that "the media, as today's principal source of visual images, powerfully shape or direct social memory" (4). It is largely through their continued repetition on television screens in the immediate aftermath of the attacks that the sight of two planes flying into the Twin Towers became iconic images. The fact that these images formed part of a news bulletin appears to have made them especially shocking. When people in New York at the time of the World Trade Center attacks were asked by journalists for their reaction to seeing two airplanes crashing into the Twin Towers, many responded that it was like something out of a Hollywood film and that it was hard to believe it was really happening. Hoskins (2004) observes that news channels exploit techniques such as the use of video graphics to add drama to replayed events, which con-stitutes a "'celebration' by network news of what it has already delivered" (25).

In refusing to recycle such footage in its original form, the direc-tors involved in *11'09"01* employ a range of different techniques. Claude Lelouch's short film centers on a deaf and mute female French photographer who is having a relationship with an American man who organizes guided tours of New York for the deaf. To reflect the woman's deafness, there is an eerie silence punctuated only by dull noises when we see her alone in her partner's flat on the morn-ing of September 11, 2001. When we see a television screen in the corner of the shot that is relaying images of the airplanes crashing into the Twin Towers, we do not hear the sounds that went with this event. A sort of symmetry is provided in the way Alejandro González-Iñárritu's short film features sounds from the attacks and the immediate aftermath against the backdrop of a black screen and only occasional glimpses of images of people jumping from the Twin Towers. The plurality of representations of the World Trade Center attacks in *11'09"01* is heightened by the fact that we hear the events being evoked in news reports in a variety of different languages; the dialogue in each director's short film is in their native language. Such an approach reflects Alain Brigand's desire for the directors who contributed to *11'09"01* to produce short films that "looked toward their own culture, their own memories, their own languages." It is precisely their emphasis on the role of the media in creating signs of war that means that *Loin du Vietnam, 11'09"01 September 11th,* and *Fahrenheit 9/11* are part of what is called counter-cinema. Hayward (2000) describes counter cinema as a genre that "is oppositional, exposes hegemonic practices, unfixes—renders unstable—stereo-types, makes visible what has been normalized or invisibilized" (76). All three films not only focus on a central conflict but also relate the central conflict to other conflicts, which helps to place the central conflict within an international context.

THE CONTEXTUALIZATION OF WAR

The central conflicts in all three films are placed within an interna-tional context in two key ways. Firstly, they are related to other con-flicts, and secondly they are related to wider social and political issues such as globalization and class struggles. In *Loin du Vietnam*, references to other conflicts such as the French war in Vietnam from 1947 to 1954 help to contextualize the American Vietnam War and indeed remind spectators that the United States of America is not the only country to have waged such a war. Similarly, *11'09"01* seeks to avoid overly emphasizing the uniqueness of conflicts or concepts relating to war. This is illustrated by evoking several events that happened on a September 11, or the eleventh of another month. For example, an Israeli journalist in Amos Gitaï's short film lists events that occurred on a September 11, which includes advances made by the British Army in the American War of Independence in 1777, the French taking Malakoff during the Crimean War in 1855, and Roosevelt and Churchill agreeing to split Nazi Germany in three in 1944. Pablo, the Chilean refugee living in London who features in Ken Loach's short film, reminds us of how September 11 is the date in 1973 when there was a brutal military coup in his native country. In Danis Tanovic's short film from Bosnia-Herzegovina, we learn that the women of Srebrenica mark the anniversary of one of the worst massacres of the Bosnian war on the eleventh of every month. Thus, *11'09"01* is reacting against the way in which "September 11" has become instantly and uniquely synonymous with the World Trade Center attacks of September 11, 2001. The refusal to adhere to near-universal concepts and ideas is further reflected by the fact that the title of the film is 11'09"01 and not "9/11." In Europe, 9/11/01 would correspond to November 9, 2001, as the day of the month comes before the month of the year when writing a dating numerically. By entitling the film *11'09"01*, Alain Brigand is refusing to adopt a term that had nevertheless become commonly used to refer to the World Trade Center attacks, including in Europe. This is in keeping with the way the film rarely shows the now iconic images of the planes crashing into the Twin Towers, an approach that Moore also adopts in *Fahrenheit 9/11* by playing sounds of this event and its immediate aftermath accompanied by a black screen. This raises questions about how and if it is in fact possible to represent such a catastrophic event, indeed one whose iconic images have been so often replayed and seen by so many people. Given this situation, it makes sense that the films not only focus solely on single events or single conflicts but also place the Vietnam War, the attacks on the World Trade Center, and the Iraq War within a wider context.

The way in which *Loin du Vietnam* does so is made particularly clear in its closing monologue in which the choice faced by the West is described in the following terms:

> Faced with this challenge, the choice for the society of the rich is quite simple. Either this society will have to accomplish the physical destruction of all that resists it, and it is a task that risks being superior to its means of destruction despite how fabulous and atomic they are. Or, it will have to accomplish a total transformation of itself, and this is perhaps also too much to ask of a society at the height of its force. If it refuses this choice, all it will remain to do will be to sacrifice its reassuring illusions and to accept this war of poor people against rich people as inevitable, and to lose it.

In turn, *11'09"01* places the World Trade Center attacks within a wider context by addressing several other conflicts, which serves to highlight how an attack on a rich Western country can attract more media attention than a war in a poorer country. While the film shows that people from countries such as Chile and Bosnia feel sympathy toward Americans following the September 11 attacks, it also demonstrates that the people of Chile and Bosnia have a sense that their sufferings have gone comparatively unnoticed due to their country being seen as less significant. The United States of America's status as a rich and powerful country is made clear in both *11'09"01* and *Loin du Vietnam*. In *Loin du Vietnam* we are told that "a country whose 200 million inhabitants spend more on wrapping paper than the 500 million people of India can spend on food can provide its army with certain resources." In Idrissa Ouedraogo's segment of *11'09"01*, a group of school children in Burkina Faso struggle to comprehend the enormity of the twenty-five million dollar reward that the United States is offering for information leading to the capture of Osama bin Laden, and they talk of how the reward could be used to pay for medication to tackle diseases such as meningitis, AIDS, and malaria. The fact that they decide not to tell anyone else that they have seen a mysterious figure that resembles bin Laden and instead plan to spend the money on villas, cigars, and women illustrates that they too are influenced by the consumerism and capitalism associated with rich western industrialized nations. In Michael Moore's *Fahrenheit 9/11* we hear an American soldier who has served in Iraq say he would not return there as he believes it is wrong to kill poor people who have never threatened the United States. In addition, the film shows army recruitment officers targeting poor areas where young people often have difficulty finding employment or being able to prolong their studies. Near the end, Moore refers to Orwell's comments about war being continuous and waged by the ruling class over its subjects in order to keep social structures in place.

Do *Loin du Vietnam, 11'09"01 September 11th*, and *Fahrenheit 9/11* Work as Films?

As has already been made clear, *Loin du Vietnam, 11'09"01*, and *Fahrenheit 9/11* all bring together a variety of issues, types of footage, and range of techniques in attempts to challenge the way people think about issues relating to war and representations of war. In assessing whether they work as films, it is necessary to assess the coherence of not only the arguments presented within the films but also of the three works as films in their own right. This sort of focus on cinematic as well as political or factual issues can often be neglected when it comes to analyzing documentary films. Zheulin (1988) argues that "documentary film makers—especially those whose work reflects a social and political commitment—are not asked to describe their creative process" and "prefer to talk about the subjects they've filmed rather than about their craft" (227). Much of the publicity surrounding *Fahrenheit 9/11* reflects this description. The vast majority of the articles about Moore's film, apart from some in specialized cinema journals, deal primarily with the arguments and issues he evoked rather than the way he went about evoking them. In addition, the bonus features on the DVD of *Fahrenheit 9/11* are all related to the political issues in the film rather than the making of the film itself despite being billed on the British DVD version as providing "unmissable insight into the making of the film." The need to simultaneously address both cinematic and political issues is encapsulated by Mike Wayne (2001), who argues that cinematic issues are of considerable importance to a film's potential political impact. He states that "cinema, like poetry must immerse itself in and generate a cultural energy and creativity if it is to act as a model and conductor of the kinds of energies required to change the world beyond the screening of the film" (58).

These films seek to have an impact on spectators that will remain with them after having left the movie theatre. The most explicitly-stated example of this comes in the closing monologue of *Loin du Vietnam*. Spectators are reminded of their distance from Vietnam both in terms of being many miles away and also potentially very far from being able to easily understand the Vietnam War and the reasons behind it: "In a few minutes, this film is going to end. You are going to leave this film theater, and for many of you, go back to a world without war. It is also our world, and we know how easy it is to forget about certain realities here. We are far from Vietnam, and the Vietnam of our emotions and our indignations is sometimes as far from the real Vietnam as indifference would be. We live in a society that has gone a very long way down the path of hiding its real goals from itself, its own fears and especially its violence."

This closing monologue illustrates how *Loin du Vietnam* uses off-screen narration (read by Maurice Garrel) to bring together the distinct shorts in the film. In contrast, *11'09"01* does not feature a narrator and the eleven short films are left to stand on their own as more discreet entities. The project behind the film is explained to spectators via an on-screen caption that appears before the first of the eleven short films that make up '11'09"01'. There is no narrator in the film, and each segment is merely preceded by a map of the world showing the name and native country of its director. Finally, Michael Moore acts as a narrator in *Fahrenheit 9/11*, generally adding his comments from off-screen but also appearing in the film itself. Numerous critics have analyzed the consequences of these different forms of narration. Field argues that "the disembodied voice of a narrator distances people from the material" in a documentary (Zheulin 1998, 232). However, one could argue that it is through the opening and closing narration that *Loin du Vietnam* makes clear its purpose as a film and is able to powerfully and directly address its spectators. Field suggests that directly addressing a film's audience in such a manner is going too far and has stated "I believe in presenting the material in an analytical structure that's accomplished in the editing room, if possible, and letting people deduce for themselves—aided by an analysis you give in the way you structure the material" (ibid.). This corresponds to the way *11'09"01* does not use any form of narration to link the individual shorts that make up the film and does not use narration to make a closing statement. Such an approach puts demands on the filmmaker in terms of structuring their film so as to make clear what they want people to take away from the film, and it also places greater demands on the spectators in terms of interpreting the images that they see. The approach adopted by Michael Moore in *Fahrenheit 9/11* regarding his narration falls between that of *Loin du Vietnam* and that of *11'09"01*. In *Fahrenheit 9/11*, Michael Moore is less present than in *Bowling for Columbine* both in terms of appearing on screen and the amount of comments he makes. Vaughan (1988) has observed that "the function of a presenter introducing a documentary—or interpolated within it—is to diminish the authority of the people filmed" (37), and Moore appears keen to allow people such as Lila Lipscombe (mother of an American soldier killed in Iraq) talk about how the ongoing conflict in Iraq has affected their lives. However, Cousins (2004) has criticized Moore's interviewing style in the film as "rather than challenging an assertion he encourages it in a chummy way, or bumbles through" (60). This illustrates how, on one hand, the intervention of a narrator or presenter within a documentary film can be seen negatively as it detracts from what the interviewees say or the message of the images. On the other hand, a lack of intervention or questioning can be seen as a sign of a lack of scrutiny on the part of the presenter. Thus, there is a fine line to tread regarding the presence or lack of presence of a presenter as a narrator or on screen in a documentary.

The way intervention by a narrator or director within a film can play a positive role is highlighted by John Else, who states that "in dealing with the overwhelmingly complex subjects which so often attract us, narration should be thought of as a friend and ally, not as a necessary evil" (Zheulin 1988, 231–32). Given the eclectic nature of the shorts that make up *11'09"01*, which were produced without the directors knowing about each other's films, it could have been extremely difficult to provide a narration that succeeded in bringing them all together and this might not have been in keeping with the film's objective of providing a diverse range of responses to the World Trade Center attacks and their treatment by the media. Since Alain Brigand was eager for the film to produce a "reflection responding to images with other images," it might have seemed inappropriate to add a narration that could have drawn attention away from the images and directed people's reflection to a greater degree. However, it has been argued that the portmanteau form of *11'09"01* draws attention to its conception in a manner that is both conceited and in bad taste given its subject matter (Matthews 2003, 32–33). In an interview that appeared with the DVD of the film, the director of one of the short films (Mira Nair) discussed the fact that every film had to last eleven minutes, nine seconds, and one frame as "French conceptual bullshit." Debates on the relation between form and content can be very long and technical. To sum up briefly, many film theorists and directors who have studied or been involved in what is considered counter cinema believe that challenging ways of thinking must go hand in hand with challenging conventional methods of representation. In this way, Jean-Luc Godard and many underground filmmakers in general have questioned the dominant methods of representation employed by Hollywood (Hayward 2000, 76). Thus, critiques of dominant ideas regarding society are constructed without regard for dominant ideas regarding appropriate methods of representation (assuming one does not take the idea that radical politics necessitate radical aesthetics to be a dominant idea). A problem with this approach is that while it might make sense to the filmmaker, it might not always be evident and comprehensible to the spectator. The fact that ideas are constructed in an unconventional framework might make it harder for the spectator to understand them and realize what the filmmaker's true objectives are even though counter cinema is supposed to be a genre that "draws attention to itself . . . and the production of meaning" (Hayward 2000, 76). Just as people approaching documentary or political film might neglect artistic and creative issues at the expense of political and factual issues, there is also the danger that an overly explicit aesthetic approach might detract from the content of a film and the message it is intended to convey.

What If No One Watches?

Despite their creative use of techniques that demonstrate how films can challenge and question the workings of the media by producing alternative images and interpretations, counter cinema faces several problems in getting its message across. Much of this stems from the dominance of the mass media. As Mermin (1999) states, "the great majority of Americans still get their foreign policy news from newspapers and television, not from specialized websites or magazines" (xi). While *Loin du Vietnam, 11'09"01 September 11th,* and *Fahrenheit*

9/11 illustrate and compensate for certain failings of television coverage of war, they have all faced battles in getting anywhere near comparable exposure to television news coverage of war. Whereas television news is beamed directly in the living rooms of millions of households around the world, for these films to be seen as close as possible to the times and conflicts they evoke, a spectator must not only leave their living room but also leave their house. In addition, on leaving their house to go to the cinema they cannot just go to any cinema. While Michael Moore's *Fahrenheit 9/11* was a box office success and shown in numerous multiplexes, *Loin du Vietnam* and *11'09"01* were largely restricted to the art house circuit. Thus, they were made accessible to a considerably smaller potential audience. While it is possible to buy a DVD of Michael Moore's *Fahrenheit 9//11* in a reasonably well-stocked video store, *11'09"01* is less widely available in commercial outlets. Therefore, those interested in obtaining a copy would likely have to order one over the Internet. Even if a large number of people do watch these films having bought them on DVD (and also to a lesser extent in cinemas), they are likely to be watching them many months after their production due to the time it takes to produce a film and the gap between it release in theaters and on DVD. Thus, films can often lack the immediacy and accessibility of news coverage and especially that of twenty-four-hour news channels.

Despite the fact that the films I have studied here have problems competing with television news in terms of immediacy and accessibility, they do nevertheless demonstrate an ability to provide a more wide-ranging and thorough analysis of war than what the mass media has provided. In relation to Vietnam, Spencer (2005) argues that "the news media were largely unreceptive to debates and articulations presented by the anti-war movement and that the nuances of argument were ignored in favor of what the movement suggested through its appearances" (69) and that peace protesters were seen as "an image of threat to social order" (186). In *Loin du Vietnam*, footage of peace protests shows the diversity of groups demonstrating (age, gender, race) and the camera's zooming in and out makes it possible to read slogans on the banners carried by the demonstrators. The chants of the protesters are clearly audible, and several people talk about why they are demonstrating and what they feel about the Vietnam War. The footage also includes interactions between antiwar demonstrators and pro-war hecklers at such marches, which gives an example of the sort of debates that went on within certain sections of American society at the time. Thus, we can see how *Loin du Vietnam* is not just portraying opposition to the Vietnam War but also illustrating debates regarding the justification for opposition to the Vietnam War.

There have certainly been political and media-related developments that have affected how the war is treated and dealt with between the release of *Loin du Vietnam* in 1967 and the releases of *11'09"01 September 11th* in 2002 and *Fahrenheit 9/11* in 2004. A whole new generation of politicians is making decisions related to war, and the consequences of these decisions are relayed to people around the world in an increasingly technologically advanced manner. Although the Vietnam War was one of the first of which images were broadcast on television into people's homes around the world, Hoskins (2004) reminds us that this came at a time when "television was a medium in its infancy" (15). He mentions that television news teams "had to rely on the military to transport their heavy equipment and were censored by their relative immobility" (58). Lighter, modern equipment such as smaller cameras, videophones, and Internet and satellite technology, has increased the ease with which the media can cover news events in a range of different locations. Despite such changes, the need to question and analyze the role of mass media in relation to war remains.

The international dimension of *11'09"01* can also be seen as responding to the failings of the American media in relation to coverage of issues of international importance. Seib (2005) argues that "it is difficult for Americans to make knowledgeable judgments about the existence of civilization-related clashes if the public knows little about the civilizations in question," also noting that "aside from their occasional spurts of solid performance, American news organizations do a lousy job of breaking down the public's intellectual isolation" (222). By taking an event of global importance—the World Trade Center attacks—and illustrating reactions to it from a variety of different cultures and contexts, *11'09"01* is illustrating the way a single event can be subject to several different interpretations. By providing a range of international reactions, *11'09"01* is making a start on breaking down the intellectual isolation, which Seib refers to. While Michael Moore's *Fahrenheit 9/11* has been criticized in relation to how it makes use of the cinematic medium in constructing its arguments, it does constitute an attempt to understand and critique the workings of the American media in the aftermath of September 11, which has succeeded in generating considerable public debate. Mermin (1999) argues that the far-reaching nature of the mass media in America means that it is "essential to understand and critique their performance" (xi). *Fahrenheit 9/11* helps to redress the balance regarding a recent trend in the American news media that Spencer (2005) identifies: "In the post-9/11 world, the exacerbation of public fear of a possible terrorist attack is an omnipresent news story. But what has become noticeable within this climate is the news media's non-critical stance toward official and elite discourse which seeks to circulate and consolidate the feats being created" (192–93).

The value of films such as *Loin du Vietnam*, *11'09"01* and *Fahrenheit 9/11* stems from the fact that they challenge ideas that are often not challenged and encourage greater reflection on important issues. The failings of mainstream news coverage create a window of opportunity for cinema to exploit and through which to challenge spectators to think differently about key issues. However, there are certain problems that cinema faces in attempting to do so. Firstly, it is necessary for there to be a certain degree of complicity between cinema and the forms of mass media that they criticize. While Michael Moore is seen as a dissenting voice within American society and is very critical of large American television networks, the television program that he owes much of his notoriety to (*TV Nation*) was broadcast by NBC and Fox, two major networks of the sort Moore is so critical of. In a similar manner, the directors involved in *11'09"01 September 11th* were determined to provide alternative images to those of the mass media, but their film was nonetheless co-produced by Studio Canal, which is part of the large multinational Vivendi Universal media group. Admittedly *Loin du Vietnam* was produced independent of traditional cinematic structures, which were seen by those involved in the film as money-dominated and thus linked to a form of censorship that they wished to avoid (Véray 2004, 26). The fact that those involved with the film were not prepared to work with traditional cinematic structures might partly explain why *Loin du Vietnam* was not a commercial success.

The commercial success of a film can also depend in part on how well it is received, for example as a result of reviews or media coverage, which further highlights how a film's relations with the media can have an influence on its success. While all three films I have studied here have enjoyed success at international film festivals, they have all been dogged by criticism due to what has been seen as their engagement with politically controversial subject matter. Despite receiving a largely positive response at the 1967 New York Film Festival, the anti-war stance of *Loin du Vietnam* meant that some American journalists were very hostile toward it. Writing in the *New York Times*, Bosley Crowther (1967) described it as a "hodgepodge" and "a fierce, unmitigated propaganda picture" (58). Likewise, *11'09"01* was seen by some as being anti-American and insensitive in its approach to the World Trade Center attacks. Anne Thompson, formerly an editor with *Premiere* magazine, said that she and others had been offended by a film that she considered to be "an outrage" (Jacobson 2002, 4D). Writing in the *Washington Post* in September 2003, Desson Howe (2003) commented that "for a great many people, and not just Americans, the tragedies of that day are still too emotionally devastating to swallow anyone's filmic interpretation—particularly if that interpretation smacks of political hostility or admonition" (T41). Michael Moore is a target for many right-wing critics, some of whom have created Web sites, written books, and made films that set out to challenge the accuracy of his representations of America.

Despite this situation, there are those who have lauded the filmmakers involved with *Loin du Vietnam*, *11'09"01*, and *Fahrenheit 9/11* for tackling the issues in the way they have done, and there are also responses one can offer to the criticisms previously outlined. One could say that Crowther's criticism of *Loin du Vietnam* fails to take into account the nuanced nature of its approach and the way it raises questions about other countries (such as France) who have been involved in wars overseas. The film also calls into question the sincerity of certain forms of opposition to war, notably in Alain Resnais's short film. Here, a character giving a monologue reminds viewers that France also fought a war in Vietnam post-World War II, and the character acknowledges that the extent of international opposition to the more recent Vietnam War was partly because America was the country waging war. It would also be wrong to write off those involved in the production of *Loin du Vietnam* as being anti-American. Several of the main French directors involved in the film, including Chris Maker, Jean-Luc Godard, and Claude Lelouch, spent considerable time in the United States and were in many ways fascinated by the country and in admiration of it. In addition, the approach of *Loin du Vietnam*, highlighted by the opening and closing narrations, illustrates that the film is about opposing the capitalism and imperialism of powerful, rich Western countries rather than simply setting out to criticize the United States. In addition, Crowther's description of *Loin du Vietnam* as a "hodgepodge" fails to take into account the way narration is used to link up the individual elements (the short films) that make up the entire film.

In response to the accusations of anti-Americanism leveled at *11'09"01*, it is worth remembering that the film begins by referring to the World Trade Center attacks as "tragic events" and the shorts feature people in locations as diverse as the United States, Iran, and Bosnia trying to comprehend and communicate the enormity of the events and the sense of loss felt by the American people. Furthermore, the short films of Alejandro González-Iñárritu and Shohei Imamura end with captions that condemn notions of "Holy War." This appears to be a direct response to the justification in Islamic fundamentalist circles of the World Trade Center attacks in the name of "jihad." Imamura ends his short film, the last of those that make up *11'09"01*, with the caption "there is no such thing as a holy war." González-Iñárritu ends his short film, the seventh of the film, with the phrase "Does God's light guide or blind us?" which also serves as a denunciation of religious fanaticism. He has also called a series of photos he took during the aftermath of the World Trade Center attacks *Blinded by the Light*, and in an interview for the DVD of *11'09"01* has talked of his short film as being a reflection of the myth of Icarus and the "dark side" of human nature. His question, "does God's light blind us?" can be related to several different issues, including terrorism justified in the name of religious fanaticism, government in accordance with religious beliefs (be they those of Islam, Christianity, or another faith), and the over-consumption of televisual images. These can be related to life in America and to those responsible for the attacks on the World Trade Center. The sensitivity surrounding the issues evoked in *11'09"01* has been acknowledged by many people, but not all would argue that it means that the film should not be shown. Faced with criticism for programming *11'09"01* at the Toronto Film Festival on the first anniversary of the World Trade Center attacks, Piers Handling (in Dwyer 2002) made the following response: "There is no question that the films are provocative and made to encourage discussion.

There is also no question that they are all measured and respectful. There is no hate in these films. Some might take issue, but arguments are healthy. People and countries that suppress arguments are, finally, totalitarian in their outlook" (54).

Handling's response could also be used against those who disagree with Michael Moore's stance in relation to George W. Bush, the "war on terror," or the ongoing conflict in Iraq. There may be flaws in his arguments and his cinematic approach, but he is participating in a debate and presenting elements that are not always examined in the mainstream media.

CONCLUSION

All three of the films studied here demonstrate a strong desire to counteract ideas and discourses relating to war and representations of war. They do so by not just showing images related to war but also by placing the images within a framework that contextualizes (and often recontextualizes) them and encourages spectators to question assertions made by their leaders. In more general terms, the work of Hoskins and Spencer helps us to further understand how the legacy of the Vietnam War has influenced the way war has been conceptualized in America ever since. Despite being made almost forty years before the recent Iraq War, *Loin du Vietnam* is a film that is relevant to understanding and interpreting conflicts such as the Iraq War. Indeed, in *Fahrenheit 9/11* we hear a news reporter speculate about the Iraq War potentially turning into "another Vietnam." Both wars were portrayed from an American point of view as being fought to combat a foreign evil; respectively that of the North Vietnamese Communists and the regime of Saddam Hussein in Iraq.

Cinematic as well as political issues provide a link between *Loin du Vietnam* and both *11'09"01* and *Fahrenheit 9/11*. *Loin du Vietnam* provides a cinematic model for analyzing signs of war that is similar to what is used in *11'09"01* and *Fahrenheit 9/11*. The three films illustrate the media's role in creating and enhancing the perceived importance of signifiers of war through their diffusion and interpretations of them. The way cinema can be a means of highlighting the selective nature of media reporting of war is reinforced by the way all three films illustrate how certain conflicts or events receive considerably more news coverage than others. All the films demonstrate how cinema is a medium that can permit a more measured and in-depth analysis of signs of war and representations of signs of war. To effectively challenge spectators, a film needs to get beyond merely embracing political subjects, it also needs to move spectators by making use of its creative and artistic potential. Cinema critics often talk about political films needing to be political in their conception and form as well as their subject matter. François Bégaudeau (2005) states that "political designates less content, opinions and watchwords than a means of stitching together and unstitching reality. It is about pursuing what could be within what is and anticipating movement in what is static" (79). This quotation fits with the way that the films studied here all set out to make political statements and do so by questioning the visions of reality put forward by the media and by creating an appropriate format in which to do so. All feature structures which highlight the way signs of war can be viewed differently by people from different countries or cultures. This is achieved by the involvement of directors from several different countries in both *Loin du Vietnam* and *11'09"01* and by the way all three films feature footage shot in both rich Western countries waging war and poorer Eastern or Middle Eastern countries suffering the consequences of such wars. In doing so, all three films challenge mainly American-based representations and perceptions of the Vietnam War, the World Trade Center attacks and the Iraq War by illustrating a range of different reactions to such events from all over the world. All the films relate such conflicts and signs of war to factors such as of globalization and also the imperialism and consumerism of rich Western society. *Loin du Vietnam*, *11'09"01*, and *Fahrenheit 9/11* all set out to be "more than just films" in the sense that they aim to provide not just a representation of the world but also a means of challenging representations of the world. They employ a variety of techniques in so doing. The range of distinct short films that make up *11'09"01* means it has a considerably more eclectic range of images and ideas than *Loin du Vietnam* or *Fahrenheit 9/11*. Similarly, *Loin du Vietnam* and *Fahrenheit 9/11* feature words spoken by a narrator to link up the range of images they show and issues they address, whereas *11'09"01* does not. In doing so, they are showing how film can use a range of techniques in creating a model for analyzing and interpreting signs of war and achieving greater understanding of how the media itself goes about doing so.

By entering into such a process, a film is embracing politics. At the same time it becomes subject to politics. As Cyril Béghin (2005) states, "the political question is not exterior to cinema. It is not a subject that cinema treats with its tools, but rather a concern that enters into every decision taken regarding the making or non-making of a work" (80). Questions of whether a work can be made or funded are even more likely to become pertinent in relation to counter cinema and independent films due to their isolation from mainstream commercial cinema. Questioning ways of thinking and actions of governments, are issues that corporate backers of films might not wish to be associated with, as is highlighted by Disney exerting pressure on Miramax not to distribute Michael Moore's *Fahrenheit 9/11*. This illustrates how film faces tough battles in challenging the media's representations of war and making sure its critiques are not marginalized. Given the size and power of large media corporations in an age of ever-increasing globalization, independent films and counter cinema do not appear to be fighting on a level playing field. Thus, while some films might become exceptions to the rule and achieve significant commercial success (like *Fahrenheit 9/11*), such films appear to be exceptions to the rule. However, even if films providing critical analysis of war do not have immediate impact in relation to a specific conflict, they can be a means to understanding war and representations of war in general.

NOTE

1. Jean-Michel Frodon is the editor of the renowned French film journal *Cahiers du cinéma*, which Godard was once a regular contributor to.

REFERENCES

Primary sources

Brigand, A. (Producer), Chahine, Y., Gitai, A., Gonzalez-Iñárritu, A., Imamura, S., Lelouch, C., and Loach, C., Malkhmalbaf, S., Nair, M., Ouedraogo, I., Penn, S., Tanovic, (Directors). 2002. *11'09"01 September 11th*. France: Galatée Films/Studio Canal.

Glynn, K., Czarnecki, J. (Producers), and Moore, M. (Director). 2004. *Fahrenheit 9/11*. United States: Dog Eat Dog Films.

Marker, C. (Producer), Godard, J-L., Ivens, J., Klein, W., Lelouch, C., Resnais, A., and Varda, A. (Directors). 1967. *Loin du Vietnam*. France: SLON.

References

Alexander, A. 2004. Disruptive technology: Iraq and the Internet. In *Tell me lies: Media distortion in the attack on Iraq*. London: Pluto, 277–85.

Bégaudeau, F. 2005. Film politique. *Cahiers du cinéma* 604 (September): 76–79.

Béghin, C. 2005. Si tu peux le filmer. *Cahiers du cinéma* 604 (September): 79–80.

Bruzzi, S. 2000. *New documentary: A critical introduction*. London: Routledge.

Burdeau, E. 2004. Double M contre W. *Cahiers du cinéma* 592 (July/August): 44–45.

Cousins, M. 2004. Fahrenheit 9/11. *Sight and sound* 14, no. 9 (September): 60.

Crowther, B. 1967. Film festival: A polemic on Vietnam. *New York Times*. October 2.

Dwyer, M. 2002. Eleven views of the day the Earth stood still. *Irish Times* (City Ed.). September 14.

Freeman, D. 2004. Misrepresenting war has a long history. In *Tell me lies: Media distortion in the attack on Iraq*. London: Pluto, 63–69.

Frodon, Jean-Michel. 2004. Une Défaite. *Cahiers du cinéma* 591 (June): 14–15.

Gauthier, G. 1995. *Le documentaire: Un autre cinéma*. Paris: Nathan.

Hayward, S. 2000. *Cinema studies: The key concepts. 2nd* ed. London: Routledge.

Hoskins, A. 2004. *Televising war: From Vietnam to Iraq*. London: Continuum.

Howard, T., and Stokes, J., eds. 1996. *Acts of war: The representation of military conflict on the British stage and television since 1945*. Aldershot, UK; Brookfield, VT: Scolar Press.

Howe, Desson. 2003. *September 11th* lacks direction. *Washington Post*, September 5.

Jacobson, H. 2002. Shining a light on Toronto film festival. *USA Today*. September 16.

Kehr, D. 2003. Film in review; *September 11th*. *New York Times*. July 18.

Knightley, Phillip. 2004. History or bunkum? In *Tell me lies: Media distortion in the attack on Iraq*. London: Pluto, 101–107.

Kuehl, Jerry. 1988. Truth claims. In *New challenges for documentary*. Berkeley: University of California Press, 103–109.

Matthews, P. 2003. One day in September. *Sight and sound* 12, no. 1 (January): 32–33.

Mermin, J. 1999. *Debating war and peace: Media coverage of US intervention in the post-Vietnam era*. Princeton, NJ: Princeton University Press.

Miller, D., ed. 2004. *Tell Me lies: Media distortion in the attack on Iraq*. London: Pluto.

Nikolaev, A. G. 2004. Misrepresentation, bias and ignorance: Can we trust what we see on TV about international politics and wars? In *Defeating terrorism/Developing dreams: Beyond 9/11 and the Iraq War. Volume one: Culture clash/Media demons*. Broomall, PA: Chelsea House, 76–83.

Philo, G., and Gilmour, M. 2004. Blackholes of history: Public understanding and the shaping of our past. In *Tell me lies: Media distortion in the attack on Iraq*. London: Pluto, 232–40.

Rosenthal, A., ed. 1988. *New challenges for documentary*. Berkeley: University of California Press.

Seib, P. 2005. The news media and "the clash of civilizations." In *Media and conflict in the twenty-first century*. New York: Basingstoke, UK: Palgrave Macmillan, 217–34.

Solomon, N. 2004. Look I'm an American. In *Tell me lies: Media distortion in the attack on Iraq*. London: Pluto, 157–63.

Spencer, G. 2005. *The media and peace: from Vietnam to the "war on terror."* Basingstoke: Palgrave Macmillan.

Vaughan, D. 1988. Television documentary usage. In *New challenges for documentary*. Berkeley: University of California Press. 34–47.

Véray, L. 2004. *Loin du Vietnam*. Paris: Editions Paris Experimental.

Virilio, P. 1989. *War and cinema: The logistics of perception*. London: Verso.

Wayne, Mike. 2001. *Political film: The dialectics of third cinema*. London: Pluto.

Zheutin, B. 1988. The politics of documentary: A symposium. In *New challenges for documentary*. Berkeley: University of California Press, 227–40.

C H A P T E R   1 0

WAR, NATIONALISM, FEAR,
CRUELTY, RELIGION:

COMPARING DEPICTIONS OF AMERINDIANS IN
NINETEENTH-CENTURY FRENCH-CANADIAN
LITERATURE AND MUSLIMS IN AMERICAN
POLITICAL CARTOONS, 2001–2006[1]

Vincent Masse

ANALOGICAL THINKING

Obviously, comparing twenty-first-century American political cartoons and nineteenth-century French-Canadian literature is both anachronistic—in the strictest sense possible—and "anaculturalistic." Yet, as soon as the incongruity is exposed, one starts "discovering" hints of tangible connections—providing, of course, one looks hard enough. For a start: although nineteenth-century French-Canadian literature was primarily influenced by French literature— for example, François-René de Chateaubriand's figure of the Amerindian or Henri-Émile Chevalier's Amerindians packed novels, printed both in France and in Québec—another important direct influence was from American literature, in the case of Amerindians depictions it was mostly through the work of James Fenimore

Cooper. The latter affiliation means that a lot of what follows, pertaining to the Amerindian imagery in nineteenth-century French-Canadian literature, would relate to the imagery of Native Americans in nineteenth-century American literature. And since there is a pronounced continuity, ranging from the nineteenth century to the twentieth and beyond, concerning the depictions of Amerindians in American culture—such as the Western cinematic genre—and since cartoonists delight in depicting Georges W. Bush as a cowboy involved in some Western-style fight against (Muslim) terrorists, surely, the similarities in depictions are more than purely coincidental.

Yet my intention is not to explore hypothetical continuities—had I wanted to, I would have been better off using nineteenth-century *American* literature—nor do I believe that such continuities are sine qua non to the whole analogical enterprise. It could even be argued that analogical insights are optimal when the leaps are taken from optimally unrelated topics, if only because anything gained through counter-intuitive comparisons would necessarily be unexpected and thus possibly enlightening, in ways unforeseen.

My foray into analogical thinking is experimental rather than theorized. However, because I will quote from Edward Said's *Covering Islam* (1981/1997), which could well be read as a vitriolic essay *against* analogical thinking, I have a certain obligation to mind the potential problem. In *Orientalism* (1978), Said argues at length that both "Orient" and "Islam" are widely and wrongly seen and understood as a "force overriding the distances in time and space that otherwise separates" events (1981/1997, 41). Imagined, widely generalizing "connections"—"Islamic thought" or the "Arab mind"—hinder comprehension and generally engender "more fear and less knowledge about Islam" (43). Said derides the experts on specific topics—"jurisprudential schools in tenth-century Baghdad or nineteenth century Moroccan urban patterns" (15)—then moving on to generalizations about the "Islamic mind-set" and the like. The question is: if leaping from historical Moroccan urban patterns to modern-day "Islamic mind-set" is not permitted, how can one hope to leap from nineteenth-century French-Canadian literature to twenty-first-century American political cartoons?

Said also highly praises a piece written by I. F. Stone, titled "A Shah Lobby Next?" which was published in the *New York Review of Books*, February 22, 1979:

I cite Stone not just because he happens to have been right in his predictions [concerning the Iran hostages crisis that would unfold less than a year later] but also because he was not, and never pretended to be, an "expert" on Iran. . . . Look through his article and you will find no references to the Islamic mentality or Shi'a predilections for martyrdom or any of the other nonsense parading as relevant "information" on Iran. He understands politics; he understands and makes no attempt to lie about what moves men and women to act in this as well as other societies; above all, he does not doubt that even though Iranians are not Europeans or Americans they may have legitimate grievances, ambitions, hopes of their own, which it would be folly for Westerners to ignore. No euphemism, no hyperbole there. If Stone cannot read Farsi, he does not allow himself the compensating luxury of generalizations about "the subtle and elusive nature of the Persian language." (98)

Stone was unique in predicting the Iran hostage crisis as a likely consequence to continuing U.S. support for the Shah after the revolution (160), so apparently insights can be the result of overlooked, well-timed, or lucky leaps. Stone got his by arbitrarily comparing Iranians' grievances to the grievances of various other, unrelated groups (160). If he has *stayed on topic* and tried to enthusiastically *connect the dots* like everyone else, he might have also ended up on a quest of forcibly fit data and delusional, grand systems, for example, "The Iranians, as all Muslims, act in such and such a way."

Thus is it for the purpose of enlightening one another rather than to offer a systemic analysis of either one that I screened the August 2001—January 2006 production of nearly sixty cartoonists[2] and the 1855–1875 production of thirty-one French-Canadian authors, most of them from Québec[3].

Sneaking, Self-invalidating Characteristics, and WMDs

— Les environs de la ville sont donc bien peu sûrs, Madame, qu'il faille s'armer jusqu'aux dents pour faire une douzaine de lieues hors de Québec?

— Oh! M. de Mornac, on voit bien que vous êtes arrivé d'hier au pays pour me poser pareille question. Mais ne savez-vous pas que pour peu qu'on s'éloigne hors de la portée des canons du fort Saint-Louis, on court risque d'être massacré par les Iroquois?

(— Are the outskirts of the city so unsafe, Madam, that one must
be armed to the teeth in order to venture just a few miles outside
of Quebec?
— Oh! Monsieur de Mornac, asking such a question truly shows
you newly arrived! Do you not know that as soon as one goes
beyond the fire range of our arsenal, one runs the risk of being
massacred by Iroquois?) (Marmette 1872, 78)

If we are to believe the precautionary, alarmist warnings constantly
exchanged by characters in nineteenth-century French-Canadian
novels, every Quebecker is permanently on the verge of attack by
marauding Iroquois, and only through luck can they survive at all:
"Ils seront fort heureux s'ils ne font pas la rencontre de quelques-
uns de ces démons enragés" (They will be quite fortunate if they do
not encounter a few of those enraged demons) (Casgrain 1875, 34).
Although many of the narrative poems and historical novels are set
within the time-settings of the Franco-Iroquois Wars, no precise
time-settings nor tribes affiliations are prerequisite: Amerindians
wage terror across regions and centuries, yielding to permanent, per-
meating war*like* circumstances affecting various aspects of the narrative: "le soldat qui s'arme en guerre a peut-être bien moins besoin de
ses armes pour sauver sa vie, que nous ici pour aller visiter un voisin"
(an armed soldier at war has less need of his weapons to save himself
than we do whenever we go to visit a neighbor) (Marmette
1872/1972, 78)

A number of novels employ the following typical scenario—a
commonplace—illustrating how *constant yet unpredictable* the
Iroquois/Amerindian menace is: a female, unaware, is sleeping while
being spied upon by a hateful Amerindian, usually through the window of some lonely cabin set in the middle of a dark forest at night.
The commonplace syntax then asks for a last-minute discovery of the
ongoing peril: "Cependant cette tête sortait toujours davantage du
soupirail, se détachant toujours de plus en plus de l'obscurité. Un
moment les rayons de la lune tombèrent en plein sur cette figure. La
jeune fille tressaillit." (All the while this head was slowly emerging
from the basement window, standing out more and more against the
darkness. Suddenly moon beams fell directly on his face. The young
girl gave a start.) (Casgrain 1875, 26)
According to Umberto Eco, a very similar cliché exists in cinema; in
his essay "How to be an Indian" (1975), he provides the following

advice to Indians wanting to play in a Western: "In preparing to attack an isolated farm, send only a man to spy on it at night. Approaching a lighted window, he must observe at length a white woman inside, until she has become aware of the Indian face pressed against the pane. Await the woman's cry and the exit of the men before attempting to escape" (1975/1994, 202).

What this commonplace is built upon is the received wisdom that Amerindians master the arts of deception: they sneak around undetected, hit quickly, and then immediately retreat. Nonetheless, such a crucial, character-defining skill is precisely what is being denied, whether via the night-time-spying scenario or any other scene involving stealth, for the Amerindian systematically ends up being discovered. It is sometimes due to his adversary's luck (e.g., someone passing by), yet more often than not, it is because of plain clumsiness, such as stumbling straight into the only moonlit spot. Only through the use of a vulnerable and gullible victim—be it a hapless, shrieking, nineteenth-century female, or, as we will see, some near-sighted UN inspectors looking for weapons of mass destruction (henceforth WMDs)—can the paradox of the *clumsy expertise* unfold. If the victims were alert, able men, there would be no deceitfulness. If the victims were simply caught of guard yet otherwise able men, there would be no ineptitude. Deceitfulness and ineptitude have to be maintained for the sake of both suspense and comical relief. Clumsy expertise is seen whenever a very dangerous, hiding Amerindian is exposed through his own fault; it could be that his feathers, sticking out where they shouldn't, betray his whereabouts (Marmette 1872/1972, 77), or that he raises his head because a white hero has tricked him into doing so by mimicking a fellow Amerindian mimicking a coyote (Eco 1975/1994, 201). Similarly, throughout the weeks leading up to the invasion of Iraq, Saddam Hussein was widely portrayed both as a "skillful" deceiver—to the extent that deceit and evasiveness became one of his defining characteristics[4] as a clumsy, mediocre deceiver. Only through the use of gullible UN inspectors,[5] two-faced Frenchmen, or slow-witted Kofi Annans could Hussein retain both his (frightening) deceitfulness and his (comical) clumsiness. Without rockets sticking out of his closet or pants[6] or from under his bed, Hussein's portrayal would violate the assumed zaniness of political cartoons. The same could be said about Iran, which is depicted as a "generic" Iranian trying to hide a nuclear missile under his cape (Combs, December 1, 2004), or under the carpet (Dick Wright, November 26, 2004). Likewise, Osama bin Laden's ability to hide, an ability tautologically linked to his cowardice, is both shown and denied by numerous cartoons depicting shady seven-feet-tall burqa-wearing "women" with manly feet sticking out, showing that he is far from being competent.[7] Despite his purportedly "invisibility," would not a cartoon in which bin Laden remains unseen simply fail at being a bin Laden cartoon?

Self-invalidating characteristics, as a rhetorical device, have uses other than simply comical. There is nothing funny about Sack's September 18, 2001, cartoon depicting a rat (terrorist) trying to hide: "You can run to the end of the earth . . . / Through the farthest valley / Behind the largest rock . . . / Into the deepest hole . . . / And burrow as far as you can. /—But we'll still find you." In the end the hiding rat is caught, and a gun is put to his head. In other words: *you hide, but you can't*. As any rhetorical figure, a self-invalidating characteristic is used to prove something, that is, to prove resolve via unlikeliness: *even though* they are sneaky Amerindians, we find them; *even though* they are terrorizing terrorists, they don't scare us. Its proving-ability ensures that what is primarily a (literary) figure of unlikeliness used for laughs (bin Laden in a dress) or suspense (will the undetectable Amerindian be detected before he kills the white maiden?) can also be used as an (argumentative) figure of *likeliness*, which offers some antithetic knowledge that could not be attained through "regular" logic and therefore that cannot be disproved. *Likely unlikeliness*: it is well known, at least since Terry Pratchett, that within the boundaries of fiction, million-to-one chances crop up nine times out of ten. As much as Amerindians, *in theory*, are unequaled, all-but-invisible stealth masters, whenever they *actually* try to sneak upon some "hero," nine times out of ten they are perceived, caught, and defeated. While it is mainly used in literary settings, it can also be used in unliterary settings in which case it is used to "prove" that what is unlikely is *actually* likely: "nothing has been found, therefore Iraq has weapons of mass destruction." "Nothing has been found," in theory, tends to prove that there is nothing to be found; yet, in *our* actual case—that is, from the perspective of the acting "hero"— it proves that it is likely.

Likely unlikeliness is precisely what underlies self-invalidating characteristics: cartoon terrorists are often depicted as various forms of vermin, ranging from germs to rats,[8] and they are represented as such precisely because of characteristics—secrecy-therefore-cowardice, great numbers—that are denied in front of our very gaze: they are seen, exposed, identified, and limited in numbers. Similarly, Saddam Hussein's weapons of mass destruction, never found in real life, are nine times out of ten "found" in cartoons. And those WMDs are present whether or not the cartoon is mocking Hussein's "slipperiness" or criticizing the Bush administration. Mocking: McCoy, December 6, 2002, features a panicked Hussein trying to flush a nuclear missile down the toilet; the missile is too big, flushing doesn't work, Hussein fails at concealing. Criticizing: Benson February 9, 2003, shows Hussein facing Donald Rumsfeld; Hussein says: "Remember me? We used to work together." This allusion to Rumsfeld's 1983 dealings with Hussein clearly intends to question the credibility of the administration's claims concerning Iraq, and yet Saddam is shown carrying under his arm the WMDs which are— or at least were—central to those claims. Effectively, the immensely-widespread leitmotiv of Hussein "hiding" *clearly seen* missiles and weaponry is a self-invalidating characteristic that became somewhat normative in cartoons drawn right before the onset of the Iraq invasion: his "missiles" were almost as typical as his beret or his moustache. Because of this convention, and whether or not cartoonists actually intended to denounce the bellicose rhetoric of the marching on to war or not, they often ended up offering visual proof of the very *menace* that was used to justify the enterprise[9].

Relevance, Muslims, and Terrorists

Leaving aside questions regarding likeliness and unlikeliness, I will not turn toward *newsworthiness* and *relevance*, mainly because the concept of *representation* alone—as in "the representation of Muslims in American cartoons"—seen as a straightforward mimetic enterprise, would not lead us very far. Starting December 22, 2001, and continuing for almost a week, many of the Muslims depicted in cartoons were Richard "Shoe Bomber" Reid, and yet obviously, in real life, for almost a week, starting 12/22/2001, many of Muslims from around the world were *not* Richard Reid. The selection and image-processing of Reid as a topic has more to do with *newsworthiness* than with fair representation. Political cartoons being part of the news, or at least related to it, have what appears to be a simple tautology: what is newsworthy makes it to the news. Nevertheless,

Edward Said's *Covering Islam* argues that newsworthiness, or currently-crucialness, is also a discerning criteria *outside* of the media. Said opposes European-style orientalism, which is concerned if not obsessed with the "all-encompassing" knowledge of everything "oriental," to American-style orientalism—now Middle Eastern studies—which deals, and teaches how to deal, with current or potential crisis situations. American scholars appear on television to gloss the news, government agencies offer scholarships to promote the study of "crucial," strategic areas (such as "Islamic thought" right after the Iran revolution; Modern Arab language skills nowadays) (1981/1997). Likewise, the "knowledge" on Muslims offered in political cartoons is a knowledge in times of crisis. It is a knowledge of what is going wrong: Muslim men wearing shoe bombs; Palestinians wearing dynamites belts; Afghan woman wearing oppressive burqas; fat, bearded, laughing Saudis sitting on top of oil barrels. Muslims in cartoons, not to mention in the media, are specifically characterized by how relevant and gaze-worthy they presently are for us. Thus it constitutes a *self-invalidating* knowledge: a knowledge that voluntarily offers no relevance or predictive ability, whenever anything *outside* of our direct, current focus is concerned. Muslims you see *here* are terrorists, but Muslims *out there* are not necessarily so. For a limited few weeks immediately following September 11, 2001, this was explicitly stated by numerous public-awareness cartoons. For example, Carlson, September 18, 2001, depicts three white Americans beating up someone lying on the ground:

> First guy: This'll show this Arab how we deal with scum who attack innocent people!
> Second guy: He's from India
> Third guy: Close Enough!!

Another cartoon (Don Wright September 19, 2001) terms "goon" and "terrorist" anyone who "attacks American mosques, Muslims and anyone else with dark skin."[10] In other words: dark skin, while being a *defining* characteristic, is not a *valid* one. Dark skin does not make a terrorist, not to mention a Muslim. Dark skin tones are rarely used to portray Muslims in cartoons, but the equally visual, telling sign of wearing a turban and a beard is as close as you can get to a sine qua non of the cartoon Muslim attire, and yet knowing that

Muslim terrorists wear beards and turbans is an instance of self-invalidating knowledge. We recognize cartoon Muslim terrorists because of their telltale beards and turbans: draw a beard and a turban on a rat and you'll turn it into a terrorist. Despite this convention, what makes them terrorists is not their turbans and beards but rather their existence as characters in a political cartoon. Terrorists may be *characterized* as being hard to identify, but within the boundaries of cartoons, million-to-one chances to spot a terrorist from his turban and beard crop up nine times out of ten. And what makes them crop up is *relevance*, cartoon-worthiness, or that *we are looking*. Unlikeliness repeated over and over again: sneaky Amerindians always ending up being exposed is what suspense is made of, and drawing cartoon Muslims wearing dynamites belts and burqas is called being witty. The knowledge being offered relies on insistence rather than on coverage: burqas and bombs, burqas and bombs, burqas and bombs.

The commonplace of the unseen enemy which is nonetheless perceived by the reader/viewer—e.g., Ohman, January 4, 2002: from behind a team of unsuspecting airport security personnel, a smiling, bearded, turbaned, and robed Mollah Mohammad Omar waves to us—is part of an atmosphere that taps right into widespread fears and apprehension concerning the outside world. Both the Vietnam War and the Invasion of Iraq coincided with discourses about impending catastrophes. According to Said, Asia having "always been endowed both with greater size and with greater potential for power (usually destructive) than the West," it is no surprise that the Vietnam War, the Iran Revolution/hostages crisis, the 1973 oil crisis, and more recently the invasion of Iraq, concurred with discourses guaranteeing impending catastrophes; each of them was assumed to point toward "an unprecedented potential for loss and disruption" (1981/1997, 4, 39). These "hypothetical urgencies" (154) need monitoring and need the United States to keep *gazing* at them, for fear of catastrophic consequences. Political cartoons, especially those featuring the commonplace described, are certainly part of that discourse: Oliphant, November 13, 2001, and McCoy, November 16, 2001, depict turbaned rats sneaking toward discarded Russian nuclear weapons. The unseen-by-everybody-else commonplace implies that if nobody is keeping watch, catastrophes will occur. In a sense, relevance *is* vigilance. Some Moebius circular logic[11] and very contorted reasoning are required. Relevance is due to unlikeliness or extraordinariness: *this* Muslim, out of all the Muslims who are not, is a terrorist, and that is why he is extraordinary enough to make the news and political cartoon. But repeated relevance tends toward likeliness—*every* single Muslim cartooned is cartooned because he is relevant, thus fishy. Therefore *all* cartoon Muslim are fishy. While all-along retaining an unlikely, for-your-eyes-only quality: we don't know who terrorists are, except for *this* one, and *this* one, and *this* one. Without this unlikely extraordinariness—otherwise known as newsworthiness or cartoonworthiness—cartoon Muslims would not be relevant here-and-now. Thus, outside of the current events, outside of our gaze, there *are* uncaught turbaned terrorists, hidden WMDs, and sneaking Amerindians. Otherwise terrorists, hidden WMDs, and sneaking Amerindians would not be characterized as hard-to-catch and hard-to-find, and unlikely turns of events would no longer be unlikely or relevant. Therefore throngs of Muslim terrorists and Amerindians with knives between their teeth are roaming the countryside, and the proof is that we do not see them. And it explains why WMDs were very *likely*—they could not be found—and why Saddam Hussein was hiding them on account that if he did not he would not have been in the newspaper.

HEROES AND VILLAINS, AND HOW TO DIFFERENTIATE FRENCHMEN FROM MUSLIMS

The domino effect theory underlying one of the many justifications for invading Iraq is self-centered and pessimistic: when "we" are not around, things always go wrong. And yet it is also "disquietingly optimistic and confident" (Said 1981/1997, 136), such as when it focuses on the Iraq invasion "entering strategy" and/or pictures democracy spreading throughout the Middle-East. Hopelessness, political clashing, political withdrawal, violent behavior, grandiosity, impaired judgment, and financial extravagance—the manic-depressive rhetoric found in political cartoons and elsewhere is somewhat similar to the manichean narrative logic of the hero surviving against all odds, which features numerous hyperboles and vicious circles pitting an increasingly "good" main character against increasingly bleak surroundings or evil opponent(s). The interlocked, proportional hero–opponent opposition is a commonly used literary device, and images and stereotypes are commonly interlocked and situational as well, according to specific genres and specific rhetorical effects, for example, there can be no suspense without odds. It would thus be difficult to study Amerindian images in nineteenth-century French-Canadian literature without considering specific literary genres—adventures and gothic novels, narrative epic poetry, and hagiographies. Generic circumstances even supersede authorial considerations: Joseph-Charles Taché's and Henri-Raymond Casgrain's imagery of the Amerindians might superficially appear as bluntly opposing one another—Taché's fascination with the "Amerindian lifestyle" and his emphasis on ethnographical details versus Casgrain's generic, devilish, murderous "Savages"—nonetheless, through the comparison of specific works by genres, the difference blurs out. Whenever the genre or the topic calls for meliorative imagery such as when the French and Amerindians side against the British or when "*coureurs des bois*" live a peaceful life amongst the "forest people" Amerindians tend to bear positive traits—for example, Taché's *Forestiers et Voyageurs* and Casgrain's *Le Tableau de la Rivière-Ouelle*. And whenever pejorative imagery is expected—e.g., relations of Catholic martyrs being tortured by Amerindians—negative imagery is expected, regardless of the author's "individual stand" (See Casgrain's *Les pionniers canadiens* and Taché's *Trois Légendes de mon pays)*. Similarly, depictions of Muslims and terrorists depends on the genre, topic, or argument, even within the short-term work of a specific cartoonist. Ramirez, September 22, 2001, and October 22, 2001, portray various Muslim figures and countries as vermin: Taliban, Iraq, and Iran are shown as three rats getting out of a barrel of vermin; a tiny, bearded, turbaned, germ-like figure held in tweezers by an American clad in his anti-contamination suit. The topic was "despicable," and the argument was that they are all in it together. In Ramirez (December 17, 2001) the opponent is now a gigantic, fearsome dragon; an armored knight facing the beast asks his squire for his shield, but the squire replies: "Sorry, Sire, but that could start an arms race." The topic was "dangerousness," and the argument was that the use of nuclear weapons should not be systematically banned. The metamorphosis had to occur: you cannot convincingly use weapons of mass destruction on rats. Neither do the rhetorical devices change from one cartoonist to the next: how else could numerous "instant-commonplaces" be explained, such as the "simultaneously invented" gag of the "new jobs opportunities for Saddam's doubles," not to mention the burqa-wearing bin Laden?

Nor are those rhetorical devices limited to the cartoon world: the *urgency* or the *impending-catastrophe* scenarios are used both in the governmental public discourse and cartoons. The Bush administration's early 2003 *urgency* scenario concerning Iraq's capacity to rapidly deploy WMDs was redirected rather than contradicted within political cartoons of the time: while there was disagreement over the actual threat, its urgency was granted. Such urgency was to be found in cartoons urging immediate action against Iraq, for example, Auth on February 7, 2003 shows Dominique de Villepin saying "We French believe the inspectors should be given more time" while Hussein, working in a lab on some chemical concoction, probably about to make a breakthrough, trumpets "Yes, mon ami!" But urgency was also to be found in cartoons mocking Georges W. Bush's failure to identify the *real* urgency. For example, Luckovich's cartoon on January 16, 2003: Bush says "I'm running out of patience with Saddam!!!" North Korea's Kim Jong-il unsuccessfully tries to distract him by poking at him with a nuclear missile. Even cartoons criticizing the rush to or need for war tended to use the "urgency" scenario—for example, Danzigner on January 26, 2003: under the headline "Mr. Bush Anxious To Get the Ball Rolling," Bush is about to push the world into a fiery pit.[12]

What hero–opponent proportions and other genre considerations underline is that some of the traits attributed to Amerindians and Muslims figures have more to do with literary and argumentative conventions than with stand-alone stereotypes. Within nineteenth-century historical books and adventure novels, the distribution of meliorative and pejorative characteristics can readily be grasped if one adopts the Vladimir Propp (1928) and Algirdas Julien Greimas (1970) nomenclature, a structuralist formula pitting the hero and his or her auxiliarie(s) against the opponent(s); the formers accumulates meliorative traits, while the latter gathers as many defects as possible. The same feature can thus be differently connoted: while the stealth of the Amerindian as auxiliary is impressive and useful and while he is frequently referred to as "cunning," the stealth of the Amerindian as opponent is fearsome, traitorous, and is often called "barbarous." Another example: the North Alliance's attacks against the Afghan's regime were deemed brave, fair, and christened "freedom-fighting," while the Iraqi insurgent attacks directed toward the occupying forces and the Iraqi regime are termed cowardly, disloyal, and ultimately synonymous with terrorism.

Within the nineteenth-century French-Canadian novels surveyed, the hero role is invariably assigned to a French-Canadian or a French character and never to Amerindians, which are relegated to the roles of auxiliaries or opponents. Whenever an Amerindian within the narrative is from the opponents group, all-negative imagery is found, but there are no cases where Amerindian auxiliaries could be found without some Amerindian opponent(s) being thrown in as well. Thus not a single narrative offers a strictly positive Amerindian imagery. In the rather common cases where the main opponent is British, Amerindians serve as the English's "special weaponry." Even if Amerindian opponents are evil, Englishmen as opponents are largely immoral and wicked. It is therefore quite methodologically tricky to find out if Amerindians are negatively portrayed because they are Amerindians or simply because they are opponents. This is why poetics must be carefully considered before one gets involved with stereotypes. So, before the conclusion that Muslims are systematically mocked and negatively portrayed in twenty-first-century American cartoons can be reached, it must be taken into account that mockery and negative portrayal *is* a large part of what the genre of political cartoons calls for. Even if cartoons usually show Muslims as playing opposing-thus-pejorative roles (waging terror, hiking oil price with a smirk, oppressing women), the same is true about French characters (childishly vetoing at the UN, cowardly obeying Hussein's will, backstabbing). Nonetheless, within the settings of nineteenth-century French-Canadian literature, what is "typically Amerindian" *can* be derived, through the comparison of Amerindian and non-Amerindian characters and role distributions. While English characters involved in the oft-portrayed 1755 Deportation of the Acadians show arbitrariness, cruelty, and heartlessness, sometimes to the point of being compared to Amerindians (Lemay 1865, v.858), they nonetheless retain some sense of "European" morality or at the very least some understandable motive such as greed, jealousy. In Joseph Marmette's *François de Bienville* (1870), the main opponents are the Englishman Harthing and his Amerindian accomplice Dent-de-Loup. They both kill and wage war, and yet Harthing has a conscience, which Dent-de-Loup does not possess. The Englishman is redeemable:

> Dent-de-Loup . . . , après avoir fait décrire à la pointe de son couteau
> un cercle rapide sur la tête de Marthe, retient entre ses dents la lame

> ensanglantée dont il vient de se servir; et, posant son pied droit sur le
> dos de la pauvre femme, la saisit par la chevelure qu'il arrache violem-
> ment par une brusque secousse, en laissant nu l'os du crâne. . . .
> Harthing n'a pu vaincre le dégoût que lui inspire la brutalité sauvage
> de son complice; il a détourné la tête. . . .
>
> (Dent-de-Loup, having traced a rapid circle on Marthe's head with
> the point of his knife, holds the bloody blade between his teeth, and
> then, positioning his left foot on the back of this hapless woman,
> holds her by the hair, which he violently tears off, leaving exposed the
> bone of the skull. . . .Harthing could not fight the disgust he felt from
> his accomplice's savage brutality. He looked away. . . .) (1907, 176)

Through large scale comparison, many such differences between
Amerindians and Euro-Americans can be deduced. Sometimes those
"findings" are surprisingly straightforward, such as animal
metaphors and comparisons with animals being commonly ascribed
to Amerindians but rarely to anyone else. Another difference is the
use of satanic imagery, which is also widely found in political cartoons of Muslims terrorists and fighters and *only* in cartoons of
Muslims. God/Allah sometimes makes personal appearances within
cartoons in order to repudiate Muslims figures, for example, terrorists denied their seventy-two virgins and sent to Hell.[13] Various
Muslim leaders are shown as affiliated with Satan, either through
direct lineage (a fatherly Devil welcoming back bin Laden or
Hussein or expelling them on the grounds that even Hell is to good
for them), through damnation (Yasser Arafat and Ahmed Yassin sent
to Hell), or through digging, (Trever, April 3, 2003: Hussein tries to
hide so deep in his bunker that he ends up digging his way to Hell).
In Horsey, June 12, 2002, Guatanamo suspects are devilized by
proxy: under the headline "When the law gets a little tricky,"
Rumsfeld stands in front of a cage containing the Devil and tells the
press "We have captured the Evil One and will be holding him in
military custody as an enemy combatant." An American Civil
Liberties Union representative shouts: "Hold it right there! We
believe the detainee may be an American citizen with a right to legal
counsel!" Obviously, not *all* Amerindians and Muslims are described
using devilish undertones, but out of all the hellish images found in
both corpora, *all* were linked to Amerindians or Muslims: not a single Englishman or Frenchman, not even a North Korean, can hope
to attain such familiarity with the Evil One.

Muslim and Amerindian figures also share a cruelty-related irrationality. Both opponent and auxiliary Amerindian figures are vicious fighters: Hurons delight as much in killing Englishmen as Iroquois do in killing French-Canadians. The Amerindian irrational attraction to spilled blood is to be found even within Renard-Noir, an important positive figure from Marmette's *Le Chevalier de Mornac* (1872) who becomes unable to contain himself whenever there is blood in his vicinity (223). The same could be said about most Amerindian auxiliaries: "J'ai assisté à bien des scènes d'horreur de la part de nos barbares alliés" (I have witnessed many horrifying scenes brought about by our barbarian allies) (Aubert de Gaspé 1863/1987, 163). Similarly, and whether or not the allegations are true, those in favor and those against the surrendering by the United States of its "enemy combatants" to allied Muslim, mostly Arab states, rest their case on the ground that *they*—that is, the Muslims and Arabs—do not mind torture and spilled blood.

Thus, the sight of blood arouses the Amerindian (Marmette 1872/1972, 117) and makes him salivate (Casgrain 1875, 50; Duquet 1866, 39), and the scale of the resulting rage cannot be foreseen or understood: "Qui pouvait prévoir où s'arrêteraient ces barbares une fois alléchés par l'odeur du sang . . . ?" (Who could predict where those barbarians would stop once they are lured to the smell of blood?) (Casgrain 1875, 23). His rage does have an onset, making his cruelty of the vengeful sort. He is in fact vengefulness incarnate:

> La seule passion qu'il nourrit et caresse,
> Qui lui donne, à la fois, le vertige et l'ivresse,
> C'est la vengeance. Il est surtout vindicatif.
> Et quand il laisse son arc et ses flèches à terre,
> C'est pour mieux attiser le feu de sa colère.

> (The sole passion he nourishes and entertains,
> And which both bedazzles and intoxicates him,
> Is vengeance. Above all else, he is vindictive.
> And when he lays down his bow and arrows,
> It is only so that he can stir his fiery anger.) (Lemay 1875, 10–11)

And yet, the onset of his vengeance is discredited: Amerindian resentment is either narratively unexplained or presented as ridiculously disproportionate to actual events. The first half of Léon-Pamphile Lemay's *Les Vengeances* (1875), titled "La vengeance indienne" (The Amerindian vengeance) relates, throughout nearly two hundred pages, the degree of persistence and the heights of excess that an Amerindian is capable of whenever it comes to avenging himself. What is this Amerindian mad about? A light, playful slap he received from a "rieuse enfant" (a merry young girl) (10). Its onset rejected, what comes to best qualify Amerindian vengefulness and cruelty is arbitrariness. Thus vengefulness is yet another self-invalidating characteristic: the act of vengeance needs a cause, yet none is possible—Palestinian terrorism needs a cause, yet none is possible. The second half of Lemay's long poem titled "La vengeance chrétienne" (The Christian Vengeance) offers a *civilized*, Christian alternative: forgiveness, via antithesis, the *irrational* cruelty of invalidated vengefulness. Both Édouard Duquet's *Pierre et Amélie* (1866), a love story, and the previously quoted Casgrain's *Légendes canadiennes* feature senseless, irrational attacks. Nothing is left save irrationality: Amerindian figures suddenly jump into the narrative for the sake of gratuitous murders. A young, uncomprehending girl asks her mother: "Maman! que leur avons-nous donc fait . . . qu'ils nous font tant souffrir!" (Mother! What have we done to them . . . that they want to make us suffer so?); the mother's answer: "ils ne savent pas ce qu'ils font" (they [themselves] do not know what they are doing) (Casgrain 1875, 51). They torture for the sake of it: they roast prisoners as a hobby, whenever they are bored (Aubert de Gaspé 1863/1987, 162). Arbitrariness means that most large-scale conflicts and many of the texts surveyed are set during the conflict-prone New-France period have, as a simple, identifiable *raison d'être*, a senseless, *causeless* aggression.

Causality: To **Do** or To **Be**?

Time and the Other (1983) is a foray into what Johannes Fabian calls the "denial of coevalness" supposedly at the core of the discipline of Anthropology. Denial of coevalness is "a persistent and systematic tendency to place the referent(s) of anthropology in a Time other than the present of the producer of anthropological discourse" (31). Simply put: we *are* right now, and they *are* ahistorical. Fabian refers to the denial of coevalness as a form of allochronism. Anachronism is "a fact, or statement of fact, that is out of tune with a given time frame; it is a mistake, perhaps an accident." On the other hand, allochronism is not a mistake, but a device, which may be existential, rhetoric, political (32). Although the specifics of Fabian's "denial of coevalness" concept cannot be readily applied to the portrayal of Amerindians/Muslims within literature and political cartoons, its general principle is: McKee's (September 21, 2001) and Menees's (September 28, 2001) argument is that Afghanistan cannot be "bombed back to the Stone Age," for Afghans already are living within the Stone Age, wearing fur, and discovering the wheel. Moreover, allochronism could be understood as being precisely what underlies both the causelessness of Amerindian and Muslim aggressions, and the logic of the attribution of roles—aggression versus self-defense—within a conflict. In Eraste d'Orsonnen's "Felluna, la vierge iroquoise" (1856), the city of Québec is continuously under the assaults of Amerindians:

> Ils dressaient continuellement des embuscades, afin de surprendre ceux qui sortaient des forts. . . . Ils torturaient leurs malheureux captifs avec les raffinements féroces que l'on reconnaît aux naturels de l'Amérique du nord. . . .
>
> (They continually ambushed the people who were leaving the forts. . . . They tortured their unfortunate victims with all the ferocious refinement that is known to North American natives. . . .) (9)

Those details are given in lieu of any other description of Québec, and they establish both the attacks and the city as a continuous process. Of course, the poetics of the genre itself calls for a continuous–discontinuous duality. Within the context of standardized literature such as adventure or historical novels descriptions call for the *imparfait* (continuous past) verb tense while the narrating calls for the *passé simple* (discontinuous past), which is assigned to *interruptive* events. Once the setting is set through descriptions, the narrative moves on to list relevant disruptive events—those extraordinary events that make it a relatable story. Amerindian attacks are not part of the causal, narrative time, but rather part of the background scenery, hence the use of imparfait. *Imparfait*-tensed attacks in "Felluna" are not part of the onflow of narrative time, namely, events leading to other events, that is to say causality, but rather part of the scenery. To quote Homer Simpson: "it was like that when I

got here."[14] Therefore, the city of Québec is *not* a colonizing enterprise disruptive of Native societies nor does it have a specific onset
and a complex history.

Lets now add the notion of 'culpability' to the mix. Said writes:

> In fact [Jimmy] Carter does seem to have viewed the [American]
> embassy seizure [in Teheran] in symbolic terms, but . . . he had his
> own frame of reference. To him Americans were by definition inno-
> cent and in a sense outside history: Iran's grievances against the
> United States [i.e., U.S. support for the Shah oppressive regime over-
> thrown by the Revolution, and its continuing support for the ex-
> Shah], he would say on another occasion, were ancient history. What
> mattered now was that Iranians were terrorists, and perhaps had
> always been potentially a terrorist nation. Indeed, anyone who dis-
> liked America and held American captive was dangerous and sick,
> beyond rationality, beyond humanity, beyond common decency.
> (1997, lxv–lxvi)

How does one get from "the hostages were already hostages when
'we' awoke to the crisis to 'therefore 'they' are beyond rationality?'"
Allochronism appears to provide the underlying mechanism to what
perhaps is the primary discursive weapon of bellicose rhetoric: the
notion of kickoff *culpability*. It is precisely because the Amerindians
started attacking us before the "narrative" even started that they are
the kickoff culprits. And from that kickoff culpability everything follows. The Iroquois are not simply foes, they are culprits, which calls
for *punishing* action. "Châtier les Iroquois" (punishing the
Iroquois) is the reason why Louis XIV sends troops to Canada in
1665, as they are guilty of "massacre et . . . devastation" (massacre
and devastation) (Marmette 1870/1883, 9). It is neither war nor
colonization; it is a duel pitting rational temperance against uncivi-
lized ferocity or (Christian) civilization against (heathen) barbarity,
good versus evil.[15] The fight against the Iroquois "reptile" is waged
against our will, we have to carry it on even if we would prefer not
to (47). To us they were not our enemies at the onset of our narrative, but since they seem to (irrationally) think that we are theirs, we
are somehow forced to join the fight. The necessity of punitive retal-
iation explains why massacres perpetrated by Iroquois are acts of
"cruauté inouïe" (astounding cruelty), inspiring "la terreur" (terror)
while massacres perpetrated against Iroquois are rational, judicial,
and even therapeutic: "Il fallait au plus tôt mater l'insolence de ces

barbares" (the insolence of those barbarians had to be put down as soon as possible) (11–12). One is a crime, the other is punishment. The punishment can *go* wrong—those wrongs are called collateral damages—but the crime *is* wrong. And it stays wrong, even if it happens *after* the punishment. How can a crime happen after its punishment? Since the offense is by nature allochronic, *continuous*, and since the punishment is circumstantial, crime and punishment do not happen within the same time. Thus, after-the-offense punishing can be *preventive*: the massacre perpetrated by the Iroquois—200 French deaths and 120 captives—took place in 1688–1689 while the punishing massacres perpetrated against them—5,400 Iroquois deaths, mostly civilian—took place in 1687 (numbers given out by the unabashed narrative itself, 11–13, 27). Our grievances against them are circumstantial and based on causality. We have to retaliate or preemptively strike, *because* they already hate us; their grievances against us are nonspecific to the point of being ontological: they simply hate. Amerindians would fight and hate even if we were not around to be their opponent. They are haters without a cause. To adopt the wording of Said's analysis of the portrayal of Islam in American media, we act, we *do*, and they simply *are:* "I am not saying that Muslims have not attacked and injured Israelis and Westerners in the name of Islam. But I am saying that much of what one reads and sees in the media about Islam represents the aggression as coming from Islam because that is what 'Islam' is. Local and concrete circumstances are thus obliterated. In other words, covering Islam is a one-sided activity that obscures what 'we' *do*, and highlights instead what Muslims and Arabs by their very flawed nature *are*" (1997, xxii).

One of the many examples added by Said for the 1997 edition of his book concerns Lebanon's Hizbollah, whose political *raisons d'être* are muted by the media and whose religion instead is emphasized to a point where Hizbollah becomes a "militant" Islamic party rather than a political and military force with a specific, identifiable— or *debatable*—political onset, that is, Israel's occupation of South Lebanon (xliii–xlvii). Hizbollah *hates* not because of circumstantial causes but through continuous, religious non-circumstances. Terrorists in political cartoons, including Hizbollah and *relevant* Palestinians, are haters without a cause. Let us use the cartoon of bin Laden as an example. Considering that real life bin Laden owes much of his relative popularity within the moderate Islamic world specifically to his discourse playing on causal grievances that the Western world, too, might have received as political rather than religious/irrational/nonexistent, had they been formulated by anyone but him,[16] it sharply stands out that, out of the thousands of surveyed cartoons portraying him and his discourse, not a single one addresses causality. One might point out that it amounts to leaving bin Laden's own causality-prone discourse unchallenged. In Matt Davies, September 18, 2001, bin Laden's monologue—"All hell is unleashed on New York City . . . causing a grief-stricken populace to take to the streets . . . & band together to donate money, food, labor . . . [and] even blood . . . & selflessly offer anything they can to help . . . in an unprecedented outpouring of unity & humanity . . . God, I hate America."—is allochronic, a-causal: bin Laden hates America because of the American reaction to his attacks.

Since cartoon Muslim terrorists are by nature opponent figures, in order to extract the Muslim from the opponent, other figures have to be called upon. Cagle, May 1, 2004, and Marlette, May 3, 2004, both depict Muslim non-terrorists, and Ramirez, February 25, 2003, depicts non-Muslim opponents. Cagle's and Marlette's cartoons feature before and after drawings of how the Arab world and Arab streets reacted to the release of photos showing the abuse of Abu Ghraib prisoners. Cagle's "before photo" shows a gesticulating, knife-wielding, mad-eyed Arab—with pupils of different sizes and colors—shouting "I hate you." The "after photo" is the exact same drawing. Marlette uses the same gag, featuring four ragingly mad Arabs watching Al Jazeera while holding signs that say "U.S. is Satan!" and "Jihad!" Neither causality nor temporality affect the irrational Arab worlds. His hate is non-circumstantial. He is mad regardless of causes and time has no effect whatsoever on him.[17] Ramirez's cartoon, titled "The French deploy troops." features heavily armed French soldiers deployed around a pile of paper labeled "Iraqi oil contracts." Contrary to *acting* Arabs and Muslims, *reacting* French follow rational reasoning; they oppose the invasion of Iraq because they want to preserve the advantageous status quo. French are opponents because they are opportunists.[18] Westerners *do*, Muslim and Arab *are*. *The* cartoon Arab and Islamic world's hate and grievances are self-invalidating characteristics: hate is there, but it is dismissed on grounds of irrationality.

What about non-Muslim terrorists? That there is an interlocked relationship between Muslims and terrorism is one of the "self-evident" tidbits of knowledge offered via cartoons. Marlette, December 20, 2002, parodies the "What would Jesus drive?" anti-SUVs campaign and asks: "What Would Mohammed Drive?" The answer is the cartoon of an angry-looking Muslim driving a Ryder Moving Services rented car of the kind used by bomber Timothy McVeigh and out of which sticks out some nuclear missiles.[19] It is as if Islam and terrorism were so intertwined that Muslims attract terrorist imagery originating from non-Muslim related news events. Portrayed Muslims and portrayed terrorists *do* share a very important, structuring commonplace linked to irrationality and to the absence of a cause. Nevertheless cartoonist Ted Rall, who likes to point out that history could readily provide "rational terrorists," such as the French Resistance during WWII, within the ambient discourse, in a Foucaldian sense, the aura of irrationality surrounding both terrorists and terrorist activities is presented as a fact. Understanding the rationale behind a terrorist's hostage taking, for example, is equated to a dramatic loss of rationality, a condition psychiatrist F. Ochberg has named the Stockholm syndrome.[20] If non-Muslim terrorists and non-terrorist Muslims both were irrational figures to begin with, it is perhaps of no surprise that Muslim terrorists should rise, above and beyond that of common stereotype, to the status of archetype. Such a status, for a foreign figure, has not often been obtained since the sixteenth- to nineteenth-century Amerindian Noble Savage.

If Stockholm terrorists (allegedly) and their hostages (clinically) were both irrational, and since Muslims *already* are culturally and religiously irrational to begin with, does it logically follow that terrorism is part of the Muslim culture? Cartoons appear to say yes: Muslim terrorism *is* an inbred cultural reality—a way of life. In McCoy, April 5, 2002, two parents are driving a car with a license plate that reads "Mid-West" and with a "Proud parents of an honor student" bumper sticker; next to them is another couple driving a car whose license plate says "Mid-East" with a "Proud parents of a suicide bomber" bumper sticker. Wilkinson, March 26, 2004, and Auth, March 28, 2004, both depict toddlers learning to be martyr bombers by learning to tie their shoes and fasten their dynamite belt. Oliphant, June 23, 2004, is more detailed as a proud father asks his son "And what did we learn in Saudi religious school today?" The son answers: "Allah says we must hate America and love terrorism. Allah says we must reject and destroy all democratic and civilizing influence. Allah says we must behead all infidels." The Saudi's son presents violence not as an unfortunate side effect, such as the inevitable "collateral damage" occasioned by American bombing, but as the objective itself. Depoliticization, the act through which grievances are lost, of the Palestinians and Muslims' motives proceeds through religionization, through culturization—such as toddlers learning "the culture of death"—and through irrational logic. As Lemay's Amerindian did because of a playful slap, Daryl Cagle's terrorist gets mad because he is offered long distance savings: "You want us to change our long distance company? Suffer and die infidel pig!" (September 22, 2001)

The commonplace of grievances without any specificity or cause explains why, even though real-life Iraqi insurgents' primary demand is the retreat of American troops, cartoon Iraqi insurgents systematically would continue fighting despite such a retreat. Cartoon insurgents do not fight against specifics; they fight either intransitively or for grotesquely hyperbolic goals, such as against freedom or the concept of democracy.

Controversial, oppositional cartoonist Ted Rall offers a striking counter-example to the a-causal Muslim terrorist, entitled "At home with Joe Terrorist" (November 20, 2003). It starts with Bush's declaration: "They can't stand the thought of a free society. They hate freedom. They love terror. They love to create fear and chaos.'" A bearded yet non-turbaned Palestinian answers: "Bush sure has *my* number. In a few hours, I'm going to board the no. 12 bus to Haifa and blow myself up. It's not because of the occupation. The Israelis are polite, the checkpoints are a breeze and all of my pals in Gaza and the West Bank are millionaires! ["Joe" is now strapping dynamites on himself] Freedom drives me *crazy!* I *hate* it! Also, I'm a total terror freak. Terror *rocks!* Before Allah, it is *eerie* how well Bush understands me. It's like he lives inside my head!!"

The last frame shows a far away explosion, and there is a letter on Joe's bed addressed to "Mom & Dad."[21] Returning to nineteenth-century French-Canadian literature, out of the thirty-one authors surveyed, only Vinceslas-Eugène Dick provides a similar counter-example to Amerindian stereotypical conventions in his *Une Horrible Aventure* (1875). A French Canadian visiting Paris provides grotesque details about his country to mock the gullible locals:

> — . . . je vois que vous ne connaissez pas mon pays et que vous ignorez complètement les moeurs de ces démons. Tenez, pas plus

tard que l'année dernière, un de mes cousins a été littéralement
dévoré vif par eux.
— Dévoré vif!
— Dévoré vif, messieurs: c'est comme je vous le dis . . . sachez,
messieurs, que, la nuit, les bois autour de Québec fourmillent de
sauvages qui guettent les voyageurs attardés ou les imprudents que
leur mauvaise étoile a conduit là.

(— I see that you do not know about my country, and that you are
completely ignorant of the mores of these demons. Why, no later
than last year, one of my cousins was literally eaten alive by them.
— Eaten alive!
— Eaten alive, gentlemen: it is as I'm telling you . . . you must
know, gentlemen, that, by night, the woods around Québec are
thronged by savages waiting for a late or imprudent traveler led
there by an unlucky star.)

His description of his homeland, where "people have their throat
cut, are massacred, tortured, even eaten, right in front of the doors
to the capital city," is long and detailed and covers many of the figures used at face value within contemporary novels and poetry of the
time (38–41). Both Rall's and Dick's reiterations of commonplaces
are satirically perverted, and yet they nonetheless borrow from the
ambient discourse, as if this discourse were all-permeating to such a
degree that, while dissidence could redirect its intent, there is no
escaping from its set of commonplaces. Always optimistic despite the
odds, Edward Said ends his *Covering Islam* with the coining of the
notion of "antithetical knowledge," "the kind of knowledge produced by people who quite consciously consider themselves to be
writing in opposition to the prevailing orthodoxy" (157); while listing such people, he includes "writers, activists, and intellectuals who
are not accredited experts on Islam but whose role in society is
determined by their overall oppositional stance" (159), amongst
whom can most certainly be included a few of the cartoonists surveyed, including Rall. Involuntarily—as Said clearly intended his
"antithetical" adjective to be metaphoric rather than purely literal—
Said offers us a seemingly apt term to describe the nearly-symmetric
act of the convention reversal.[22]

Indians, Muslims, and Ghosts

Lastly, I would like to comment on the discursive use of Muslim figures rather than on the figures themselves. Within a metaphor-prone medium such as cartooning, it should be of no surprise that the use of Muslim imagery goes well beyond the direct portrayal of Muslim figures. Through its systematic use by cartoonists such as Ann Telnaes, the burqa has become an immediately recognizable symbol of oppression, to be used in a variety of non-Muslim contexts, for example in her December 20, 2002, use of a burqa to denounce the Bush administration's rejection of contraception and endorsement of abstinence, and in her December 3, 2001, critique of Japanese imperial succession rights. Dick Cheney has been compared to bin Laden and Saddam Hussein: a running gag features them stumbling one upon the other(s) while hiding in caves or bunkers. John Ashcroft has been compared to a mullah, Michael Jackson to Saddam Hussein, and Michael Moore to turbaned terrorists. Telnaes's Japanese burqa apart, Muslim imagery is thus often used in order to illustrate national issues, usually for the sake of humor. A common side-effect of this analogy technique is trivialization, usually to the detriment of the foreign issue, such as the taxpayers' plight being compared to the torture of Abu Ghraib prisoners in Luckovich, May 6, 2004. DickWright, December 26, 2003, reviewing the year 2003, mentions the Iraq War and the Middle East alongside Martha Stewart, the Chicago Cubs, and the Boston Red Sox.

Since Michael Moore has also been derided through the use of a French imagery—berets, poodles, cowardice, betrayal—the subtracting and comparing of imageries is once again called for. Out of the tens of thousands of cartoons surveyed, while several hundreds use Muslim figures or imagery to convey fear, neither French figures nor French imagery were ever used to a similar end. And although North Korean figures were often used as bogeymen in the early months of 2003, North Korean *imagery* never really kicked off. Conveying fear and terror seem to be the specialty of twenty-first-century Muslims, and it brings us back to the opening epigraph about fearsome marauding Iroquois.

Most of the nineteenth-century French-Canadian novels I have surveyed were directly or partly written using elements from the European gothic genre featuring ghosts, castles, and scenic cemeteries.

In its French-Canadian avatar, the gothic esthetic uses dark forests instead of castles—both because nineteenth-century authors were struggling to invent a local, nationalistic, non-European literature, and because there simply weren't any abandoned castles in Québec—and instead of ghosts we have Amerindians. Henri-Raymond Casgrain explains: "dans un pays comme était alors le Canada, couvert d'immenses forêts inexplorées, peuplées de races étranges et à peine connues, tout était propre à entretenir et à fomenter les idées superstitieuses" (in a country as big as Canada was at the time, covered by immense, unexplored forests filled with strange and little known races, everything was in place to maintain and create irrational thoughts) (1861/1875, 37). Sudden appearances by lurking Amerindians had a ghostly feel: "Une clarté plus vive, et apparaît le visage d'un Indien tenant entres ses dents un couteau." (A flash, and then there appeared the face of an Amerindian holding a knife between his teeth) (12). Although similar comparisons were widely used, Amerindians did not *really* appear and disappear at will: they were ghastly, not ghostly. Nevertheless, they were able to provide a similar fantastic backdrop. If no ghost was around to do it, they could fill the air with the "bruit incessant de quelque énorme chaîne" (incessant sound of some large chains) (Chapman 1876, 90), no narrative role asked in return. Although the main incidents related within the 1864 narrative poem "Le braillard de la montagne (The howler of the mountain)" have nothing to do with Amerindians or Amerindian-related themes, it opens on an array of dancing, howling, demonic, and will o' the wisps-like Amerindians strictly in order to conjure up the horror genre.[23]

Oliphant's and McCoy's rats/terrorists sneaking upon Russian missiles cartoons mentioned earlier (November 13, 2001, and November 16, 2001) both rely on the use of Muslim figures and imagery as *ghosts* in order to sustain the micro-argument of the hypothetical-yet-imminent threat. Russian missiles stockpiles have been decaying, unattended, for decades, and yet, with the simple addition of a rat in a turban, the *mood* is set, suspense is created, and immediate attendance is required. During the brief anthrax-related cartoons fad in 2001, willing cartoonists could add an edge to any spore with the inclusion of a Muslim *ghost*, e.g., Breen, October 14, 2001: a turbaned, bearded character named "Terrorists" reads a copy of Introduction to Germ Warfare "cleverly" hidden inside the cover of a Koran. Telnaes's December 3, 2001, critique of Japanese imperial succession rights, with its inclusion of a burqa, turns the issue into something that *has to be dealt with*, preferably *now*. Her May 24, 2003, cartoon is another good example. We first see the silhouette of a man—is he a Republican?—holding a book and demanding: "Put prayer back in our schools and public institutions." Then we get to see who that man was: a bearded Shiite holding the Koran. Whether Telnaes's argument is that "we shall not become as fanatical as foreign fanatical Shiites" or "religion and state should not mix, lest we be vulnerable to American Muslim demands." in both cases it rests upon the Muslim as a threatening rhetorical device. A widely-used technique: Alcaraz, October 26, 2001, Day, June 12, 2002, and Conrad, March 1, 2004, make a nuclear symbol even more menacing by respectively adding to it a beard, a turban, and a chador. To a skull, Conrad, April 8, 2004, adds a ghutra. Even the shark from the *Jaws* movie poster can be improved upon by the addition of a turban, a beard, and an al-Qaeda name tag (Breen, May 27, 2004).

At the closure of our analogical brainstorm and of the counterintuitive comparing of twenty-first-century American cartoon Muslims with nineteenth-century French Canadian literature Amerindians, we are left with a few finds that perhaps would otherwise have eluded us. Dialogic theorizing concerning self-invalidating characteristics taught us how to catch sneaking Amerindians or laugh at terrorists while likely unlikeliness possibly explains why Saddam Hussein likely possessed the WMDs that he didn't have. Also chanced upon were: relevance (or why every Palestinian is a terrorist), self-invalidating knowledge, the comparative derivation of specifics (or how to take the terrorist out of a Muslim), kickoff culpability (or how "they" started it), a-causality (or why leaving Iraq would not stop the insurgency), depoliticizing (or how to turn any Resistance fighter into a religious freak), and rhetorical ghosts (or how to spice up gothic novels or nuclear menaces). As these concepts were encountered through off-topic reasoning by essence if not practically, they could hardly be used out of context, and thus this author hopes that they help enlighten third topics, especially those he could not foresee.

Notes

1. I would like to thank Michelle Troberg for her help with this chapter.
2. The following cartoonists, and more, were covered from September 2001 to January 2006: Lalo Alcaraz, Eric Allie, Nick Anderson, Chuck Asay, Don Asmussen, Tony Auth, Clay Bennett, Steve Benson, Chip Bok, Steve Breen, Daryl Cagle, Stuart Carlson, Paul Combs, Paul Conrad, Jeff Danziger, Matt Davies, Bill Day, John Deering, Bob Gorrell, Bruce Hammond, Walt Handelsman, Jack Higgins, David Horsey, Clay Jones, Kevin Kallaugher, Mike Keefe, Steve Kelley, Mike Lester, Dick Locher, Chan Lowe, Mike Luckovich, Doug Marlette, Glenn McCoy, Rick McKee, Jim Morin, Jack Ohman, Pat Oliphant, Jeff Parker, Henry Payne, Joel Pett, Dwane Powell, Ted Rall, Michael Ramirez, Steve Sack, Ben Sargent, Drew Sheneman, Kevin Siers, Scott Stantis, Ed Stein, Wayne Stayskal, Dana Summers, Paul Szep, Ann Telnaes, Tom Toles, John Trever, Gary Varvel, Kerry Waghorn, Dan Wasserman, Signe Wilkinson, Larry Wright, Dick Wright, and Don Wright. Most of the cartoons quoted can be found at http://www.ucomics.com/editorials/ or http://www.cagle.com/.
3. Ten novels, four short stories, sixty-one poems, and one anthology of popular songs; complete references are available in Masse, 2002.
4. For example, Sargent, January 2, 2003: under the headline "World's slipperiest substances" is shown (a) a scientist slipping over the content of a spilled barrel of polytetra-fluoro-ethylide, (b) an egg flying out of a Teflon frying pan, much to the surprise of the cook, and (c) Saddam Hussein, smiling slyly.
5. For example, McCoy, January 18, 2003: Hans Blix, as the Inspector Clouseau, holding a magnifying glass, having just fallen down, his foot caught in a nuclear missile, says "Sacré bleu [sic]! How am I supposed to do my investigation with all these odd canisters lying around?!"
6. For example, Sack, January 29, 2003: a bending down Hussein splits his pants, revealing WMD-themed boxers.
7. For example, Handelsman, September 19, 2001; Conrad, October 21, 2001; Lowe, November 16, 2001; Marlette, November 20, 2001; Ramirez, November 19, 2001; Oliphant, November 21, 2001.
8. McCoy, November 19, 2001, under the headline "vermin," offers the following possibilities: snakes, worms, lizards, rats, spiders, bats, flies, vultures, and various insects.
9. Around Colin Powell's February 6, 2003, address to the UN Security Council regarding alleged Iraqi WMDs, the use of "smoking gun'" metaphors in political cartoons was another instance of strictly *literary*, yet *visual*, "evidence." The question as to whether or not the evidences laid out amounted to a definite proof of the existence of said WMDs

was widely sidestepped within cartoons, in order to make way for literal smoking guns, for example Cagle, February 4, 2003; Huffaker, February 5, 2003; and L.Wright, February 5, 2003. The "smoking gun," from a metaphor standing in for an *outcome*—a *result*—morphs into a metaphor—but is it still a *metaphor?*—standing in for an *evidence*. If only for the sake of the visual gag, a smoking gun certainly looks more appealing than a drab caricature of Powell, the gun *is* there. And once the gun is visually there, it becomes rather difficult to turn it into a gag that would question its very existence. Instead of "is there a gun?," it is both easier and punchier to ask "what kind of gun is it?," like in L.Wright, February 5, 2003, depicting a man being mugged by a gun-holding criminal, while a policeman nearby says "Call me when the gun is smoking."

10. See also Auth, September 14, 2001; L.Wright, September 15, 2001; Alcaraz, September 17, 2001; Sheneman, September 18, 2001; Ohman, September 18, 2001.

11. Moebius circular logic: same as circular logic, but each time you go round you end up on the opposite side.

12. *Urgency* is obviously linked both to *relevance*—it would not be mentioned if it did not require immediate attention—and to the general fast-paced media, and specifically of the news and political cartoons. Bush's May 1, 2003, declaration of the end of hostilities in Iraq was widely deemed, if only a posteriori, to have been rushed in, at the same time, many, if not most of the surveyed cartoonists had long ago stopped cartooning about the Iraq invasion. It would also explain why Afghanistan disappeared not long after the publication of arguably premature "final" cartoons depicting the fall of Kabul (Afghan men shaving off their beards, women throwing out their burqas). Paradoxically, many political cartoons mock the short-attention span of the American public and the media.

13. For example, Ramirez, September 19, 2001, and Alcaraz, September 21, 2001: highjackers entering an "afterworld" lobby with airport security undertones are directed to Hell. The similarity in both those cartoons is a case in point of the spreading of imagery and commonplaces across political affiliations: Ramirez and Alcaraz otherwise disagree on a strong majority of issues.

14. "One Fish, Two Fish, Blowfish, Blue Fish," *The Simpsons*. Wolverton, October 1, 2001, with his before and after set of Afghanistan depictions, precisely and preemptively illustrates the it-was-already-destroyed-when-I-got-here argument: either before or after, only rubble can be seen.

15. The literary convention pitting Heroes/Auxiliaries against Opponents is partly maintained through *relevance*: characters that would neither help nor hinder the hero have no narrative reason to exist.

16. His use of the widely unpopular stationing of thousands of foreign troops in Saudi Arabia would be a chief example of causal, political grievance. Although the complete list of Bin Laden/ al-Qaeda grievances is long indeed, Saudi internal, politically-related griefs, chronologically and publicly, seemed to have played a forefront discursive role, starting in the early 1990s, and they still do. The rhetoric of his December 2004 audio message plays heavily on local "political rights," "I address this short message to the Riyadh rulers and decision-makers—there is a contract between the ruler and his subjects entailing rights and obligations on both parties. One of its main features is that the ruler protects his people. But the truth is otherwise. You have oppressed the people without their agreement. The people have woken from their slumber and realised the extent of the tyranny and corruption that you exercise. The Muslims in the land of the two mosques insist on regaining their rights, regardless of the cost." http://news.bbc.co.uk/2/hi/middle_east/4103137.stm.

17. For similar gags, aimed at the Arabs/Muslims's irrational handling of international news, see Bok, May 6, 2004, McCoy, May 11, 2004, and Horsey, July 3, 2004. Bok's cartoon shows a Muslim watching news on television: "Al Jazeera brings you rare footage of an American having his throat slashed" elicits no reaction, neither does "special coverage of burned and mutilated Americans," but when images "naked Iraqi prisoners" is aired, he starts screaming "How humiliating!" Marlette, August 9, 2004, hints that such inability to use rational comparative thinking may be due to anti-Semitism: "If we can't blame Israel it's not a crisis!"

18. Only Saudis stand apart, concerning rationality, as they are widely depicted as opportunists: cashing in on American oil demand, playing complex political games (that is, offering one hand to the Americans and another to terrorists), or controlling the whole of the American internal politics (e.g., the cartoons following the April 2005 Bush-holding-hands-with-Saudi-Crown-Prince-Abdullah incident).

19. As the infamous Danish Muhammad cartoons would a few years later, Marlette's cartoon gave rise to controversy. Marlette later declared that he never intended to represent the prophet Muhammad but rather aimed for a "generic" Muslim-looking character. See http://www.worldnetdaily.com/news/article.asp?ARTICLE_ID=30197. Marlette's complete declaration can be read here: http://dougmarlette.com/page19.html.

20. If it was possible to analyze paper-and-ink figures through psychiatric criteria, many of the "leftists against War," as they are portrayed in early 2003 cartoons—not to mention the French/German or the Democrats during the 2004 elections—would qualify as sufferers.

21. Two other examples of Rall's use of convention reversal, one titled "Wishful thinking, American style," two Afghans discuss, "Sure—the Americans dropped a bomb that killed my wife and maimed my kid. But hey—no biggie." "You know what would be really cool? A repressive, corrupt, U.S.-backed puppet dictatorship. That would totally rock!!" (November 22, 2001); the other shows in front of a completely destroyed Afghanistan with nothing but ruins and hanged bodies around them, two Afghans talk: "The Americans are going to liberate Iraq too." "Lucky bastards!" (March 4, 2003).

22. One could nonetheless argue that Rall's *analogical* humor—of the *analogical* family that was described earlier—gives much more than simple reversals. Out of the cartoonists surveyed, Dan Asmussen is the one who uses the most sophisticated analogical humor.

23. Amerindian imagery used in order to build horror upon can also be found in twentieth-century American cinema, such as in Stanley Kubrick's *The Shining*, which features a haunted hotel supposedly "located on an Indian burial ground." In *Dawn of the Dead* (2004), a post-9/11 remake of Georges A. Romero's *Dawn of the Dead* (1978), features beefed-up opponent zombies, a more strictly secured frontier set between "us" and "them," and even more irrational logic of the opponent—we are no longer told why the zombies try to get inside the secured mall—which has strictly nothing to do with Islam or Muslims, Muslim imagery is nonetheless called upon, near the onset of the movie, for dramatic effect. While we hear Johnny Cash's *Apocalypse*-themed "When The Man Comes Around," a series of extremely brief clips are shown: vandalized buildings, riots and anti-riot troops, breaking glass, crashing cars, dead people lining the streets, screaming, blood-covered zombies, microscopic shots of rapidly developing viruses, and a large group of praying Muslims. For dramatic effect, I put the Muslims at the end of the enumeration, but in the movie, for dramatic effect as well, the Muslim clip opens the sequence. *Dawn of the Dead* needs not actually feature religious fanatics, terrorist activities, Iranian nukes, or even a few Palestinians: the simple, *generic threat* of praying Muslims suffices at being the opening act to the Apocalypse.

References

Aubert de Gaspé, Philippe. 1863. *Les anciens Canadiens*. Montréal: Stanké, 1987.

Casgrain, Henri-Raymond. 1875. *Légendes canadiennes et oeuvres diverses*. Québec: C. Darveau.

Chapman, William. 1876. La vengeance huronne. *Les Québecquoises*. Québec: C. Darveau.

Dick, Vinceslas-Eugène. 1875. *Une horrible aventure*. Sainte-Foy: Éditions de la Huit, 1998.

d'Orsonnens, Éraste. 1856. Felluna, la vierge iroquoise. *Felluna, la vierge iroquoise; Une épluchette de blé d'Inde; Une resurrection*. Montréal: Senécal et Daniel.

Duquet, Édouard. 1866. *Pierre et Amélie*. Montréal: C. Darveau.

Eco, Umberto. 1975. How to play Indians. *How to travel with a salmon and other essays*. London: Secker and Warburg, 1994.

Fabian, Johannes. 1993. *Time and the other—How anthropology makes its object*. New York: Columbia University Press, 2002.

Greimas, Algirdas Julien. 1970. *Du sens—Essais sémiotiques*. Paris: Seuil.

Lemay, Léon-Pamphile. 1865. *Évangéline. Essais poétiques*. Québec: G. E. Desbarats.

Marmette, Joseph. 1870. *François de Bienville; Scènes de la vie canadienne au XVIIe siècle*. Québec: Léger Brousseau.

———. 1870. *François de Bienville; Scènes de la vie canadienne au XVIIe siècle*. Montréal: Beauchemin and Vlois, 1883.

———. 1872. *Le chevalier de Mornac*. Montréal: Hurtubise HMH, 1972.

Masse, Vincent. 2003. *Figures de l'Amérindien dans la littérature québécoise, 1855–1875*. McGill University: M.A. Thesis.

Propp, Vladimir. 1928. *Morphologie du conte*. Paris: Seuil.

Said, Edward W. 1978. *Orientalism*. Afterword. New York: Vintage, 1994.

———. *Covering Islam—How the media and the experts determine how we see the rest of the world*. New York: Vintage, 1997.

Taché, Joseph-Charles. 1863. *Forestiers et voyageurs*. Montréal: Fides, 1981.

CHAPTER 11

WAR AND PEACE IN CHRISTIAN PRAYER

Andrew Thomas
Susan Berg
Tor Berg
David Nice

Although all major religions have enduring principles and concerns, the issues and events of the day often trigger responses from religious leaders and organizations (Ahlstrom 2004; Butler, Wacker, and Balmer 2003; Gaustad and Schmidt 2002; Harvey 2001). When people face the possibility or reality of warfare, they are likely to press for some form of response from many social institutions, including religious institutions. Given the value of peace and its fragile nature, many people are also likely to expect religious institutions to discuss and support peace much of the time—although many people also experience warlike feelings at least occasionally, such as immediately after September 11, 2001.

One part of that response in many religions is prayer (Moore 2005). Prayers take many forms, but they usually offer a communications link between people and a divine being or presence, between religious leaders or organizations and their members, or among members of a group. In addition, prayers serve as vehicles for individual reflection and self-examination.

For much of American history, intensive wars occupied fairly limited spans of time, although more limited battles took place between major wars. Beginning with World War II, however, the United States entered an era of nearly continuous mobilization for war with periods of active warfare, albeit at varying levels of severity. With the collapse of communism in the Soviet Union and Eastern Europe, some observers hoped for an extended period of relative peace. However, the world has remained mired in military conflicts, and the United States has been directly involved in conflicts of various sizes, including the recent invasions of Afghanistan and Iraq.

Since the terrorist attacks of September 11, 2001, Americans have also faced the specter of attacks on American soil.[1] Terrorism presents the added stresses of violent conflict that may erupt virtually anywhere and that may be quite open-ended. Moreover, some of the combatants are not clearly identifiable and may make no distinction between military and civilian targets (see Howard, Forest, and Moore 2006; Sauter and Carafano 2005). All of those dynamics make terrorism particularly frightening and confusing. In that environment, many people are likely to turn to religion as a source of guidance and reassurance.

In the following, preliminary analysis, we will explore war and peace in Christian prayer with particular emphasis on prayers linked to the United States. We limit our analysis to Christian prayer because Christianity has by far the largest number of adherents in the United States (Gallup and Jones 2000) and due to resource constraints. We plan to extend the analysis to prayers of other religions in the near future.

The Uses and Purposes of Prayer

Virtually all religions incorporate some form of prayer. The types of prayer vary considerably. They may be long or short, spoken or sung, spontaneous or written in advance, focused on a single topic or spanning a number of topics (for an overview of the considerable diversity of types, see Water 2004). Prayers may be uttered by an individual who is alone or in a large group. Prayer is used for a great many purposes, and when several people utter the same prayer, they may interpret it in a number of different ways (Buckley 1986, xvii). Even a single individual may use a prayer for a number of different purposes or even without any conscious goal in mind at the time. Assessing the contents of any prayer should, therefore, be approached with caution.

One major purpose of many prayers is bringing about changes in the people who are offering the prayer (Zaleski and Zaleski 2005, 6, 11, 335). In some instances these changes may be the direct result of praying, but in other cases the prayer asks for divine assistance in changing some aspect of the person's own life. Prayers can help to focus people's attention on particular issues and to express feelings and thoughts that many people may have difficulty articulating or, in some cases, may not even be consciously aware of (Acker 1970, 11–12; Buckley 1986, xvii-xix; "Preface" 1993, 5).

Prayers that highlight particular issues can serve as part of the political system's agenda setting process by drawing people's attention to some problems or issues and not emphasizing others (on agenda setting, see Anderson 2006, 86–103; Dye 2002, 33–40). In addition, the manner in which a prayer treats an issue may influence people's thinking about it. For example, a prayer may present a war as a moral duty or a wrongful action; a prayer may call for the destruction of an adversary or express sympathy for the suffering endured by all sides of the conflict. One prayer may depict a war as being a matter of self defense while another prayer emphasizes the possibility of replacing a dictatorial government with a more democratic one or the opportunity to replace one religion with another.

Prayers, whether offered individually or as part of a group, may provide a sense of companionship or solidarity for people who fell lonely or isolated (Fosdick 2001, 8–9). War may heighten that feeling for combatants who are far from their families and friends, for relatives and friends who miss someone serving in the war or killed by the war, and for refugees and displaced persons.

Praying can also help to relieve fear, grief, stress, and anxiety (Fosdick 2001, 4–7; Roberts and Amidon 1996, x). Many prayers call attention to events and circumstances that generate emotional pain and ask for some sort of relief. In some cases, the act of praying itself may provide relief; in other cases, people may ask for divine aid. War and the threat of war both generate enormous emotional turmoil and distress, which may continue for many years after the war ends, and many prayers regarding war and peace address those emotional issues. Although research on the health effects of prayer has produced mixed results, some studies find evidence of benefits (see Zaleski and Zaleski 2005, 342–46).

In a related vein, praying is sometimes a process of reflecting on one's life and confessing failings and wrongdoing (Job and Shawchuck 1983, 9–10; Suter 1940, xxxvi), this is a process that is often painful and difficult. War can make that process even more difficult as people reflect on the violent pain and suffering that they may have inflicted, the anger they have felt, and regrets over many things, from blunders to panic. Note, too, that people in combat zones are likely to face the same environment and the same demands repeatedly. They are likely to encounter regular reminders of their failings, and failures to correct them can mean additional pain and suffering.

With or without reflections on past actions, prayers may ask for guidance to help people understand confusing or ambiguous situations or to help them think and act appropriately in accordance with the teachings of their faith (Batchelor 1992, xiii; Boulding 1997, xix–xx; Buckley 1986, xviii; Stookey 2004, 21). That guidance may have little impact, however, unless people are willing to make the effort to follow it (Boulding 1997, xix–xx; Buckley 1986, xviii; "Preface" 1993, 2–4). Prayer in this case may be less a matter of calling for divine action and more a matter of helping people unite with their religious principles and acting on that basis (Fosdick 2001, 11).

Following religious guidance may be particularly difficult in wartime when people may be ordered or pressured by circumstances to do things that almost all major religions normally forbid—killing, injuring, destroying, lying, and stealing (see Moses 2002)— although many religions allow some exceptions to those guidelines, as in the case of a "just war" (see Wasserstrom 1970). Moral considerations aside, wars also generate an increased need for guidance because warfare often involves considerable confusion and uncertainty. Many factors contribute to that state of affairs, but one important source is the tendency for all sides in war to try to mislead one another (Sun 1963, 66). Hostile leaders may appear to be friendly; an enemy may have concealed military assets. Military forces may circulate false information in hopes of fooling adversaries, as the Allies did in World War II regarding the likely site of the D-Day landing. In that environment, people are likely to feel the need for guidance from any number of sources, including religion.

Prayers may also be a way for people to express their feelings without necessarily expecting any concrete action to result. The feelings expressed span the full range of human emotions, from love, devotion, pride, and gratitude to anger, fear, sorrow, and exhaustion (Batchelor 1992, xiii; Buckley 1986, xviii; "Preface" 1993, 2–4; Suter 1990, xxxvi; Zaleski and Zaleski 2005, 6, 12–15, 353). Some of the people offering these prayers may implicitly hope that some sort of relief or help will result, but the primary emphasis in the prayer (or a particular part of a prayer) is simply expressing a feeling. War may heighten the need for expression, because warfare can produce very strong feelings and many of the participants are separated from the loved ones to whom they would normally express their feelings. In addition, combatants are often encouraged or required to limit what they communicate about their thoughts and actions for security reasons ("loose lips sink ships") and by the hierarchical nature of military organizations, which normally discourage overt criticism of superiors.

Other types of prayers include direct appeals for divine intervention to change the course of events or influence other people. One of the more famous examples of this type of wartime prayer was offered by General Patton during World War II. In that prayer, he called on God to provide better weather in order to help the Allies turn back German forces during the Battle of the Bulge (Zaleski and Zaleski 2005, 7–10). Much earlier, in some of the Psalms of the Old Testament, people called on God to destroy Israel's enemies or to offer protection from them (for examples, see Psalms 3, 18, and 27). The warlike spirit of some Psalms makes them unappealing for some people in the modern era (Stookey 2004, 165–66), but warlike feelings still exist.

In addition to calling on divine aid to defeat adversaries, prayers may also ask for divine help in bringing a war to a quick end, helping wounded soldiers and civilians recover, minimizing suffering, protecting people from their enemies, maintaining a state of peace, or meeting many other human needs (Buckley 1986, xviii). The problems created by wars sometimes appear too large and complex for human comprehension and management. In that situation, divine assistance may seem essential.

A Focus on Written Prayers

Prayers can be expressed in a number of ways, including speaking, singing, and silent reflection. At this preliminary stage, our study will focus on written prayers for a number of reasons. First, we have very little ability to retrieve prayers that are spoken, sung, or thought silently unless some sort of record is made. In addition, many written prayers began as silent or spoken prayers that were eventually written down, and many spoken and silent prayers are read from a service book or collection of prayers.

Second, written prayers have the potential to reach and influence large numbers of people (Buckley 1986, xviii–xxii), whether through regular use in religious services, recitation at a public or private gathering, appearance in publications read by people who do not regularly attend religious services, or some combination of all three. Many Americans who pray regularly do not belong to any religious organization and do not attend religious services on a consistent basis (Gallup and Jones 2000, 178, 180). Written prayers can reach large numbers of people and have a continuing impact, although there is no guarantee that any particular written prayer will reach a large audience. In addition, although some religious groups place considerable emphasis on using an officially approved liturgy, other groups attach a higher value to more spontaneous expressions of faith (Buckley 1986, xiii). The latter inclination is likely to reduce the influence of written prayers somewhat.

In our analyses, we have tried to focus on written prayers since 1900 that explicitly address issues of war and peace in terms of military or terroristic combat, the threat of that combat, or the absence of it. We have excluded prayers that use the terminology of warfare, fighting, combat, and peace in more metaphorical terms, such as the battle of good versus evil, fighting temptation, and spiritual peace. In this preliminary analysis, we will also focus on Christian prayers because Christianity is the most common religion by far in the United States (Gallup and Jones 2000, 180), although some Christian prayers have been adapted from other faiths, especially Judaism. We hope to expand our analysis to include other faiths in the near future.

Analysis of the First Sample

Our first sample of prayers comes from twelve prayer and devotional books that met at least one of three criteria: they were indexed or organized by subject area, they were comparatively brief (which made an examination of the entire contents practical), or they were devoted to people serving in the armed forces and/or their families.[2] Only two of the books met the last criterion. Of the twelve books, eleven were nondenominational and one was devoted to a single denomination. Two of the books did not contain any prayers devoted to issues of war and peace (except for duplicates of those contained in at least one of the other books examined). A total of eighty-seven prayers contained clear references to military or quasi-military conflicts, members of the armed forces, or peace (indicating the absence of military or quasi-military conflicts).

Not surprisingly, more than 90 percent of the prayers in the sample contained one or more requests to God (see Table 11.1). The nature of the requests varied considerably. Roughly 70 percent of the prayers included one or more requests for the person praying; a slightly larger proportion included requests for other people, including loved ones far away, comrades, and adversaries. In addition, approximately half of the prayers asked for the creation of a specific condition or situation, with or without a clear indication of the presumed beneficiary or any human agents being called upon to act. Finally fewer than two-thirds of the prayers expressed a sentiment, assessment, or belief. Some of those expressions emphasized the conditions that people were facing or expecting to face; others discussed personal feelings or even the attributes of God.

A comparison of the prayers from the two books developed for the military and their families with prayers from other sources revealed two striking differences. First, prayers from the sources designed for more general audiences were considerably more likely to include requests calling on God to directly create a condition or situation—victory, peace, or others. Prayers from the more militarily related sources were unlikely to contain request of that type. Instead, their requests were more likely to be directly linked to people—such as requests to give my comrades and me more courage or to instill a greater love of peace in all people. The greater emphasis on requests to change people (rather than conditions directly) in military-related prayers may reflect a view that human action is needed in order to change conditions or circumstances. A good indication of the importance of that human action emphasis in military thinking is found in the U.S. Army's field manual, *Military Leadership* (1990), which emphasizes the importance of teaching subordinates, being a good listener, motivating others, considering emotional needs, and treating soldiers with dignity and respect, among other concerns.

A second major difference between the prayers from the militarily-oriented books and the others lies in the expression of sentiments, beliefs, and assessments. Contrary to expectations, prayers from the militarily-related sources were considerably more likely to include expressions of one or more types than were the prayers from general sources. Given the strong feelings that close involvement in wars creates, a need for expressing them is not altogether surprising. We found admissions of fear, weakness, loneliness, and a reluctance to fight. In addition, the stresses of war may create an increased need to reaffirm basic beliefs and principles. For example, the prayer "For a Dying Service Member" (*Armed Forces Devotional Book* 2003, 17) mentions Christian beliefs in divine creation and redemption, both of which may provide some comfort for the survivors and for the dying. Other prayers express beliefs in a divine moral order, divine forgiveness, and the value of repentance.

The requests included in prayers related to war and peace span a wide range of topics and concerns (see Table 11.2). Not surprisingly, one of the two most frequent requests is for peace or, less directly, a stronger desire for peace in the hearts and minds of people. The relative frequency of peace requests is consistent with the finding that relatively democratic leaders and societies, such as the United States, have a general preference for peace rather than war, at least in their relationships with other democracies (see Dahl 1998, 57–58; Ludwig 2002). The other most frequent request is for guidance; given the confusion, uncertainty, and cruelty that often accompany wars, people may very well feel a need for guidance, either for themselves or for others. The complexity and difficulty of maintaining peace or bringing an end to a war may seem beyond the range of human capacity, in which case divine guidance may also seem necessary.

The third most numerous group of requests involves moral principles (including concepts such as ideals, righteousness, and right and wrong). The pressures and stresses of war, along with the hatred often associated with warfare, make moral principles particularly necessary. At the same time, some of the authorities that have influenced thinking about warfare have suggested or stated outright that moral principles do not necessarily apply in at least some wars (see Nice 1998). That contention has won renewed attention with the George W. Bush administration's mixed signals regarding the treatment of prisoners and allowable interrogation methods, including torture (see Espo and Sidoti 2005, 13A; Johnson 2007: 201–2). When moral principles are ignored, war can bring torture, the murder of civilians, and even genocide.

The final type of request among the top four is for protection. Modern warfare features a wide array of weapons that can strike from virtually any direction, from distances at which the enemy is not visible, and at speeds exceeding the speed of sound. Weapons capable of killing or harming a considerable number of people can be concealed in an attaché case or under a teenager's jacket. In addition, the threat of terrorist attacks on civilian targets has multiplied the number of potential danger zones. Many people feel a need for protection and may doubt the ability of human actions to provide that protection.

Almost one-fourth of the prayers requested some form of knowledge, information, or wisdom. Some of these requests emphasized making leaders wiser or more knowledgeable regarding their decisions affecting war and peace. Others asked for assistance in knowing how to perform their missions or carry out their duties successfully. An important distinction between these requests and the requests for guidance (some requested both) is the requests for knowledge—wisdom sought to enhance the decision-making capacity of human actors. Requests for guidance alone did not make that request—at least not clearly.

Seventeen prayers requested courage, usually to enable the petitioner to function effectively in the context of war or if war should occur. Some of these prayers were for military personnel facing the prospect of active combat. Other prayers were for people who needed courage because their loved ones were in or likely to be in combat. Several other prayers in this group requested courage to face the general dangers of war and could be for military personnel or civilians.

A dozen prayers in the sample requested some form of solidarity, including feelings of brotherhood, mutual goodwill, and friendship. Some of these requests involved humanity in general in hopes of maintaining or restoring peace or restraining the brutality of war. Others were more selective in scope, typically asking for unity among the people in one country or for strong bonds among members of a military unit.

Each of the remaining types of request appeared in fewer than a dozen prayers, but each is significant in the context of issues of war and peace. These requests included comfort—often for people who have lost loved ones, military personnel who have been wounded, or refugees displaced by warfare. Ten prayers asked for strength; some of the requests were for military personnel, but others were for civilians needing strength to carry out their own responsibilities or to endure separation from loved ones. An equal number of prayers were for faith, often for religious faith. A few of the requests were possibly more secular, asking for faith in a successful outcome or in leaders or comrades.

The last two types of requests (aside from a scattering of unusual types) were for justice (or a spirit of justice) or for a reduction in the level of hatred among various nations or the people of the world more generally. The justice-related requests often indicated the belief or hope that justice would help to maintain or restore a lasting peace.

The types of requests noted in Table 11.2 can be combined in a variety of ways in order to cast additional light on prayer dynamics. A large number of requests deal with the psychological needs likely to be generated by war or the threat of war. Among those requests are guidance, protection, courage, comfort, and forgiveness. The requests of psychological or emotional significance, which include a number of the scattered requests, amounted to 239 altogether.[3]

Almost as numerous (210) were requests that, broadly speaking, address factors that might affect the likelihood of war versus peace. Among these requests are those for peace (however achieved) or a greater love of peace, feelings of kinship or brotherhood, justice or a spirit of justice, and a reduced level of hatred. Implicitly or explicitly, these requests seem to reflect the view that conditions of war and peace are rooted into other causes that need to be addressed.

Analysis of the Second Sample

The second sample was more narrowly focused and includes two prayer collections. The first is *The Book of Common Prayer*, which is one of the most influential Christian prayer book ever written, in part because of the wide global reach of the Anglican Communion and in part because early editions helped to influence the development of the collect type of prayer used by many denominations in the United States and worldwide (see Suter 1940). The second is *A Peace Treasury* and includes prayers and meditations devoted to the issue of peace and taken from sources all over the world.

Social psychology can offer us much insight into the structure and purpose of all sorts of messages, including prayers. Among the many social psychological concepts that may be useful here are complexity, rigidity of argument, priming, and framing.

Complexity of thought has many facets, but one significant element is captured by the relative preponderance of black and white (absolute) thinking (which indicates rather simple thought) and more subtle, relative thinking (Preston 2000). In the former type of thought, the world is divided into dualistic categories, such as good versus evil; the latter type of thought assesses degrees of good and evil. Another important aspect of complexity is integrative complexity, which involves the ability to assimilate a variety of factors into an overall, integrated conclusion (Tetlock 1985). Individuals who have a high degree of integrative complexity are generally more likely to engage in relative thinking as well, for their assessments of goodness, strength, wealth, and so forth are likely to include a number of different elements, some of which might point in different directions. High levels of integrative complexity might also help individuals incorporate new information into a novel synthesis of ideas. A prayer that attributes evil to enemies but also expresses forgiveness for them implies a complex belief system.

Priming occurs when a stimulus encourages people to think about a topic (Iyengar and Kinder 1987). People are not likely to need priming to encourage them to think about a major war involving their own country, but priming might affect whether they think about wars in which their own country is not involved. In addition, priming could increase thinking about peace during peacetime, when a host of other issues are clamoring for attention, and might encourage thinking about peace during chronic or low-intensity conflicts.

Framing occurs when a topic or issue is presented within a particular frame of reference or in connection with other issues, beliefs, or images (Cottam, et. al. 2000); the type of frame used may influence public thinking regarding the issue. For example, a prayer might present a war as a moral crusade, a necessary evil, or as absolutely wrong. The prayer might include the premise that a war is inevitable, no matter what we do, or the premise that we may still choose between war and peace.

A variety of factors may influence the choice of frames used in any given communication, including prayers. If a war is very unpopular with the public or with church leaders, it may be more likely to be framed in ways that encourage additional skepticism or criticism regarding the war. A prayer might frame a war in terms of the larger battle of good versus evil, as an unpleasant but necessary duty, or as a sign of divine disapproval.

Another important aspect of framing involves the definition of in-groups and out-groups. Especially when conflicts develop, people often feel a need to know who is on which side. Some analysts believe that drives rooted in kinship and social identity encourage people to perceive the world, in part, by dividing it into groups to which they belong and groups to which they do not. Those drives may be inherent parts of the human personality and help provide the basis for social cognition (Buss 2002). On a more fundamental level, the ability to perceive in-groups may enhance genetic survival (Axelrod 1984). A wealth of political research shows that many people perceive the world through group affiliations and that many of those affiliations are powerful influences on political behavior and thinking (for examples, see Dalton 2002, 46–56, chapters 7–9; Erikson and Tedin 2001, chapters 3–7, 11; Flanigan and Zingale 2002, chapters 2–5, 8).

More intensive conflicts, especially wars, may enhance the tendency for thinking in terms of in-groups and out-groups. People may be actively encouraged to unite to support the war effort, and internal dissent may trigger complaints that the dissenters are helping "the enemy." In addition, propaganda may depict the enemy as less than human (see Struch and Swartz 1989), in part to make wartime actions against the enemy seem more acceptable on a moral level. Moreover, creating cognitive distance between allies and enemies may help solidify in-group identity among allies.

Characterizations of good and evil represent another aspect of conflict dynamics that may form part of a frame, possibly in conjunction with in-group and out-group labeling. Good and evil are sometimes assessed in secular terms, but religious principles often help to guide judgments of goodness and badness. In some wars (such as the Crusades) the judgments have been partly along the lines of religious affiliation; the enemy has a different religion and is, therefore, evil. In other cases people may define an adversary as evil due to violations or misinterpretations of a shared religion. In those circumstances, war may appear to be a moral necessity.

Not all attempts at framing are necessarily divisive. A peace frame may encourage people to move away from thinking of a divided world (friend versus enemy, our side versus their side) and toward a world of peace. Emphasizing peace may help both sides recognize the existence of a goal that can benefit both sides—by ending battlefield casualties, for example. An implicit peace frame might present the adversaries as people like us, with similar feelings, needs, hopes, and fears. Another implicit peace frame might appeal to the religious beliefs of adversaries in hopes of increasing their receptivity to a peaceful settlement. Conversely, a peace frame might be countered by a frame emphasizing the incompatibility of the two sides' goals or by staking out a position demanding an outcome that is unacceptable to the other side. Another countering frame might downplay the cost of the war in one or more ways; a successful war might give the country access to resources that would more than pay for the cost of the war (as some people apparently believed prior to the second Iraq War; see Johnson 2007, 79). People killed while fighting for our side might gain immediate entry into "Paradise" in which case we have less reason to mourn their deaths.

The context within which messages are developed and sent is likely to influence what types of frames are chosen, other things being equal. Wars that are unpopular, have produced heavy casualties, or have dragged on for a very long time are likely to encourage the use of peace frames or frames that try to minimize the cost of the war. Conversely, if or when a war is popular or produces few casualties, frames justifying or recommending war may be more acceptable.

One other important aspect of context is the level of stress or threat. Research on messages from political leaders finds that when levels of stress or threat are higher, leaders' messages become simpler and less abstract (Tetlock 1993). One possible reason for this pattern lies in evolutionary biology: the fight or flight response. When danger is near, an animal must decide whether to flee from the danger or fight against it, and the decision must often be made quickly.

There is little time for a complex assessment of the situation. If the ability to decide quickly and simply in times of imminent danger enhances the odds of survival, that trait may be passed on to future generations. In addition, high levels of stress or threat may simply render many people unable or unwilling to think in complex terms and, therefore, enhance the appeal of relatively simple messages and simple frames.

In the analysis of this sample of prayers, we categorized them according to whether they made relatively specific or relatively general appeals to a higher power and according to whether the appeals were primarily practical/secular or spiritual in nature. Most of the prayers in this sample are of American or European origin, but some come from other parts of the world.[4] A large majority of the prayers are Christian, although a limited number come from other religions. This sample included 110 prayers.

The analysis of this sample tended to confirm the expectation that the context in which prayers are developed and offered affects the types of prayers that emerge. One group of prayers made relatively abstract or general requests; many of these were for spiritual guidance. By and large, these prayers came from relatively stable, well-educated, prosperous societies, particularly the United States and Western Europe, which have usually had relatively modest levels of conflict since World War II. A second type of prayer also made relatively general requests but of a more practical and secular nature. These requests often call for an end to all conflicts or for greater kindness among people in general (see Table 11.3).

A third type of prayer made a relatively specific request, often focused on a specific situation, of a primarily practical/secular nature. These prayers tended to come from areas with relatively high levels of conflict, a finding consistent with the notion that higher levels of stress or threat tend to encourage simpler thinking and a greater emphasis on tangible, immediate needs. For example, "A Prayer for all of Those Involved in Reconciliation" asks for peace in Northern Ireland. However, the relatively small number of cases of abstract prayers that could be classified by point of origin makes that conclusion tentative.

Many of the prayers in this sample, as well as in the first sample, make use of the peace frame (note, however, that one of the two sources in the second sample is explicitly oriented to peace: *A Peace Treasury* 2000). Even the prayers that acknowledge the need for war at times hold out the hope for a return to peace before long. The frequent occurrence of the peace frame is consistent with basic Christian teachings.

SOME PRELIMINARY CONCLUSIONS

Our analysis of war and peace in Christian prayers found that many prayers address war and peace in fairly clear terms. A great many of these prayers include some expressive passages, especially for prayers that are most closely linked to the military. Given the strong feelings that war helps to create, the need to express feelings and thoughts is hardly surprising.

In addition, many prayers include one or more requests, which take many forms. One of the most frequent requests is for peace or for conditions likely to be favorable to peace. Many of the prayers also requested guidance or understanding, the strengthening of morality or ideals, or protection. Especially in an era when terrorist attacks can strike anywhere, many people at least occasionally feel a need for protection.

We also found that in countries where warfare was present or imminent, prayer requests tended to be simpler and more concrete. More general and abstract requests tended to occur in more prosperous countries that were at peace.

Table 11.1 Prayers Related to War and Peace: Preliminary Content Analysis, First Sample

One or More Prayer for:

	Expression	Requests	Self	Others	A Condition
Full Sample	92%	69%	72%	47%	63%
(n=87)	(80)	(60)	(63)	(41)	(55)
Sources Tied					
To Armed Forces	81%	62%	67%	19%	86%
(n=21)	(17)	(13)	(14)	(4)	(18)
Other Sources	95%	71%	74%	56%	56%
(n=66)	(63)	(47)	(49)	(37)	(37)

Note: Some prayers included both requests and expressions; some prayers contained more than one type of request.

Table 11.2 Types of Request Made in Prayers Related to War and Peace, Second Sample

Peace, love of peace, commitment to Peace	41*
Guidance (for self and/or others)**	41
Adherence to moral principles, ideals, justice, righteousness	32
Protection	29
Knowledge, skill, wisdom	19
Courage, bravery	17
Solidarity, feelings of kinship, brotherhood, or similar	12
Forgiveness	12
Comfort	11
Strength	10
Faith	10
Justice, spirit of justice	9
Less hatred	9

* Note: the numbers in the table refer to the number of prayers making a particular type of request.

** Some requests for guidance were relatively general. When a specific type of guidance was requested (toward greater wisdom, for example), the prayer was coded as requesting both guidance and the specific type of guidance.

Table 11.3 Environmental Context and Types of Appeals Made, Sample 2

	Abstract Appeals	Appeals for a Specific Action	General Appeals
Conflict Ridden	6% (2)	38% (12)	54% (17)
Non-Conflictual	50% (5)	20% (2)	30% (3)
Total Sample*	25% (28)	41% (45)	34% (37)

* Many prayers in this sample could not be classified regarding their origin.

Notes

1. The September 11 attacks were not the first terrorist acts committed in or against the United States. A number of domestic terrorist groups, including the Ku Klux Klan, have been active over the years, and American targets overseas, including embassies, have been attacked on a number of occasions.

2. The twelve prayer books included in the first sample are: *Armed Forces Devotional Book* (2003), Brandt (1980), Collins (1999), Counsell (1999), *Lutheran Book of Prayer* (1970), McCauley and McCauley (2001), *Pray for Our Nation* (1999), *A Prayer Treasury* (1998),

Rikkers (2003), and Warburton (2004). A number of other sources were examined but did not meet one or more of the inclusion criteria.

3. A complete list of the types of requests included in this calculation is available from the authors.

4. Bear in mind that many Christian prayers that have become part of American and European prayer traditions have been adapted from early Christian and Jewish prayers from the Middle East, North Africa, and Eastern Europe, as well as more contemporary prayers from other parts of the world. The patterns of requests, however, suggest that the process of adapting prayers has been relatively selective.

REFERENCES

Acker, J. W., ed. 1970. *Lutheran book of prayer*. St. Louis: Concordia.

Acker, J. W. 1970. "Preface." In the *Lutheran book of prayer*. St. Louis: Concordia, 11–12.

Ahlstrom, Sydney. 2004. *A religious history of the American people. 2nd ed.* New Haven: Yale.

Anderson, James. *Public policymaking*. 6th ed. Boston: Houghton Mifflin.

Armed Forces devotional book. 2003. St. Louis: Concordia.

Axlerod, Robert. 1984. *The Evolution of cooperation*. New York: Basic.

Batchelor, Mary, ed. 1992. Introduction. In *The Doubleday prayer collection*. New York: Doubleday, xiii–iv.

1979. *Book of common prayer*. New York: Seabury.

Boulding, Maria. 1997. Discerning God's Will. In *The complete book of Christian prayer*. New York: Continuum, xix–xx.

Brandt, Leslie. 1980. *Book of Christian prayer*. Minneapolis: Augsburg.

Buckley, Michael. 1986. Introduction, and How to use the prayer book. In *The Catholic prayer book*. Ann Arbor, MI: Servant, xii–vi and xvii–xix.

Buss, David. 2000. *Evolutionary psychology*. In *Encyclopedia of Psychology*, ed. A. H. Forman. Washington, DC: American Psychological Association.

Butler, Jon, Grant Wacker, and Randall Balmer. 2003. *Religion in American life*. Oxford, UK: Oxford.

Collins, Owen. 1999. *Classic Christian prayers*. New York: Testament.

Cottam, Martha, B. Dietz-Uhler, E. Mastors, and Thomas Preston. 2004. *Introduction to Political Psychology*. Mahwah, NJ: Lawrence Erilbaum.

Counsell, Michael. 1999. *2000 years of prayer*. Harrisburg, PA: Morehouse.

Dahl, Robert. 1998. *On democracy*. New Haven: Yale.

Dalton, Russell. 2002. *Citizen politics*. 3rd ed. New York: Chatham House.

Dye, Thomas. 2002. *Understanding public policy*. 10th ed. Upper Saddle River, NJ: Prentice-Hall.

Erikson, Robert, and Kent Tedin. 2001. *American public opinion*. 6th ed. New York: Longman.

Espo, David, and Liz Sidoti. 2005. Cheney appeals to senators for CIA exemption to torture ban. *Moscow, ID./Pullman Daily News*. November 5–6, 13A.

Flanigan, William, and Nancy Zingale. 2002. *Political behavior of the American electorate*. 10th ed. Washington, DC: Congressional Quarterly.

Fosdick, Harry. 1959. *A book of public prayers*. New York: Harper.

———. 2001. The strength of personal prayer. In *The book of prayers*, ed. Leon McCauley and Elfreda McCauley. New York: Portland House, 1–13.

Gallup, George, and Timothy Jones. 2000. *The next American spiritually*. Colorado Springs: Cook.

Gaustad, Edwin, and Leigh Schmidt. 2002. *The religious history of America*. Rev. ed. San Francisco: HarperSanFrancisco.

Grevstad. 2005. *Red state, blue state*. New York: Universe.

Harvey, Paul. 2001. The Christian doctrine of slavery. In *Religions of the United States in practice*, vol. 1. Princeton: Princeton, 466–482.

Hollihan, Thomas. 2001. *Uncivil wars*. Boston: Bedford/St. Martin's.

Howard, Russell, James Forest, and Joanne Moore, eds. *Homeland security and terrorism*. New York: McGraw-Hill.

Iyengar, Shantar, and Donald Kinder. 1987. *News that matters*. Chicago: University of Chicago.

———. 1989. Intergroup aggression: Its predictors and distinctness from in-group bias. *Journal of Social and Personal Psychology* 56:364–373.

Job, Reuben, and Norman Shawchuck. 1983. *A guide to prayer*. Nashville: Upper Room.

Johnson, Loch. 2007. *Seven sins of American foreign policy*. New York: Pearson Longman.

Josephy, Alvin. 1991. *The Indian heritage of America*. Boston: Houghton-Mifflin.

Ludwig, Arnold. 2002. *King of the mountain*. Lexington: University of Kentucky.

Martin, Joel. 2001. The green corn ceremony of the Muskogees. In *Religions of the United States in practice*, vol. 1, 48–66.

McCauley, Leon, and Elfreda McCauley. 2001. *Book of prayers*. New York: Portland House.

McNally, Michael. 2001. Ojibwe funerary hymn singing. In *Religions of the United States in practice*, vol. 1, 150–157.

Military leadership. 1990. Washington, DC: Department of the Army.

Moore, James. 2005. *One nation under God*. New York: Doubleday.

Moses, Jeffrey. 2002. *Oneness*. New York: Ballantine.

Nice, David. 1998. The warrior model of leadership. *Leadership Quarterly* 9:321–332.

Peace treasury. 2000. Oxford, UK: Lion.

Pray for our nation. 1999. Tulsa: Harrison House.

Prayer Treasury. 1998. Oxford, UK: Lion.

Preface. In *Book of common worship: Daily prayer.* 1993. Louisville: Westminster/ John Knox, 1–6.

Rikkers, Doris. 2003. *Praying for those we love as they serve our country.* Grand Rapids, MI: Zondervan.

Roberts, Elizabeth, and Elias Amidon. 1996. *Life prayers.* San Francisco: HarperSanFrancisco.

Sauter, Mark, and James Carafano. 2005. *Homeland security.* New York: McGraw-Hill.

Sider, Ronald. 2005. *The scandal of the evangelical conscience.* Grand Rapids, MI: Baker.

Stookey, Laurence. 2004. *This day: A Wesleyan way of prayer.* Nashville: Abingdon.

Sun Tzu. 1963. *The art of war.* Oxford: Oxford University Press.

Suter, John. 1940. The Anglican communion and the collect form. In *The book of English collects.* New York: Harper and Row, xv–li.

Tetlock, Phillip. 1985. Integrative complexity of American and Soviet foreign policy: A time series analysis. *Journal of Personality and Social Psychology* 49:1565–1585.

———. 1993. Cognitive structural analysis of political rhetoric: Methodological issues. In *Explorations in political psychology.* Durham, NC: Duke.

Van de Weyer, Robert. 1993. Introduction. In *The HarperCollins book of prayer.* San Francisco: HarperSanFrancisco, 9–11.

Water, Mark, ed. 2004. *Encyclopedia of prayer and praise.* Peabody, MA: Hendrickson.

Zaleski, Philip, and Carol Zaleski. 2005. *Prayer: A history.* Boston: Houghton-Mifflin.

CONTRIBUTORS

Susan Berg is the family and youth minister at Trinity Lutheran Church in Pullman, Washington.

Tor Christian Berg is pastor of Trinity Lutheran Church in Pullman, Washington.

Michael J. Butler is an assistant professor in the Department of Government and International Relations at Clark University, Worcester, MA. His research interests converge in the areas of international security, foreign policy, and global governance, with a particular emphasis on studying the impact of international norms and institutions on state behavior. His most recent research has appeared in the *Journal of Conflict Resolution*; the *Canadian Journal of Political Science*; *Global Change, Peace, and Security*; *International Journal*, and a variety of other peer-reviewed journals and edited volumes.

Jonathan Ervine is originally from Dundee in Scotland and is currently a doctoral researcher and teaching assistant in the Department of French at the University of Leeds, England. He specializes on relations between politics and cinema. His research has included a particular focus on the theme of opposition to war in the 1950s and 1960s French cinema and also how contemporary filmmakers have represented issues of social and racial exclusion in modern France.

Ernest A. Hakanen (PhD, Temple University) is an associate professor in the Department of Culture and Communication at Drexel University. His books include *Leading to the 2003 Iraq War: The Global Media Debate* (with Alexander G. Nikolaev, Palgrave Macmillan, 2006), *Mass Media and Society* (with Alan Wells, Ablex, 1992), and *The Branding of the Teleself: Mass Media Effects and the Self* (Lexington Books, forthcoming). His research interests include public affairs reporting, media effects history, and media and emotions.

David J. Koch just earned his BA in anthropology from Drexel University and is currently investigating graduate study in sociology. His interests include tourism research and the ways in which culture affects human development.

Harry Littell is Instructor of Photography at Tompkins Cortland Community College, Dryden, NY. He specializes in fine art photography and photographic history. He received his MFA in sculpture degree from Alfred University, Alfred, NY; his BFA in photography and sculpture from Cornell University; and his AAS degree in photography from the Rochester Institute of Technology, Rochester, NY.

Vincent Masse is a graduate student at the University of Toronto, currently writing a thesis on the constructing of proto-colonial stereotypes on newly discovered lands in early sixteenth-century French writings. He also works on nineteenth-century Québec literature.

Maríadelaluz Matus-Mendoza is a language educator and sociolinguist and an associate professor of Spanish at Drexel University. Her research explores Spanish language variation and geographical and social movement. She is also interested in language in the media, bilingualism, and second-language acquisition. She is currently working with attitudes toward language and ethnic groups among Mexicans residing in Philadelphia, Pennsylvania. She is the author of *Linguistic Variation in Mexican Spanish as Spoken in Two Communities—Moroleón, Mexico and Kennett Square, Pennsylvania.*

David Nice is a professor of political science at Washington State University.

Anne-Marie Obajtek-Kirkwood is an associate professor of French in the Department of Culture and Communication at Drexel University. Her specialization is in post-1968 and current French and Francophone literature. She has published on the German occupation of France, the Algerian War, conflict in the French suburbs, the Iraq War, and French and Francophone twentieth- and twenty-first-century writers. Her research interests also include minorities in France, autobiography, and feminist issues.

Ronald E. Ostman is professor of Communication at Cornell University, Ithaca, NY. His specializations include the history of photography, mass media effects, and public opinion. He received his PhD and MA degrees in journalism and mass communication from the University of Minnesota and his BA in English from Bemidji State University, MN.

Douglas Porpora, a sociologist, is head of the Department of Culture and Communication at Drexel University. His previous books include *How Holocausts Happen: The U.S. in Central America* (Temple, 1990) and *Landscapes of the Soul: The Loss of Moral Meaning in American Life* (Oxford, 2004). He is currently working on how the attack on Iraq was morally debated—or not—in the American public sphere.

Priscilla Ringrose is a post-doctoral research fellow at the Norwegian University of Science and Technology, Trondheim. She has published articles on post-colonial francophone literature, feminist theory, contemporary fundamentalist Islam, and on new media. Her book *Assia Djebar: In Dialogue with Feminisms* was published by Rodopi in 2006.

Paul A. Taylor is a senior lecturer in Communications Theory at the Institute of Communication Studies, University of Leeds. He is general editor of the online *International Journal of Zizek Studies* and his research interests focus upon critical theories of mass culture. His recent work includes *Hacktivism & Cyberwars: Rebels with a Cause?* (with Time Jordan, Routledge, 2004); *Digital Matters: The Theory and Culture of the Matrix* (with Jan Harris, Routledge, 2005); and the forthcoming *Critical Theories of Mass Media: Then and Now* (with Jan Harris, Open University Press, 2007).

Andrew Thomas is a doctoral student at Washington State University. He received his master's degree from the University of Northern Illinois.